THE ENGAGED SPIRITUAL LIFE

THE ENGAGED SPIRITUAL LIFE

A Buddhist Approach to Transforming Ourselves and the World

•

DONALD ROTHBERG

Beacon Press, Boston

Beacon Press
25 Beacon Street
Boston, Massachusetts 02108-2892
www.beacon.org

Beacon Press books
are published under the auspices of
the Unitarian Universalist Association of Congregations.

15   14   13   12   11   9 8 7 6 5 4 3

This book is printed on acid-free paper that meets the uncoated paper
ANSI/NISO specifications for permanence as revised in 1992.

Text design and composition by Yvonne Tsang
at Wilsted & Taylor Publishing Services

Library of Congress Control Number: 2006925997

To my mother, Bernice,
and
in memory of my father, Simon

Thank you for your big hearts, wisdom,
generosity, amazing support, and
guidance over so many years.

CONTENTS

FOREWORD

Anyone whose eyes and heart are open can see the troubles facing humanity. We find in the news and in our communities the effects of continuing warfare, racism, injustice, and environmental destruction; of greed, hate, and ignorance. As people of conscience, how best can we respond? How do we fashion a spiritual life that has both inner wisdom and integrity, as well as compassionate care for the world around us?

The key message of *The Engaged Spiritual Life* is that this is possible because inner and outer development are intimately connected. With an engaged understanding, inner work can transform the world. Zen master Thich Nhat Hanh describes how naturally this can happen: "When the crowded refugee boats met with storms or pirates, if everyone panicked, all would be lost. But if even one person on the boat remained calm and centered, it was enough. It showed the way for everyone to survive."

This book, *The Engaged Spiritual Life,* is a practical new guide, a handbook that pulls together theory and practice to join the inner meditative life and outer activism. It presents these understandings in a systematic, inspiring, and user-friendly fashion. With the clarity of a classic, it offers a rich palette of teachings, exercises, and understandings gained over decades to guide the reader to integrate activism with inner maturity.

Donald Rothberg has spent his adult life in this quest. His work is in the lineage of Joanna Macy and Mahatma Gandhi. For almost twenty years, he has been an active participant in the development of the Buddhist Peace Fellowship and the International Network of Engaged Buddhists. He has helped craft and mentor the Buddhist Peace Fellowship's BASE (Buddhist Alliance for Social Engagement) program for those linking spiritual practice with social service and social change work, particularly young Buddhist activists. He has taught years of retreats, workshops, and university classes on engaged spirituality, all the while being active and deeply engaged in social issues.

In these pages, Donald invites us to get in touch with our highest aspiration, our basic goodness, and bring the sacred into our modern lives. He invites us to embody these spiritual values in body, speech, and mind. The way to do so, he instructs, is to let our body be the local monastery and the community around us the greater temple. He teaches us to set our intentions, and to act from integrity and compassion, no matter what. He shows us how to release our attachments to views, whether political or spiritual, transform our anger, and avoid burnout. Donald shows us how to balance the way of commitment and compassion, to listen with our hearts as we ask, *Am I acting out of love and wisdom for all concerned, including myself?*

The world needs activists who are strong, compassionate, and wise. We must understand that only by facing our inner limitations can we bring forth a pure, strong energy to transform and inspire others. As Albert Camus explains, "We all carry within us our places of exile, our crimes, our ravages. Our task is not to unleash them on the world; it is to transform them in ourselves and others."

The Engaged Spiritual Life shows us how to do this. May its good teachings and wise medicine help all who read it to shine their compassionate hearts on the world and serve all beings.

With Blessings,
Jack Kornfield
Spirit Rock Center
Woodacre, California
2006

EXERCISES

Introduction

CONNECTING INNER AND OUTER TRANSFORMATION

I could not be leading a religious life unless I identified myself with
the whole of mankind, and that I could not do unless I took part in
politics. The whole gamut of man's activities today constitutes an
indivisible whole. You cannot divide social, economic, political, and
purely religious work into watertight compartments.[1]

MOHANDAS GANDHI, 1935

By the time I was in my early twenties, I knew that I had two vocations.
I wanted to dedicate myself to justice and social change, and I wanted to
commit myself to exploring the depths of human consciousness, to an
awakening to my and our deeper spiritual nature.

Yet for a long time I was not at all clear about how to bring these two
vocations together, or even whether I could. It seemed as if somehow I
had to choose one or the other. Over time and with some difficulty, I came
to see how they might be more and more part of a seamless whole, in
which our more "inner" lives and our more "outer" lives are connected
and deeply inform each other.

This book is about walking a path of *both* inner and outer transformation. It is also about coming to see that our real work is the same whether
we attend to ourselves, to our families, to our communities, or to our
larger society and ecosystems. This work is to be aware and present to
what is happening, responding compassionately to suffering, understanding our interdependence, and acting with grace, equanimity, and passion
in difficult circumstances. I offer this book as a guide and manual, suggesting a number of basic principles and concrete practices that can help
make this integration of spiritual and social transformation come alive.

My first initiation into a life attuned to social transformation started while
I was still a teenager, during the turbulent and revelatory 1960s. I grew up

in Maryland, and I had seen the poverty of African Americans firsthand in the unpaved roads and dilapidated houses and shacks a mile away from my home. As I grew older, I became more aware of the social structures and cultural attitudes that helped to perpetuate racism, evident in the divisions of school districts and pressures against developing interracial friendships. I learned the details of our often imperial and militaristic foreign policy, our support of brutal dictators, and the suppression of democratic movements in other countries; my eyes were opened especially by the Vietnam War. On our family television set, we watched the 1968 Chicago "police riot" at the Democratic National Convention. And I became attuned to the realities of domestic repression, becoming personally familiar with police harassment of young people with certain appearances (particularly those belonging to the counterculture and those with dark skin).

Increasingly aware of this shadow of injustice, violence, and suffering, while in college at Yale I turned from an early preoccupation with science as a vocation to a deepening study of politics, history, and social theory. I also participated in many local and national demonstrations, worked in the U.S. Congress, lived in Paris and studied the French student and worker movements, went to numerous political talks and meetings, and helped form a campus political group dedicated to social change.

My commitment was sealed. The intention to form my life in response to suffering, oppression, injustice, and the promise of a better society felt clear and unwavering. The needs were great; the needs were obvious. How could I do anything but have this be the focus of my life?

Yet in my late teens and early twenties, a second and equally (if not more) compelling path opened up. At first, while still in college, the quest to understand the roots of injustice and suffering brought me to the study of what philosophy and psychology have to say about human nature and human potential. I read Plato and Aristotle, Hegel and Marx, Kierkegaard and Nietzsche, Freud and Maslow, Sartre and de Beauvoir, Arendt and Habermas. I also read the poetry of Walt Whitman, Allen Ginsberg, and Gary Snyder, took several long backpacking trips in the Appalachians and Rockies, and began reading about the exploration of consciousness, meditation, Western mysticism, and Asian spiritual traditions. When the spiritual teacher Ram Dass, formerly a Harvard psychologist, visited Yale, I sat with him and a small group of students in a chapel for hours. Something was drawing me to listen, even though I saw myself primarily as an activist and hardly understood what he was saying.

In the next few years, I was particularly drawn to learning more about

Buddhism. I soon met a number of prominent Buddhist teachers, began a daily meditation practice that has continued to this day, and read everything I could find about meditation, consciousness research, and Buddhism. A short time later, I started attending meditation retreats lasting one to two weeks.

These retreats deeply touched my heart and my most basic aspirations for my life. I felt in a new sense as if I were finally at home, knowing what I wanted to do, how I wanted to be. I was completely captivated by the intensity and learning I found possible in meditation. In the simple act of paying attention to my own experience, moment after moment, day after day, I felt alive and committed as perhaps never before. At times, I wanted to do nothing other than to keep meditating, to explore the wonders of a silent mind, to peel away all the layers of repetitive thoughts and rigid reactions. I saw more clearly the inner and often unconscious sources of cruelty and hatred, the will to dominate, the fear and greed. Yet I also felt myself continually opening to yet deeper experiences of peace, understanding, and compassion.

Here, too, my commitment felt deep and unwavering. It seemed utterly compelling to follow this path—to awaken, to come to know the profound truth of the meaning of being alive, to transform my being, to come increasingly to manifest wisdom and compassion in my life. Why would I or any other human being want anything else with our short time on this earth?

Now, almost twenty-five years later, we can still make the case for the importance of both paths—of social and spiritual transformation—perhaps even more strongly than before.

The need to commit to what Jews call *tikkun olam,* "healing and repairing the world," seems, if anything, *more* urgent. The problems of poverty, racism, and injustice have remained very much with us, even as they have assumed new forms in the context of economic globalization, and even as we have come to be more aware of oppression based on gender and sexual orientation. Militarism and imperial ambitions have intensified in the United States following the fall of the Soviet Union and the attacks of September 11, ushering in prospects of perpetual war, further episodes of terrorism within our borders, growing fear and cycles of reaction, civil liberties being revoked in the name of security, and a tremendous economic burden that threatens our general prosperity. Some observers, seeing routine lying by our public figures, the disregard of domestic and international law, and in many instances a lack of concern for the economically disadvantaged, wonder whether our democracy will lose its very soul.

As if these problems weren't enough, mounting ecological crises, especially global climate change, threaten to overwhelm our ability to meet our basic needs for food, clean air and water, and fuel. Long ignored, particularly in the United States, these crises may have profound and even unimaginable social, economic, and political consequences, both locally and globally. In the face of such problems, who can stay on the sidelines?

Yet the call to spiritual exploration, to a life committed to opening to love and wisdom, to spiritual insight, is also heard more and more—in many lands, in a million contemporary voices. These voices are everywhere—on the Internet; in the sacred texts of the world, now available on an unprecedented scale; and in the growing number of those who consider themselves spiritual. The voices come from the revival of indigenous spiritual traditions; from the explosion of interest in Asian spiritual practices; from the renewed emphasis on the contemplative dimensions of Judaism, Christianity, and Islam; and even, if we look deeply, from the upsurge in fundamentalism.

To follow a spiritual path, however, sometimes seems to demand all of one's free time and energy. To cultivate love, compassion, courage, and wisdom in a deep and lasting way in one's life, to work through one's self-centeredness, hatred, fear, and confusion, seem to require an intense focus and dedication, which may preclude getting overly involved with the social world. Furthermore, we sometimes hear from spiritual teachers, as I often have heard, that working for social change places a Band-Aid on human suffering, that it doesn't address the deep existential roots of the problems, and that it distracts us from the real spiritual work. This mirrors the comments of many of my activist friends that inner work is at worst a fundamental delusion and at best an escapist luxury—as Marx proclaimed, religion is the "opium of the people." To really address the roots of suffering, they say, we need to change economic, social, and political structures and ideologies.

The premise of this book is that we don't have to make an impossible choice between these two paths. We *can* bring them together. We *can* link deep inner work with action in the world, in which our spiritual values infuse our response to the needs of the world, whether we are community organizers, teachers, activists, lawyers, or parents.

However, I would go much further. *The two paths deeply need each other.* And our times desperately call for *both* spiritual *and* social commitments. Without spiritual development, well-meaning attempts to change the world will probably unconsciously replicate the very problems that we believe we are solving. Unfortunately, we can see this all too clearly in the history of revolutions, where so often after an oppressor was toppled, the purported liberator was soon revealed as a new oppressor. Violent "solutions" all too frequently only beget further violence. Without transforming ourselves and coming to know ourselves deeply through sustained spiritual inquiry and practice, we may only make things worse. We also run the risk of not having the kind of resources of wisdom, compassion, equanimity, and perseverance necessary to respond to the great needs of the times without being quickly burned out by anger and frustration. Outer transformation thus entails inner transformation.

But if the path of spiritual transformation is not socially informed, it too is at risk. There is the irony of attempting to overcome self-centeredness through spiritual practice while ignoring the cries of the world, of living in a protected spiritual home while the rest of the world is burning. And there is the danger of not seeing how the world is not just "out there" but also "in us," internalized through our self-images; our social constructions of gender, class, and ethnicity, among others; and in our behaviors as consumers, parents, partners, and coworkers. Without transforming the world that is in us, we maintain, usually unconsciously, its patterns in ourselves and our spiritual communities. And when we do attend to the world "in us," we join in the act of social transformation. In that sense, inner transformation entails outer transformation.

So how do we connect spiritual and social transformation? What perspectives, tools, and practices are helpful? How can we draw from the resources of *both* approaches and bring them together? How can we learn from those who have brought together the spiritual and the social— from indigenous traditions, the Jewish prophets, and Jesus; from Gandhi, King, liberation theology, Dorothy Day, and the Dalai Lama; from contemporary figures like Thich Nhat Hanh, Starhawk, Julia Butterfly Hill, Cornel West, bell hooks, Joanna Macy, and Michael Lerner? How can there be an integrated path that we walk in our lives?

My intention in this book is to help present the basic contours of such an integrative path, with an emphasis on ten core spiritual principles that frame the journey, and specific practices, linked with these principles, that we can do on a daily basis. Through these practices, we both learn about and come to embody the principles.

My hope is that these principles and practices are general enough to be accessible to those who identify themselves as participating in one or more of a variety of spiritual traditions, or who claim no tradition at all. I believe that many of the *contemporary* issues and concerns of this path look very similar, if not identical, across traditions and approaches, especially when we focus more on our lived, practical experiences than on theologies or spiritual doctrines.

Although I draw stories, teachings, and perspectives from a number of different traditions and from a variety of individuals, I ground this book to a large extent both in my own personal experience and in my own practice of Buddhist-based mindfulness and lovingkindness meditation. Through this emphasis on my own experience, and on the experiences of others exploring this socially engaged spiritual path whose stories I have collected, partly through interviews, I hope to make real and tangible many of the questions and dilemmas, as well as insights and triumphs, of the path. For those who are drawn to such a path, here are some friends and signposts along the way.

Mindfulness practice has been called the heart of Buddhist meditation and is central to all forms of Buddhist meditation. The practice involves cultivating the ability to be directly aware, moment by moment, of what is occurring in one's experience—including both the inner experiences of bodily sensations, thoughts, and emotions, and the outer experiences of being with our world, with objects, or with other human beings. When such mindfulness is sustained over time, wisdom, the clear seeing into basic inner and outer patterns of experience, arises, guiding us in our choices. My own spiritual lineage is that of the Theravada ("the way of the elders"), presently found in southern Asia—in Sri Lanka, Burma, Thailand, Cambodia, and, to some extent, Vietnam. My own training, however, has occurred primarily in the West, as I have been guided by a host of generous Westerners, most of whom trained in Asia: Joseph Goldstein, Jack Kornfield, Sharon Salzberg, Christopher Titmuss, John Travis, Sylvia Boorstein, and Gil Fronsdal.

Yet mindfulness practice, as the open and direct investigation of experience, has proven surprisingly accessible to those who do not necessarily consider themselves Buddhists or even spiritual. It is neutral and light enough in terms of what we might call "doctrinal baggage" that it has been regularly practiced in synagogues and Catholic monasteries, as well as by those who do not identify with any specific tradition. In the last few years in particular, a number of meditation teachers have offered training in mindfulness practice in retreats for social activists. Some Western philosophers and scientists have even embraced mindfulness practice as a fundamental and universal mode of broadly "scientific" inquiry into human nature, which can be added to the contemporary repertoire of disciplined, systematic ways of knowing.

The practice of lovingkindness *(metta)* involves the continual intention to open our hearts—both to ourselves and to others—in all situations. As a practice, it provides the warmth, caring, kindness, compassion, and joy that balance with the development of mindfulness and wisdom —a balance that is particularly important for those connecting spiritual and social transformation. Lovingkindness practice too in recent years has been taken up by those from many traditions, including rabbis and ministers, Christian monks and nuns, as well as those from no particular tradition. And the long-term effects of such practice have been increasingly studied by psychologists and by scientists studying the brain.

I also intend this book to be a resource for those presently on one side or the other of the split between the spiritual and the social. For those who have been committed to social service or activism, and who now feel drawn to linking their action in the world with spiritual practice, the book offers perspectives and tools that can support these commitments in a more sustainable, skillful, and heartfelt way. For those who want to extend their spiritual practice farther into the world, the book offers a bridge. It presents concrete ways of bringing the ten spiritual principles into the many outer dimensions of our lives, strengthening our ability to act compassionately in the world.

My deeper intention is further to provide a guide for young people who may not yet have felt the pressure to choose between spiritual and social vocations. My hope is that the book may help them join these commitments together *from the beginning,* without having to experience some of the struggles and tensions between the two that I and others have known.

THE PLAN FOR THIS BOOK

In each of the ten chapters of this book, I identify a guiding principle, linked with specific practices, for connecting the spiritual and the social. These principles and practices apply across three broad domains: (1) the *individual*; (2) the *relational* (from couples, friendships, and families to groups, organizations, and communities); and (3) the *collective*—namely, larger systems (social, cultural, political, economic, and ecological). This basic framework, which grew out of a number of years of collaboration with my colleague in teaching meditation and engaged spirituality, Diana Winston, makes clearer the need for an *expanded* sense of spiritual practice, beyond a purely individual practice, and invites the creativity of the reader to contribute to developing such an expanded practice.

Having this broadened understanding of spiritual practice can help us find our personal niche, our own way of connecting our action in the world and our spirituality, depending on our own gifts, strengths, interests, and aspirations. We don't have to "do everything," always be on the frontlines, or model a specific socially engaged spiritual path. Aware of the links between the individual, the relational, and the collective, our engagement might be focused on working to develop an alternative community school, on teaching a new way to be with our bodies in movement or yoga, on acting as a counselor, or on working full-time against the death penalty.

I ground each chapter in an account of what the given principle looks like in terms of individual practice and then suggest ways of extending the principle into the relational and collective domains. Throughout these chapters, I also point to the varied ways in which the three domains interpenetrate, how, for example, the collective (manifest in social structures and cultural attitudes) is internalized in the individual, at the same time that individuals collectively determine social structures and cultural attitudes. Although the main reference point is Buddhist practice, I also bring in resources from other spiritual traditions, ancient and contemporary, as well as the riches of contemporary democratic and progressive political approaches to the "good society" and social change.

My aspiration throughout the book is also to point to how this integration of the inner and the outer, of the spiritual and the social, of practice in the different domains, might manifest itself in the very acts of writing and reading. To challenge the separation of the spiritual and the social has implications for how we communicate, for how we explore concerns and issues. My intention here is to bridge ways of knowing that are often separated, some ways of knowing being more identified with the spiritual, others with the social. And so I invite a variety of modes: personal stories, both my own and those of others (in some cases with identifying details changed); spiritual teachings, both traditional and contemporary; practical exercises, both individual and relational; and poetry as well as social analysis and history. May the steps of our path deeply resonate with our goal, our means with our ends!

Chapter One

ESTABLISHING THE CONDITIONS
FOR SAFETY NEAR AND FAR:
ETHICAL PRACTICE

Our spiritual practice and our work in the world commonly begin with an ethical commitment to help, and not to harm, ourselves and others. Such a commitment is central to establishing a "container" of safety for ourselves and those around us, facilitating the inner work of opening body, heart, and mind, and guiding and protecting us in our outer actions. We extend a zone of caring, what Martin Luther King Jr. called the "beloved community," outward into the world, into all the domains of our lives. In this sense, ethics is at the center of both spiritual practice and social transformation. Without a strong ethical foundation, we inevitably fall into contradictions—between means and ends, between our actions and our ideals.

We may think of ethics as a simple matter: "I'm ethical. I don't do bad things. I don't kill or steal. My ethical training is complete! Next subject!"

Yet ethical practice can be extremely challenging and complex and take us far beyond this initial understanding. In the three traditional training areas of Buddhist practice—ethics, meditation, and wisdom— ethics is often seen as foundational for development in meditation and wisdom. However, greater awareness and wisdom also spur further ethical development. As we see more deeply into the nature of our own suffering in meditation, for example, compassion for others who are suffering in similar ways naturally arises, becoming more and more the basis for relationships and action. As we deconstruct our narrow self-images and sense of separation from others, recognizing our interdependence, we strongly influence our ethical sensitivity both to ourselves and to others. I may come to see that harming another is as unthinkable as my right hand harming my left hand.

Such perspectives invite us to expand our ethical lives more fully into the relational and collective domains of our lives, becoming more subtle in our ethical awareness. We may think that we are following the ethical guideline about not killing, but how do we relate to a government that kills in our name? We may believe we are far from even the idea of stealing, but do we use work time for surfing the Internet or exaggerate on our tax returns? Do we enjoy economic and social privileges by participating in a system in which some have been unfairly exploited? We may identify ourselves as honest, as always telling the truth. But how do we relate to a lack of honesty in our own organizations or in public places, whether originating from public officials, the media, or our educational systems?

TRADITIONAL ETHICAL TRAINING GUIDELINES

The Buddha established a series of rules for monks and nuns, which were codified into a set of more than two hundred precepts, making up one of the three canonical Buddhist collections of texts, the Vinaya (literally, "that which leads away from remorse").[1] The Vinaya contains a large number of precepts, mostly relating to the minor vagaries of daily life for monastics, including the handling of money, the type of bedding allowed, and so on.

But the five most basic ethical precepts are offered for lay practitioners living in the outside world. Here is a translation of them from Pali, the language of the Buddha:

> For the sake of training, I undertake the precept to abstain from the taking of life.
> For the sake of training, I undertake the precept not to take that which is not given.
> For the sake of training, I undertake the precept to abstain from sexual misconduct.
> For the sake of training, I undertake the precept to abstain from unwise speech.
> For the sake of training, I undertake the precept to abstain from intoxicants that cause heedlessness.

The emphasis on these as guidelines for *training* is particularly important, in at least three basic ways. First, the precepts are not understood as the pronouncements of an external authority to which we must adhere. Rather, they are expressions of how a wise and compassionate person acts; we carry the seeds of such wisdom and compassion in ourselves and aspire to let them grow to maturity. The precepts water these seeds. Following the precepts helps us grow toward this way of being, toward it becoming more and more our ordinary mode.

Second, this suggests that although the precepts are expressed negatively, they can also be articulated more positively. Following the precepts means not just abstaining from certain activities but also actively developing particular qualities. For example, the first precept is an antidote especially to hatred and inclines the mind and heart toward love. The second precept counters greed and grasping and helps us to develop generosity. The third and fifth precepts transform compulsive desire and self-centeredness, leading toward caring and at times renunciation. The fourth precept works particularly against grasping, aversion, and delusion as we cultivate kindness, wisdom, integrity, and skillfulness in action.

Third, we recognize that we will typically fall short of full adherence to a given precept, yet the precepts can nonetheless guide us, can support our learning. Indeed, it was known in the Buddha's time, as we know very well in our time, that we are typically killing very small beings unintentionally all the time, whether microorganisms or insects. The spirit of following the precepts when we have fallen short is not to chastise ourselves or others harshly for transgressions, but to recognize what has happened, reflect on what we might learn, and begin again. Both traditionally and in contemporary settings, practitioners often gather in groups or communities regularly (typically every two weeks or every month) to renew their dedication to the precepts and to reflect together on the past weeks' experiences.

ESTABLISHING SAFETY

I like to think of the ethical precepts as providing training guidelines in another way as well, *as establishing the very conditions of safety that make training and learning possible.* It is very hard to learn when feeling unsafe or threatened. The five precepts are essentially about not harming others (or ourselves) and not causing suffering, whether through hatred and physical harm, through greed and taking what belongs to others, or through lack of care with our sexuality, speech, and use of intoxicants. Following the precepts thus helps us *not* to go down certain paths that typically lead to behavior that harms.

In following the precepts, I offer safety both to myself and to others. It is as if I am gradually creating a peace zone around me. Like the signs in my hometown of Berkeley, California, that read "Now entering Berkeley, nuclear-free zone," people who are in ethical training might wear T-shirts that read "Now entering a zone of (relative) peace and safety."

This kind of safety is also very important for most of us to be able to open up to the immensity of life and to ourselves. We need such safety when we explore, often precariously and with difficulty, our suffering, fears, and grief and open to greater joy, beauty, and insight. Thomas Merton speaks of our inner awakening as resembling the process of a shy animal that emerges only when it feels safe.

> The inner self is precisely that self which cannot be tricked or manipulated by anyone.... He is like a very shy wild animal that never appears at all whenever an alien presence is at hand, and comes out only when all is perfectly peaceful, in silence, when he is untroubled and alone. He cannot be lured by anyone or anything, because he responds to no lure except that of the divine freedom.[2]

This sense of safety that the practice of the precepts offers is well expressed in a number of traditional metaphors. To keep to the precepts is like "seeing the light of a fire in a dark place" or "returning home."[3]

APPLYING THE PRECEPTS TO OUR LIVES

The precepts both help support a training environment and strongly incline us toward developing the positive qualities linked with them. Yet in their relatively general formulation, they also invite us to inquire deeply into how to apply them in the concrete circumstances and different domains of our lives. For there is no definitive compendium of *how* to apply the precepts, and of course our postmodern social conditions differ substantially from the premodern Asian, rural, and agrarian societies that existed at the time of the Buddha.

My intention here is to suggest some of the contours of such a contemporary ethical practice. I will focus on the first, second, and fourth precepts because of their centrality in linking spiritual and social transformation.

Practicing the First Precept: Non-Harming

Although all of the five basic precepts can be understood as variants of the injunction not to harm, and hence to offer safety to others and to oneself, to follow the first precept is *explicitly* to commit not to harm others, in the most basic sense of not intentionally taking the lives of sentient beings.

Thus the precept is applied not just to human beings but to all beings. We abandon, according to the Buddha, "violence in respect of all beings, both those which are still and those which move."[4] Tendencies toward violence are catalyzed especially by various forms of aversion, particularly hatred, but also anger and fear. To practice the precept is to work to uproot hatred. According to a Mahayana text, "One must not hate any being and cannot kill a living creature even in thought."[5] To follow the precept, says the Buddha, is to "abandon the onslaught on breathing beings... without stick or sword, scrupulous, compassionate, trembling for the welfare of all living beings."[6] In other discourses, the Buddha more broadly characterizes the precept in terms of non-harming (ahimsa), a principle well established in the Hindu and Jain traditions of his time, and later to become the center of Gandhi's interpretation of nonviolence.

Historically, Buddhists have considered non-harming as the most fundamental of the five precepts. For the Buddha, it is "the distinguishing mark of dhamma" (the teachings of liberation).[7] It is also striking that the precept gives its name (through "nonviolence") to a whole major approach to social change, found in many spiritual and secular traditions.

Practicing in the Individual and Relational Domains

We often begin practicing the first precept by noticing when and how we and others seem to violate it in more obvious ways in our daily lives. It is particularly helpful to set an intention to work with the precept for a fixed time, perhaps a week as a start, and to establish one's intention regularly, perhaps every morning during meditation, prayer, or reflection, or even several times a day.

When the members of an ongoing meditation group that I lead in the San Francisco Bay area worked with the precepts over a number of months, they soon found several problematic areas. We reflected, for example, that although we may never have come close to killing a human being (whatever our thoughts might have been), most of us have deliberately killed other beings, including animals and insects, in the past. Several members were inspired to look carefully at their diet and question whether eating meat violates the first precept. Others were very aware of their tendencies to harm others, particularly through their speech, when they were angry or upset or reacted to something that was said to them. They gave more attention to the various conflicts in their lives and to their own tendencies to intend to harm, at least verbally, those with whom they were in conflict. Sometimes the person with whom one is in conflict is oneself! One person focused especially on her tendencies to harm herself in subtle and not-so-subtle ways.

The inner work with the first precept is to cultivate mindfulness and wisdom in relation to tendencies to harm ourselves and others and to cultivate lovingkindness as an antidote to hatred and aversion. We especially study the tendency to "pass on" the pain when we are in emotional or physical pain ourselves; this tendency is at the root of the harm we inflict on others or ourselves. As we shall explore in chapter 4, this compulsive and often unconscious *reaction* to pain constitutes "suffering." We therefore examine, over and over again, how, when we are in pain, we react with fear, anger, or blame and act in ways that we think will somehow alleviate the pain.

One way to understand the precept's centrality is to see how *it guides us to respond to pain of any kind (our own and that of others) — even if the pain was born of injustice and oppression — as much as possible without inflicting further pain on others or ourselves.* At the same time, we respond as fully as possible both to the pain and to the conditions of pain. This suggests that we might consider the first precept as fundamental to social transformation.

The practice of the first precept can occur in several stages, stages that apply to the other precepts as well. *First, we take a kind of inventory of our patterns,* looking carefully at our tendencies to harm others or the self. We attempt to notice our various patterns while refraining from actually harming as much as possible. A regular mindfulness practice helps this process tremendously, because, while we are suspended from immediate action, we can witness many of our various reactive patterns. Such a practice helps us to know when we have thoughts and emotions that *may lead* to harm.

Second, as we become more familiar with this inventory, *we give more focused attention to these patterns,* eventually becoming, we might say, connoisseurs of our own reactivity. We look at the different components of our reactions, separating out the moments of pain, or being startled, from the judgments, fear, blaming, and the actions themselves.

We may initially do this in meditation or in some protected environment, but eventually *we bring mindfulness of reactivity into everyday activities,* into the midst of action, doing inner work while engaging in conversations, meetings, or other activities, or while on our own. In this third stage, I may see myself as "in training." I may take a special interest in attending to difficult moments. Whereas in the past I might in such moments typically have sought to harm others or myself, now I can view these moments as "wake-up calls." Such moments (when I am the target of aggression, when I am angry, when I feel not recognized or "seen" clearly, when I feel dismissed) also become chances to practice nonreactive responses.

Practice in each of these three phases can be deeply transformative. One of my own insights (and surprises) at the beginning of my mindfulness practice, in my mid-twenties—related to the first phase of "taking inventory"—was about how much aggression I found in myself when I studied my mind and heart closely. I thought of myself (and others thought of me similarly) as a "nice," "kind," and "gentle" person who did not express anger frequently (or easily). To my surprise, more often than I would have acknowledged earlier, I discovered thoughts within me of wanting to harm others.

My recognition of such tendencies to harm others, although at times troubling and sobering, yielded many fruits. It helped me to give more room for my anger and aggression, to bring these qualities, as it were, "out of the shadows." It led me to see that the difference between myself and those who harm others in more obvious ways might be smaller than I had previously thought. This difference might arise more from life circumstances than from some supposed absolute moral disparity between us. Had I experienced different stimuli and conditions, my inner makeup might well have led me to harm others much more readily than I had done.

Practicing in the Collective Domain

Practicing the social or collective aspect of the first precept can occur in two major ways. First, *we more fully take as part of our commitment to non-harming our intention to end harming and violence associated with the social, political, and economic systems in which we participate.* We extend the reach of the precept by going beyond an interpretation of it as focused solely on our face-to-face interactions.

In *For a Future to Be Possible,* Vietnamese Buddhist teacher, activist, and poet Thich Nhat Hanh reworks the first precept in ways that suggest not just an individual but also a social ethics:

> Aware of the suffering caused by the destruction of life, I vow to cultivate compassion and learn ways to protect the lives of people, animals, plants, and minerals. I am determined not to kill, not to let others kill, and not to condone any act of killing in the world, in my thinking, and in my way of life.[8]

He goes on to explain the injunction to stop others from killing:

> We cannot support any act of killing; no killing can be justified. But not to kill is not enough. We must also learn ways to prevent others from killing. We cannot say, "I am not responsible. They did it. My

hands are clean." If you were in Germany during the time of the Nazis, you could not say, "They did it. I did not." If, during the [First] Gulf War, you did not say or do anything to try to stop the killing, you were not practicing this precept.[9]

Robert Aitken, Zen teacher, activist, and the cofounder of the Buddhist Peace Fellowship, maintains that following the first precept requires one to question forms of socially legitimated violence—from stockpiling nuclear weapons to environmental degradation and the killing of animals. Similarly, Thai Buddhist organizer, activist, and author Sulak Sivaraksa, twice nominated for the Nobel Peace Prize, writes:

> We must look at the sales of arms and challenge these [economic and power] structures which are responsible for murder. Killing permeates our modern way of life—wars, racial conflicts, breeding animals to serve human markets, and using harmful insecticides. How can we resist this and help create a nonviolent society? How can the first precept and its ennobling virtues be used to shape a politically just and merciful world?[10]

This articulation of a social ethics is not simply a modern innovation. We find a social aspect in the teachings of the Buddha. In the *Sutta-Nipata,* for example, the Buddha summarizes the first precept: "Let him not destroy life nor *cause others* to destroy life and, also, not *approve* of others' killing."[11] He himself at one point intervened to attempt to stop a looming war. In the time since the Buddha, many Buddhists have given decidedly social interpretations of the precept, from the rulings of the great Buddhist king Asoka (third century CE) prohibiting the killing of animals and capital punishment to the Burmese monks who regularly would spirit away prisoners about to be executed.

To help us understand that there is indeed a social aspect to our ethical practice and intentions, it is sometimes helpful to use historical analogies, as our imagination often seems quite limited in regard to our own historical period. We might see clearly that being ethical in Nazi Germany or apartheid South Africa or Mississippi in the 1930s would have demanded action. We would probably question the ethics and spirituality of someone who did not act in these circumstances.

However, it is often harder to see many contemporary forms of suffering as related to clear ethical issues. This is, I believe, also partly because contemporary problems increasingly come out of the operations of complex economic and political systems requiring many faceless managers as well as the collaboration of citizens and consumers. The challenge, though, is to hold that we are ethically required to respond, even if it is often difficult to know how to respond.

A second way of ethical practice in the collective domain is *to connect the inner work described earlier with our action in the world.* Here Buddhists and other contemplative practitioners can make a significant contribution. They can point to the reciprocal causality of individuals and the collective, the interpenetration of domains—how the systemic forces that harm living beings are rooted in the often unconscious reactivity of many individuals that has in various ways crystallized into institutions, policies, and ideologies. Analyses of the forces of racism or militarism, for example, disclose what we might call the common depth psychologies of individuals who are racist or who support militarism. Yet these individual psychologies are in large part produced by a variety of cultural and social forces, including long-standing ideologies, propaganda, education, and cultural images, as well as concrete life experiences within various institutions. Ethical practice in the world in relation to the first precept helps to clarify and transform hatred and aversion that have been activated by these cultural and social forces.

Inner spiritual work makes clearer that all of us have internalized these systemic forces. When reactive, we tend to manifest culturally sanctioned forms of aversion, hatred, and actions that harm. Furthermore, this often happens in the midst of our spiritual communities or social change organizations. We tend to replicate the sexism, racism, and ecological blindness of the society. What seems required are ways to work through the individual and social aspects of these problems simultaneously.

This inner work in the collective domain is particularly vital as we attempt *to transform the conditions of harming and violence while still following (as much as possible) the first precept not to harm.* In other words, we commit to non-harming in the process of transforming the conditions that support harm.

Such inner practice rests on the teaching of the Buddha—echoed by Jesus, Gandhi, Martin Luther King Jr., and many others—that without awareness of reactive patterns, even those who think they are doing good commonly recycle the pain and suffering generation after generation, producing what Hegel called the "slaughter-bench of history."[12] The spirit of the first precept is the spirit of nonviolence; it is to end such cycles through non-harming or, positively expressed, through love. For the Buddha in the *Dhammapada,*

In this world
Hate never yet dispelled hate.
Only love dispels hate.
This is the law,
Ancient and inexhaustible.[13]

EXERCISE: Practicing Non-Harming in Daily Life

For a week, give special emphasis to the practice of the first precept, following many of the suggestions given above. If possible, do this with another person or within a group. Each morning or evening, read the precept and set your intention for the next twenty-four hours, perhaps reading about the meaning and practice of the precept. Be aware of any tendencies to come close to violating or actually to violate the precept. Explore the sequence of first taking an inventory of your patterns, then examining these patterns more deeply, particularly in meditation, and, finally, bringing attention to your patterns as they occur, in the midst of daily life.

If you have not worked before with the precept, you might take an inventory of your behavior and patterns for the first two or three days, before moving to the more inner work for the next few days, and the social aspect perhaps the last two days. Take notes during each day, and reflect at the end of the day on what you've explored. At the end of the week, reflect on any ways in which you might integrate the continued practice of the precept into your life.

Practicing the Second Precept: Transforming Greed

Whereas the first precept is about limiting the expressions of *hatred and aversion* by refraining as much as possible from harming other beings, the second precept directs us to limit the most obvious expressions of *greed* by refraining from taking that which is "not given," by not "stealing." In the traditional interpretation of the precept, in the context of rural Asian societies, this meant that monks and nuns should accept the four requisites (food, clothing, shelter, and medicine) only when they were offered. For laypersons, this meant both not to take directly what belongs to others and not to engage in fraudulent or deceptive means in order to take something from someone.

But interpretation of this precept in contemporary Western societies is, like the interpretation of the first precept, seemingly more complex. Am I going against the precept when I use my work time to do errands? When I borrow my roommate's shampoo without asking? When I exaggerate in filling out expense reports? When I enjoy traveling and use large amounts of gasoline, although such travel collectively creates pollution and depends, for a steady supply of oil, on my country's attempt to control the supply of oil from other countries, in many cases through violence and coercion? Sulak Sivaraksa continues discussing such questions:

> We may not literally steal in our face-to-face interactions, but do we allow the rich countries to exploit the poor countries through the workings of the international banking system and the international economic order? Do we allow industrial societies to exploit agrarian societies? The First World to exploit the Third World? The rich to exploit the poor generally?[14]

Practicing in the Individual and Relational Domains

How do we practice the second precept? For six weeks, members of my meditation group agreed to set a strong intention to remember the precept in everyday life; some also did readings on the precept. Regular meetings gave the group energy and inspiration for keeping the precept in mind, strengthening their intentions.

In this context, everyday activities served as wake-up calls to look more deeply, as when one would find oneself having violated the precept in an obvious way or having entered a "gray area." One member had actually taken something from another person without permission and was troubled by that; she reflected at length on the incident and its roots. Several looked carefully at their balance of giving and taking in general and explored how to strengthen their generosity in concrete ways: giving more to charities, reviewing their finances and finding ways to give more, and so on.

Monitoring one's actions in the light of the precept was a starting point for inner work, for the threefold process of taking an inventory of our patterns, examining the patterns more deeply, especially in meditation, and then working with the patterns in the midst of everyday life. This meant especially noticing and looking in depth at greed and craving, typically the inner impetus for stealing, and actively developing such qualities as generosity, renunciation, moderation, contentment, and the ability to let go when appropriate. Ultimately greed and grasping may be dependent on delusion; we somehow think that our well-being is dependent on getting this object, that experience, or this relationship. Yet the teaching in Buddhist (and other) traditions is clearly that greed and grasping are not only *not* necessary for deep happiness but actually prevent such happiness. Our very being, our very nature, as it were, gives us enough when we see clearly. This doesn't mean that we don't desire or act to change things, but we can do so, somewhat paradoxically, with equanimity, compassion, and wisdom rather than because of greed and grasping.

In our group, we encouraged each other to be attentive to moments of strong wanting. We studied the dynamics of desire, greed, craving, and grasping, both in the moment of wanting and afterward—in reflection, contemplation, and discussion. We found how greed and the moments of "stealing" were typically characterized by extreme self-centeredness (accompanied by thoughts such as "My desires matter more than those of others" or even "Others' desires don't count"), a lack of sense of connection to others, feelings of being "out of balance" and "out of control," an obliviousness to consequences, and at times a sense of entitlement.

One question that arose was how to distinguish "legitimate" desire from greed. Am I greedy when I want to own a home or maintain job security? Isn't this the equivalent of having an updated version of the monks' and nuns' four requisites? We explored these questions in part by reflecting on the point at which desire starts to turn into greed, especially when there is fear (as when we start grasping or hoarding). We also noted the importance of compassion for each other in our practice of the precepts, since we are clearly all vulnerable to such fear and greed.

Practicing in the Collective Domain

The second precept, like the first, has been expressed in both contemporary and traditional settings in ways that suggest not just an individual ethics but also a social one. For example, in 1964 Thich Nhat Hanh developed, in the crucible of the Vietnam War, fourteen ethical guidelines for the Tiep Hien Order (Order of Interbeing), several of them related to the second precept. The thirteenth begins, "Possess nothing that should belong to others," but then goes on, "Prevent others from enriching themselves from human suffering or the suffering of other beings." The fifth Tiep Hien guideline tells us, "Do not accumulate wealth while millions are hungry.... Live simply and share time, energy, and material resources with those who are in need."[15] In the *Sutta-Nipata,* the Buddha summarizes the second precept in this way: "Let one not cause to steal, *nor approve of others' stealing.*"[16]

In my group, we reflected on how deeply our thinking, beliefs, and habits were influenced by the entrenched greed of our social, political, and economic systems (we also recognized some of the merits of these systems). Indeed, many would say that our economic system as it currently operates, while succeeding in meeting a number of material needs for some people, also crystallizes and institutionalizes greed and even theft on a massive scale. The practices of WorldCom, Enron, and the energy companies that manipulated the California energy markets may reflect more the norm than the exception.

What might it mean to practice the second precept in the challenging contemporary context of corporate dominance and economic globalization? As Thich Nhat Hanh suggests, it can mean to live simply, to be as aware as possible of the assumptions, belief systems, and privileges associated with greed and grasping, and to decondition ourselves as much as possible. It might also mean to work actively, locally and/or globally, to develop social, political, and economic systems and a relationship to the earth that is less rooted in greed and grasping and more rooted in moderation, sustainability, and even generosity and renunciation. It doesn't mean somehow not to consume, but rather to be more aware of our consumption and the consequences of our consumer choices. In our group, we discussed a number of different choice points, ranging from how and where we procure our food, to "socially responsible investing," to devoting time and energy to enhancing community life. One person saw a film on diversity issues and was drawn to deepen her reflections on privilege related to class and ethnicity and how we are often ignorant of what we take from others.

EXERCISE: Practicing Not Taking That Which Is Not Given

Follow some of the same suggestions made earlier for practicing the first precept, especially in regularly setting intentions, but this time work with the second precept for a week. As suggested in the discussion of the first precept, explore the sequence of first taking an inventory of your patterns, then examining these patterns more deeply, particularly in meditation, and, finally, bringing attention to your patterns just as they occur, in the midst of your daily life.

You might also, near the end of the week, go to a location or situation that typically brings out your greed and craving, especially a place that you frequently visit—such as a store, the home of a friend who has material things that you very much like or want, or a restaurant. Practice mindfulness before entering and then as much as possible notice the patterns that emerge when you are there, in the spirit of nonjudgmental mindfulness. (Several years ago, I cotaught a five-week class called "Greed Management," for which our "final exam" was to do silent walking meditation for thirty minutes in a newly opened Bed, Bath & Beyond superstore.)

Practicing the Fourth Precept: Cultivating Wise Speech

Whereas following the first precept may be ethically most weighty, and whereas working with the second precept is in part a response to powerful economic institutions, working with our speech and communication is most obviously applicable in our day-to-day ethical lives and in our transformative work in the world.

We all know that words can potentially cause both great harm and immense good. Unskillful words can start wars or feuds and lead those who are close to us to suffer deeply. Skillful speech can open hearts, lead to deep insights, and promote healing and transformation. In the texts of the Buddha, we find many reports of practitioners having experiences of awakening after hearing the words of the Buddha. Skillful, compassionate speech can become "holiness in words," in the phrase of Abraham Joshua Heschel, the twentieth-century socially engaged rabbi and writer who walked with Martin Luther King Jr. in the South at the height of the civil rights movement. In such speech, we may remember the traditional Japanese saying that every word we speak has spirit; when we speak a word, we share its spirit with others.

The practice of wise speech is also crucial for us because most of us speak *so much* in our everyday lives, both verbally (including to ourselves) and in written communications. If we can render our speech an alive and powerful part of our spiritual practice, all of a sudden we can be dedicated to our spiritual practice not just for a brief period of sitting meditation or prayer every day but for a large part of the day. We may have to give up the complaint that we supposedly don't have "enough time" for spiritual practice.

As with the other precepts, interpreting and practicing the fourth precept in our times demands great creativity and experimentation. The Buddha gives general guidelines for "right" or "wise" speech, which help us to monitor our behavior and direct us to be mindful of the states of mind and heart behind our speech. He also often speaks about wise speech in the relational context of a community, although little about the broader social or collective aspect of speech.

Practicing in the Individual and Relational Domains

The Buddha often identifies four main dimensions of what he calls "right speech" *(samma vaca)*, which I will call "wise speech" (avoiding some of the dogmatic connotations in the English word *right*):

> Giving up false speech and abstaining from false speech, one speaks truth, adheres to truth, is trustworthy and reliable, deceiving nobody in the world. Giving up malicious speech and abstaining from malicious speech, one does not create division between people by repeating what was heard in other contexts. Instead one reunites those who are divided. One is a promoter of friendships who enjoys concord, rejoices in concord, delights in concord, who speaks to promote concord. Giving up harsh speech and abstaining from harsh speech, one speaks words that are gentle, pleasing to the ear, and lovable, that reach the heart, that are courteous and agreeable to others. Giving up gossip and abstaining from gossip, one speaks what is timely, fact, and good. One speaks to the Dharma and the Dharma life with words that are timely, worth remembering, reasonable, moderate, and beneficial.[17]

In another discourse, the Buddha more succinctly summarizes the nature of wise speech, using "positive" terms: "It is spoken at the right time. It is spoken in truth. It is spoken affectionately. It is spoken beneficially. It is spoken with a mind of good-will."[18]

Bringing these two accounts together, we can identify the qualities of such speech more simply and positively as

1. truthfulness,
2. helpfulness,
3. kindness and goodwill, and
4. appropriateness (including timeliness, non-distractedness, and clear intention).

What is the meaning of these four guidelines? *Truthfulness,* we might say, is the outer expression of mindfulness and wisdom, of clear seeing. It is generally taken as the most important of the four qualities listed. In fact, in Mahayana Buddhist tradition, it is sometimes said that the *bodhisattva,* who aspires for both his or her own awakening and that of others, can, in the interests of skillful means, break any of the precepts but that of truthfulness, of not lying.

In taking truthfulness as a guideline for our speech, we immediately begin to notice the extent to which we are not always so truthful, both in obvious and more subtle ways. We find out, of course, if there are outright lies, but we also become more aware of the more nuanced ways in which we are not being entirely truthful. Although we may not often lie overtly, we can become much more familiar with the gray areas—our exaggerations, half-truths, omissions, and denials. We notice how we exaggerate, often in order to create or sustain a self-image, to make a point, to get something that we want, or to avoid something that we don't want. We explore how we very often utter half-truths or omit mentioning the truth for various reasons. We notice how sometimes we are not even necessarily truthful to ourselves, trying to avoid certain truths about our lives, our relationships, and our intentions.

Yet even if we were typically highly truthful, at times this would be insufficient for wise speech. For, as we know, we can sometimes be very truthful out of an intention to hurt others, as when we "vent" or "dump" truths on others, or when we tell truths that will make others look bad. Hence, it is vital that we balance truthfulness with the three other qualities: helpfulness, kindness, and appropriateness.

Taking the guideline of *helpfulness* particularly instructs us to be careful about our motivations in speaking, to look into whether our intentions are to harm or to create enmity. This invites us further to identify the roots of nonhelpful speech, discerning moments of ill will, self-centeredness, and even hatred. We can again notice both the more obvious and the more nuanced ways in which we are not helpful in our speech; the latter might include acts of omission, subtle disparagement (such as "damning with faint praise"), and passive aggression. And we can particularly cultivate speech that is helpful, that promotes friendship, long-term harmony, a sense of connection, and compassionate response.

Speaking with *kindness and goodwill* counters what the Buddha calls "harsh speech." For it is possible to be helpful in some ways while still remaining somewhat cold, seeing ourselves as superior, or lacking an empathic connection. Practicing by intending to speak with kindness and goodwill brings quickly to our awareness the many ways in which we lack such warmth in our communication, as well as lets us see when our speech is more overtly unkind (and even harmful). We may notice our sarcastic comments, our self-righteousness, our nagging comments that come out of irritation, our harsh judgments of others (or ourselves), our cynicism and negativity, our tendencies to make jokes at the expense of others, and so on. We also cultivate speech that is purposely kind. We might intend, as much as possible, for example, to "speak from the heart," or to bring forth kindness and goodwill as we speak. We can ask ourselves: What is the spirit behind what I'm about to say? We can also use the body as a reference point and ask: How does what I'm saying or about to say feel in my body?

There can be a tremendous transformative power in helpful and kind speech. My mother, Bernice, tells the story of hearing a lecture on human rights issues by the psychiatrist, activist, and author Robert Lifton. Right at the beginning of the question-and-answer period, a woman asked the proverbial "dumb" question, appearing to many in the audience not to have understood the most basic points that Lifton was making. A soft collective groan emanated from the hall after the question. Most seemed to be waiting for Lifton to correct her, letting her know where she was wrong and where she had distorted what he was saying. Instead, he responded with great warmth and considerable compassion as if to a close friend, appreciating her way of seeing things. He then mentioned how his understanding was somewhat different, but that he had learned something by being able to clarify the difference between the two views. Many years later, when I talked about wise speech with my mother, she immediately recalled this interaction. The memory of a minute of kind speech from more than ten years ago was still fresh and present in her mind. The impact on her had been profound.

The fourth guideline is having *appropriate* speech. It includes a good sense of timing and an appropriate topic for our speech, as well as being careful about overly distracted talk. We can think of the Buddha's criticism of what is translated as "gossip" as not so much a criticism of what we might call the communication of "local news," which serves important functions, but rather a questioning of our distracted "chattering." The problem of this latter kind of speech is that it often starts stirring up greed, hatred, and delusion if we are not mindful and careful. Small talk about another person may suddenly turn envious and vindictive, resentful and judgmental.

Practical experiments in this last area can be extremely illuminating. The meditation teacher Joseph Goldstein recommends the practice of committing oneself not to speak about a third party for a week. While doing this practice himself, he noticed the many times in which he was about to talk about a third person in less than helpful or kind ways. He also found that when he didn't talk about a third person, he sometimes had little to say! Similarly, for a week we can explore not having the radio or TV on in the background and notice what that is like; part of the practice of wise speech is to be careful about those with whom we talk and what we take in. Or, third, for a week, we might not pay attention (or minimize the attention) to some area with which normally we would be highly preoccupied and overly compulsive in ways that would lead to distraction. We might, for example, not read about sports or movie stars or politics, or temporarily cease reading certain types of novels or magazines or visiting particular Web sites. The aim of these experiments is not to become ascetic but rather to investigate how we normally act, what our motivations are, and how we tend to distract ourselves.

When we practice these four guidelines of wise speech, not only do we learn a great deal about how we are less than truthful, helpful, kind, and appropriate, but we may also notice that we are stronger or weaker in some of the guidelines. We may want to put more effort into some areas. For example, when I practiced wise speech regularly in a more focused way for three months along with the members of my meditation group, I found that I was pretty good with truthfulness and helpfulness but not always so kind in my communications. It became important to me to bring the intention to be more friendly and warm to my speech, especially on very busy days, when I was interacting with a lot of people and often trying to be "efficient" with my time, sometimes at the expense of basic warmth and empathy.

Members of my group developed a number of ways to support wise speech. One person prone to difficult interchanges with her teenage daughter wrote the four wise-speech guidelines on her hand before certain discussions. She reported that it helped her considerably to avoid habitual negative dynamics with her daughter. Others worked especially to remember the guidelines before answering the telephone, in some cases placing the guidelines on a wall near the phone. I experimented with writing the guidelines on a piece of paper that I placed in front of me at meetings, visible to me but not to others. On another sheet of paper, I took notes on what was happening moment to moment, to give me the energy to pay attention. I remember once noting, toward the end of a meeting, "Getting tired. Sarcastic thoughts developing." That helped me to choose to keep those thoughts to myself.

It is important to note that committing oneself to truthful, helpful, kind, and appropriate speech does not mean being overly "nice." There is an important place for speech that is direct, firm, and critical (without being judgmental). Among the discourses of the Buddha, we find numerous instances of speech of this nature, which particularly address confusion and problematic behavior with little saccharine coating. The key, as always, is the intention and motivation, grounded in understanding, which is why there is such an emphasis on helpfulness and kindness. Of course, it is often very challenging, particularly when there is conflict or injustice, to articulate speech that combines being truthful, direct, firm, and critical with being helpful, kind, and compassionate. It is all too easy to move quickly into the grooves of judgmental, polarizing speech, whether in the midst of interpersonal conflicts or when questioning social or political policies or institutions. This is why cultivating wise speech is a *practice,* a learning process, in which we investigate both the outer expression and the inner patterns of body, heart, and mind.

Practicing in the Collective Domain

How do we practice wise speech and follow the four guidelines—aware of some of the subtleties of wise speech—in relation to the collective aspects of our lives? Here, I give some general suggestions that can help orient us in this complex area.

It is important initially to reflect on how wise speech helps to establish *safety* by providing good conditions not only for spiritual practice but also for community and social life in general. Without truthfulness, which involves not just the absence of outright lying but also the absence of much of the gray area of exaggerations, half-truths, omissions, and so on, it is hard to have trust in others. Furthermore, when we are not truthful, we often have to expend huge amounts of energy, spinning vast webs of thoughts, speech, and actions to protect an original untruth or half-truth, and often feeling anxious and agitated—vulnerable to being found out. Without speech that is primarily motivated by helpfulness, kindness, and goodwill, we similarly feel less safe and may be on edge, guarding against both our own and others' harmful or self-centered motivations and behaviors.

Without such trust and safety, social relationships tend to become strategic rather than cooperative, increasingly full of skepticism and even anxiety and fear about others' intentions. In a community or society in which I can't really trust or feel safe in relation to many others, I tend to look out for "number one," whether number one is my nation, my small community, my family, or even just myself.

In carrying out this collective practice, we may, as in individual practice, start by taking a social inventory of how we collectively do or do *not* follow the four guidelines, and what kind of procedures, norms, policies, or laws support the guidelines. For example, one way of understanding *truthfulness* in a democratic society is in terms of such criteria as accuracy of public information, disclosure of information, transparency of decision making, clarity and depth of public discussion, and openness. Much of the struggle toward a more democratic society can be understood in terms of steadfast work to enhance truthfulness by establishing procedures to ensure that these criteria are met, whether in attempts to give more access to governmental information, to protect whistle-blowers who tell the truth at great personal risk, to safeguard various expressions of freedom of speech, or to support an independent and vigorous media. In this sense, we may understand our work in these areas as a direct expression of our ethics and spirituality, informed by our work in this area in the personal and relational domains.

On the other hand, there are often strong governmental pressures to limit truthfulness. Some people have even made the legal and philosophical claim that it is sometimes appropriate for government leaders and officials to lie to citizens, typically in the interests of some "higher good." In 2002, for example, Theodore Olson, the solicitor general of the United States, addressed the Supreme Court, countering a suit that had been brought by Jennifer Harbury against former high-ranking U.S. officials. Harbury had charged that these officials had lied and covered up the torture and execution of her husband, Efrain Bamaca Velasquez, by the Guatemalan military and CIA. Olson "warned the court to use 'utmost caution' before interpreting the Constitution as guaranteeing citizens a truthful response to informal inquiries of the government." He added that it was "easy to imagine an infinite number of situations...where government officials might quite legitimately have reasons to give false information."[19] (The Supreme Court sided with the government and ruled that individuals could not sue government officials for lying.)

The conventional political uses of half-truths, exaggerations, selective omissions, and propaganda, where they are not outright lies, are pervasive, particularly regarding foreign policy, whether in the United States or elsewhere. Such aspects of unwise speech in particular are often seen as necessary in order to justify violence. And so the U.S. government refuses to pay attention to the number of people that it kills (for example, in Vietnam, Central America, Afghanistan, and Iraq) and provides fabricated evidence and fear-arousing exaggerations in order to start invasions or wars (Vietnam, Nicaragua, and Iraq, among others). It is as if governments fear that the initiation of violence would not be possible if the citizens knew the truth.

We similarly may notice the extent to which public speech does or does not follow the other three qualities of *helpfulness, kindness,* and *appropriateness.* We can see, for example, that much of our public speech, particularly in some of the mass media, has become more mean-spirited. Many commentators have pointed out the growing lack of civility in political discourse in the United States, a trend exacerbated by Web sites that are only minimally guided, if at all, by ethical agreements. This explosion of information also threatens to distract and overwhelm us, making timely and appropriate public dialogue about important issues more difficult.

Spiritually grounded activists may especially benefit by considering the four guidelines and using personal and relational speech practice as a kind of laboratory. How do we tell the truth without demonizing the opponent in judgmental, polarizing, and self-righteous speech—without, in other words, forgetting the final three guidelines? How do we use speech skillfully to help cut through delusion, denial, or deliberate obfuscation while remaining grounded as much as possible in compassion? How can we use language in situations of tension and conflict? How can we, as Thich Nhat Hanh suggests, learn to write not just letters of protest but also "love letters" (presumably sometimes "tough love" letters) to our politicians, using a language that shows some understanding of their situation?[20] In later chapters, I will continue to explore these questions.

Here, I mention one particularly inspiring example of skillful speech along these lines that occurred in Nashville, Tennessee, in 1960, at the height of the civil rights movement. After a number of weeks of student sit-ins to protest segregated lunch counters, coupled with boycotts of downtown stores, tensions were high, but there had been little violence. On the morning of April 19, the home of Z. Alexander Looby, the leading African American lawyer in Nashville, was bombed. A spontaneous march began shortly thereafter, eventually growing to some four thousand participants and ending at the courthouse steps, where a delegation met Ben West, the white mayor.

C. T. Vivian, a young black minister, soon got into a heated argument with Mayor West, criticizing him sharply for failing to condemn the violence and for the actions of the police, while the mayor spoke of what he had done for black people. At that point, Diane Nash, one of the student leaders, intervened:

> Rather than attack West, she appealed to his sense of fairness (which he liked to think of as one of his virtues), asking the mayor if he felt "that it's wrong to discriminate against a person solely on the basis of his race or color." West tried "to answer it frankly and honestly," he said later; "...I could not agree that it was morally right for someone to sell them merchandise and refuse them service." Then she asked if he thought the lunch counters should be desegregated.

First he hemmed and hawed, but Nash was not going to let him off the hook, and she asked again: "Then, Mayor, do you recommend that the lunch counters be desegregated?" West, finally, said, "Yes." The crowd erupted in applause, and West and the protestors hugged each other.[21]

On the basis of one very firm but respectful question to an "opponent" whose humanity was respected, and with the support of a social movement, a large piece of the edifice of segregation in Nashville suddenly fell.

EXERCISE: Cultivating Individual Wise Speech

Work with the four general guidelines for wise speech for a week or longer. As suggested in the discussion of the first and second precepts, first take a general inventory of your patterns, then examine these patterns more deeply, and, finally, bring attention to your patterns as they occur in daily life. Also focus on practicing wise speech in particular activities. Make a commitment, for example, to use the guidelines when answering the telephone, responding to e-mails, talking to a family member, or participating in a meeting. Consider using some of the techniques mentioned, such as keeping a list of the guidelines visible near the phone or computer, or inconspicuously at a meeting table. Set your intention to cultivate wise speech before a given activity. Then notice what you find, where you go into gray areas with speech, where you violate the precept, and what your thoughts and emotions are in these gray areas.

EXERCISE: Cultivating Wise Speech in Groups, Organizations, and the Larger Society

Observe the extent to which groups and organizations of which you are a part follow or don't follow these guidelines. Consider what you might do to help establish intentions, policies, and agreements in these settings that would support relational and collective wise speech.

When you are aware of public speech and discourse—for example, while listening to radio or television or reading newspapers and magazines—notice the extent to which wise speech is followed. When you act in the collective domain, particularly when there is conflict or polarization, how do you speak? How does your speech change when you remember the four guidelines? How might you use your *personal* and *relational* practice as a guide to your *collective* practice? Is there a way that you are drawn to act more publicly to support wise speech in the larger society? What particular issue might you take on?

Practicing the Third and Fifth Precepts: Not Harming Ourselves and Others through Our Sexuality and through the Use of Consciousness-Altering Substances

The third and fifth precepts guide us in relation to two areas, sexuality and the use of substances that shift consciousness, where we often harm ourselves and others with compulsive behavior. Such harmful behavior is, in a number of ways, conditioned and supported by many of our dominant institutions and cultural attitudes.

Yet sexuality and some of the substances that shift consciousness also at times open us up to some of the most profound human experiences possible—to deep intimacy, ecstasy, interconnection and communion, love, self-knowledge, and spiritual insight. How can we approach sexuality and such substances skillfully and wisely (if we choose to enter these territories at all), establishing general safety with the aid of the precepts? Here I give a brief overview concerning the practice of these two precepts.

The traditional interpretations of these two precepts focus almost entirely on preventing harm. Historically, the *third precept* has been understood somewhat narrowly to refer to avoiding socially prohibited forms of sexuality—for laypersons, avoiding sexual intercourse outside of marriage, and for monastics, remaining celibate.

Contemporary *individual and relational* practice of the third precept usually is based on respecting our own and others' commitments to intimate relationships, including but not restricted to marriage. Such practice tends particularly to illuminate and work through qualities that often lead us to harm others and ourselves through our sexuality—greed (strongly wanting to have certain experiences or to "possess" another), self-centeredness (thinking that satisfying *my* desires matters more than honoring the intentions of others), and delusion (reflected in compulsive and relatively unconscious patterns of behavior). More positively, the precept supports the further development of a sense of connection with and caring for others, contentment with what is, and at times restraint and renunciation (in the face of strong desires). It helps us develop mindfulness, wisdom, compassion, and clarity about intentions in our sexuality.

As we practice in the *collective* domain, we become more aware of how our society commodifies and exploits sexuality, particularly young women's sexuality, in large part to sell products, from automobile batteries to chewing gum to alcohol. This commercialization of sexuality, although seemingly also linked to its freer and more open expression in formerly sexually repressive cultures, also has a number of harmful effects. It is connected to the objectification by men of women's bodies, to a high degree of violence against women, and to women typically feeling unsafe and afraid in many situations, particularly when alone and at night.

As when we take on the other precepts, we take responsibility to work individually, relationally, and collectively to establish conditions of greater safety. In the context of the third precept, this might mean working to transform the attitudes, cultural values, and institutions that lead to objectification, violence, and other forms of harm, whether on the street or among friends and partners. It means clarifying values and developing alternative contemporary visions, institutions, and practices of sexuality that support not just greater safety but lives of wisdom, caring, and spiritual exploration.

Traditionally, the *fifth precept* in the Asian context was particularly related to abuses committed by those imbibing alcoholic drinks. Counseling abstinence, the Buddha speaks of the dangers of such drinks: "Fools commit evil deeds as a result of drunkenness and cause other people, who are negligent, to act accordingly."[22] He points to the safety given to oneself and others by following the precept; a practitioner "gives freedom from danger, freedom from animosity, freedom from oppression to limitless numbers of beings."[23]

In contemporary settings, working with this precept is vital in societies where there is so much harm connected with the abuse of various kinds of intoxicants and consciousness-altering substances. Indeed, Thich Nhat Hanh gives a considerably broadened account of the fifth precept, offering guidance about "mindful consumption" of what is helpful or harmful to both mind and body in general, including our conversations and the information we take in from the mass media: "A proper diet is crucial for self-transformation and for the transformation of society."[24]

Individual practice helps us to be aware of the urge to use intoxicants (or to take in other substances). We can be mindful of a wide variety of states that may lie beneath the surface of such urges: whether dissatisfaction, tension (physical, emotional, or mental), or sadness from which we are trying to escape, or more pleasant states, such as joy, happiness, or relaxation, which we are attempting to produce, maintain, or amplify. There may be a number of habitual tendencies, some passed down over generations, to seek to control experience in these ways. Working through these habitual tendencies may reveal deep patterns, which can take considerable time and energy to transform.

When we practice in the *collective* domain, especially in the United States, we may become aware of the great harm, as well as considerable confusion and social hypocrisy, related to consciousness-altering substances. Hundreds of thousands of people die prematurely from the effects of cigarettes and alcohol, both of which are legal. Hundreds of thousands are imprisoned for possession of illegal substances such as marijuana and cocaine, which kill a small fraction of the total number of people killed by legal drugs. Those so imprisoned make up the bulk of the current prison population in the United States, a disproportionate number of them poor and young African Americans and Latinos.

Practicing the social aspect of the fifth precept might mean acting to diminish the harm caused by intoxicants. It might mean working with those who are or have been addicted, reducing the great harm caused by legal drugs, establishing a saner and less hypocritical national drug policy, or developing better educational programs, especially for young people, about the whole range of intoxicants.

EXERCISE: Practicing Care in Your Sexuality

For a week, give special attention to the third precept. Remember it each morning (and evening), and let the precept closely guide your behavior and awareness. Notice what draws your attention. Notice also when you come into a gray area involving sexuality. In these kinds of situations, be especially mindful of your body, heart, and mind. Reflect on whether your behavior is harmful to another or to yourself, and reflect on your basic intentions. Within the context of sexuality in a committed relationship, what supports or does not support greater safety, intimacy, and love? Further, how might part of your practice be to become more active in helping to establish collective safety in relation to sexuality?

EXERCISE: Developing Care in the Use of Consciousness-Altering Substances

For a week, abstain from alcohol and other "recreational" drugs. Be mindful of your experience when you are around those using drugs (including alcohol) or when you have the urge to use drugs. What occurs in your body, heart, and mind at these times? Notice your experience when you use other substances that shift consciousness, perhaps cigarettes or coffee or chocolate. Also, how might you respond personally to the great suffering related to drugs, as part of your practice of the fifth precept?

EXERCISE: Activism and the Ethical Precepts

For many of us, it is very helpful to be selective about our activism and to stay focused on one major concern or issue over a sustained period, rather than try to do too many things at once. That one concern might be related to your organization, your community, or the larger society. If you are not already involved with a particular issue, working with the precepts can help you clarify the area in which you are drawn to act.

In exploring the social aspects of the five precepts, to which concern or issue related to which precept(s) were you most drawn? Is there a concern that "calls" you to make a commitment? If so, what steps might you take to be involved? And how might you link your actions with your personal and relational practice of the precept? If you are already working on an issue, how does it help to connect your action with your understanding and practice of the relevant precept?

Chapter Two
MINDFULNESS IN ACTION

In Sri Lanka in early 2002, the grass-roots organization Sarvodaya, grounded in Buddhist practice, and its director, Dr. A. T. Ariyaratne, "Ari" to many of his friends, called for a mass "peace meditation" to take place in March of that year at the sacred city of Anuradhapura. Their intention was to support the cease-fire of February 2002, which had ended two decades of civil war. The conflict had been rooted in tensions and inequities in the relationship between the minority Hindu Tamils of the north and the majority Buddhist Sinhalese, but it had been fanned by extremists on both sides. It had led to the loss of sixty-five thousand lives, grave damage to the political and economic systems, and ongoing trauma in the life of the land.

On the day of the meditation, it became apparent that a massive number of people had come, eventually estimated at 650,000. Joanna Macy gives a moving account of what transpired:

> I arrived at Anuradhapura on the day of the meditation.... When I got there, people were streaming in from all directions.... Everyone was dressed in white and moving in silence. They had arrived from all over the country on foot and on trains, bicycles, and, according to one person's count, four thousand buses....
>
> The meditation ceremony took place at 3 p.m. Members of the clergy of all the religions of Sri Lanka were gathered on a platform, and each said a few words. In front of them on a slightly lower stage,

surrounded by flowers, was Ari. After the spoken prayers, he began to lead us all in *anapanasati,* mindfulness of breathing in and breathing out. The silence was the most exquisite sound I've ever heard. It was the sound of . . . 650,000 people being quiet together, in the biggest meditation ever held on planet Earth. I said to myself, "This is the sound of bombs not exploding, of land mines not going off, of machine guns not firing. This is possible."[1]

Engaging in mindfulness practice and other forms of meditation has become increasingly frequent at public events and demonstrations. These practices serve as a helpful preparation for being more attentive, less distracted, wiser, and more open-hearted in these activities. Such innovative uses of the 2,500-year-old practice of mindfulness point to a vital way in which there can be a deep integration between inner and outer transformation, through the cultivation of a "mindfulness in action" that can build on and complement our "mindfulness on the cushion."

THE TRADITION OF MINDFULNESS PRACTICE

The cultivation of mindfulness (*sati* in the Pali language) is the distinctive spiritual practice taught by the Buddha, offering a "direct path" toward awakening, as spoken in his "discourse on attending with mindfulness," the *Satipatthana Sutta.*[2] Mindfulness practice complements a number of practices that develop concentration and deep absorption; in large part these are inherited from the Indian yogic repertoire of the time of the Buddha. Although both kinds of practices have been seen as vital for most practitioners in Buddhist traditions, mindfulness practice has been understood to be the primary source of the liberating insights that transform the roots of confusion and suffering and that open us to the "deathless," to *nibbana* (or *nirvana,* in Sanskrit).

What is mindfulness? In one of the ancient Buddhist commentaries on this discourse, it is said that mindfulness means "presence of mind, attentiveness to the present. . . . It has the characteristic of not wobbling, i.e. not floating away from the object. Its function is absence of confusion or nonforgetfulness."[3] Meditation teacher Sylvia Boorstein speaks of mindfulness as "the aware, balanced acceptance of present experience." She goes on, "It isn't more complicated than that. It is opening to or receiving the present moment, pleasant or unpleasant, just as it is, without either clinging to it or rejecting it."[4]

So mindfulness is a way of being attentive to whatever is predominant in the present moment of experience, whether of our inner experiences of body sensations, emotions, thoughts, and so on, or of our outer experiences of external objects and other beings. What is distinctive about this way of attending is, on the one hand, its directness, focus, fullness, and ability to penetrate deeply and, on the other, its nonjudgmental, nonpreferential, and nonreactive quality. To be fully mindful is to approach one's moment-to-moment experience freshly, as much as possible not bringing the cognitive and emotional baggage of the past, which leads us as well to project into the future. (It is possible, however, to look freshly at how the past and future are present in our experience.) With this openness, there can be a great sensitivity to and curiosity about what is occurring in the present moment, even a sense of attending to a wondrous and awesome mystery.

This suggests that mindfulness tends also to have what we would call an emotional or affective quality—a quality of interest and even warmth. In other words, clear seeing may come in its maturity with kindness and caring. In Asian Buddhist languages such as Sanskrit, Pali, and Chinese, there is not a rigid separation of the mental and the emotional in the same ways that we generally find in Western languages—especially in the last few hundred years—through the Western emphasis on an "objective" knowing disconnected from the emotions. Indeed, my favorite understanding of mindfulness is suggested by the Chinese pictogram used to translate *sati*. It is composed of two symbols. The first is "present moment." The second is a combination of "heart" and "roof" (or "home"). So we might say that mindfulness is a way to find a home for our hearts in the present moment.[5]

Typically in contemporary settings, the practitioner learns mindfulness first by focusing on his or her individual experience, undergoing an initial training separate from the more relational and collective aspects of experience and from ordinary actions in the world. On the basis of this training, it becomes possible to sustain mindfulness in more complex actions and interactions, in a variety of settings. And so the Buddha speaks of first finding a quiet place and starting with mindfulness of breathing:

> Having gone to a forest, the foot of a tree, or an empty building, a practitioner sits down with legs crossed and body erect. Establishing mindfulness in the present, one breathes in mindfully, breathes out mindfully.[6]

The Buddha teaches four main ways to cultivate mindfulness, linked to four different aspects of experience. The first way is *mindfulness of the body,* often beginning with mindfulness of breathing, and commonly understood as the development of present-centered awareness of bodily sensations, including the sensations of the breath. In a highly mind-oriented culture such as ours, this kind of practice is particularly valuable in helping to cut through the mental "cloud" of repetitive thoughts in which many of us live much or most of the time, bringing us back, so to speak, to our senses.

The second way, *mindfulness of "feeling-tone" (vedana),* involves paying attention to the quality of pleasant, unpleasant, or neutral that is present with every moment of experience, on a scale that ranges from ecstasy to agony. Attending to the feeling-tone is particularly important because when we are relatively unconscious of feeling-tone, we tend to grasp pleasant experiences, push away unpleasant ones, and "space out" with neutral experiences. Such tendencies are the roots, on the Buddha's analysis, of suffering, of the so-called three poisons of greed, aversion, and delusion. Reginald Ray, a teacher and scholar of Tibetan Buddhism, once said that the entirety of Buddhist practice occurs in the interval between feeling-tone and grasping (or pushing away), over and over again, moment to moment.

The third way, *mindfulness of the "mind and heart" (citta),* is usually interpreted to mean the clear awareness of the presence of particular "mental and emotional formations" *(cittasamskara).* Here, we identify and are present to various formations such as desire, anger, distractedness, concentration, joy, peace, planning, remembering, and so on (the quality of pleasant, unpleasant, or neutral is also a mental formation but because of its importance is treated separately, as the second way of attending). In the contemporary practice of mindfulness, the usual instruction is first to know that a particular formation is occurring, which helps us to begin to notice the range of our basic patterns of mind and heart and the details of our experience perhaps as we may never have noticed them before. Then we are invited to investigate more deeply the qualities of these states.

The fourth form of mindfulness is *mindfulness of the broader patterns of experience* (of *dhammas*). In the *Satipatthana Sutta,* the Buddha mentions several teachings that provide lenses to help us see more clearly the nature of experience. So, for example, a practitioner might work with the core teaching of the Four Noble Truths: (1) we all suffer in life to a significant extent; (2) the cause of suffering is the compulsive grasping or pushing away of aspects of our experience; (3) peace, or the overcoming of suffering, is possible; and (4) there is a practical path toward such peace. The practitioner might try to note when there is suffering, examine its nature, and look for how there might be *compulsive* grasping or pushing away. Similarly, one might explore the nature of peace and what leads to it.

One way to interpret this fourth way of training is to understand it is a second-level study of the more complex patterns and dynamics of our experience, based on having learned first, in the first three foundations, to identify more clearly some of the basic constituents. We are particularly instructed to examine those dynamics that lead to suffering and those that lead to freedom. This helps to deconstruct, as it were, the seeming solidity of our patterns of reactivity, to bring awareness and clarity where there previously was automatic, relatively unconscious behavior.

We then extend this fourfold training, which occurs initially in the simplified "laboratory" of meditation, to the further complexities of ordinary day-to-day actions and interaction. Since the intention of mindfulness practice is simply to be aware of what predominates in our experience, such a practice is particularly suited to any ordinary "informal" moment of our lives.

Yet perhaps surprisingly there is fairly little in the discourses of the Buddha on the further specifics of such "mindfulness in action," for example, on training in mindfulness in such areas as speech, relationships, work, and community. It has been left to later Buddhist traditions (and to other spiritual traditions) to clarify more specifically the nature of this further mindfulness training. In the development of the Zen traditions of China and Japan, for example, there has been a strong emphasis on cultivating awareness of the details of everyday life, with a particular focus on mindfulness during various forms of manual labor; such work had been generally prohibited for monks and nuns in India.

However, the present and future generations of mindfulness practitioners in the West, the vast majority of whom are not monastics, have, I believe, a special calling: to explore new forms of training and practice that support mindfulness (and spiritual development generally) in the very midst of everyday life, including social action.

THE CONTEMPORARY CHALLENGE OF CULTIVATING MINDFULNESS IN ACTION

So what does it take to be mindful in the midst of our everyday lives, in the midst of action? We may be able to be relatively mindful on the meditation cushion or during retreats, but we often find ourselves out "in the world" without much support, feeling somewhat lost, sometimes feeling as if we have been "kicked out" of paradise. I remember how in my initial years of meditation practice in my twenties I would often experience wonderful depths of mindfulness, concentration, and peace during retreats, typically more than I had ever experienced previously, only to return to a shared household with roommates, sometimes soon finding myself in conflict or distraction, wondering where those states of mind and heart had gone. Of course, this is a common experience—near the end of a retreat he cotaught, Jack Kornfield looked over some fifty radiant faces and reflected, "It's so peaceful in here. Of course, you haven't opened your mouths yet!"

We may somehow expect that we will magically grow to be mindful, wise, and loving all or most of the time simply because we have done retreats or are meditating thirty minutes every day. Yet in the teachings of the Buddha, the emphasis is on the need for a strong effort and clear intention in order to develop a consistent and ongoing mindfulness. Indeed, when we find ways to be present to more and more of our ordinary experience, our practice takes off and our learning accelerates.

How then can we find effective ways to cultivate mindfulness and wisdom in our relationships, communities, work, and political lives? Our work, that which we do during most of our waking lives, is central. As the poet, activist, and Zen practitioner Gary Snyder put it in 1977, "I wouldn't sit ten hours a day [every day]...because there's too much other work in the world to be done...if we're going to have a democratic world that isn't fueled with nuclear energy.... We damn well better learn that our meditation is primarily going to be our work with our hands."[7]

In the remainder of this chapter, I identify three main contemporary ways of developing mindfulness in action. The first focuses on the inner work of individual mindfulness practice. The second is a central *relational* mindfulness practice related to speech. The third involves developing mindfulness in the *collective* domain, in relation to the larger society.

FINDING THE THREAD OF AWARENESS OF BODY, HEART, AND MIND

Cultivating the ability to be mindful in action often begins with the basics of mindfulness practice, setting time aside to develop mindfulness of the core constituents of experience—of body, heart, mind, and the broader patterns of our experience. Indeed, many contemporary psychologists understand maturity to involve the development of each of these three main aspects of ourselves—somatic, emotional, and cognitive—as well as their integration. Yet each of us is usually more developed in one of the aspects than in others; development is typically uneven, and sometimes quite unbalanced—both individually and culturally.

In strengthening mindfulness of body, heart, and mind, a similar process often occurs. While ultimately we need, I believe, to be deeply mindful in each of these areas of experience, manifesting a kind of presence that integrates the three areas, we often "lead" with mindfulness of one area. This occurs in much the same way that the Hindu tradition offers four kinds of "yogas," or spiritual paths, for persons of different temperaments: a path of knowledge *(jnana yoga)* for more intellectual or "mind-oriented" types, a path of devotion *(bhakti yoga)* for more emotional types, a path of work and service *(karma yoga)* for more active types, and a path of "psychophysical" exploration *(raja yoga)* for those interested in exploring "experimentally" the nature of the self.[8]

What is particularly required for mindfulness in action is to go deeply enough in our mindfulness of a particular area, so that it provides us with a *thread* that weaves our moment-to-moment experience together. To do this is to cultivate a mindfulness of body, heart, or mind that is available to a significant extent in the midst of action. Such mindfulness can serve as a touchstone that helps us to come back to ourselves continually, returning from a state of being on automatic pilot.

How might we train and practice further so that we can increasingly "lead" with body, heart, and/or mind in our everyday lives, in our mindfulness in action?

Leading with the Body

For many of us, some awareness of our bodies is the key thread to being mindful while active, particularly in such a highly mind-oriented culture as ours. One of my main mentors, meditation teacher John Travis, was once talking to me about how many of the great Asian teachers lived in protected environments such as monasteries, where they had constant reminders to be mindful, as well as lives entirely oriented toward spiritual practice. Few of us in the everyday world have such favorable conditions. So what can we do? John went on to talk about the importance of awareness of our bodies. Our bodily sensations are always present and can ground our mindfulness. Then he added, "Let your body be your monastery. Let awareness of your body support your mindfulness as strongly and continually as a monastery might."

Somehow that sentence electrified me. My early years of meditation had brought me back to the life of my bodily senses in ways that had dramatically changed my experience. I loved to listen for long periods to the wind or a creek, using sounds as meditation objects. Hungry for more meditation time as a graduate student, and without a car, I delighted in doing walking meditation through the streets of Boston when doing errands or going to school. On retreats, I was moved to live more and more in the body, through both sitting and walking meditation, often going for weeks primarily aware of bodily sensations. Later, John guided me to ground yet more fully in body awareness, particularly through awareness of the whole body and of the "center" (or *hara*), the area of the belly just above the abdomen, which is often seen as a place of grounding in the martial arts.

In a wide range of daily life activities, I practiced body awareness, endeavoring to keep tangible the thread of mindfulness of body during meetings, on walks, in interactions, while talking with friends, and even while on the computer. I found it a very skillful tool, particularly in environments centered on thinking and information, such as meetings, where the somatic and emotional dimensions of experience are often ignored. Grounding myself in the body was also helpful when I had strong and sometimes difficult emotions, helping me remember to be mindful of the emotions. Being aware of my body (whether through a focused awareness of breath, of a particular part of the body in contact with a chair, or of the whole body) helped me to remember that I was experiencing an emotion —as a person, embodied, in a particular space and time. This made it easier to avoid simply staying locked in mental and emotional reactivity.

Some of us have good initial mindfulness of body and can find this thread of mindfulness more quickly. Others, like me, need sustained practice, often over a period of many years, before the awareness of the body becomes like a mostly constant companion who eventually doesn't usually need to be reminded to come along. For some of us, such training might also take the form of a body discipline, such as yoga, the martial arts, and other forms. Such disciplines stress training in present-centered body awareness, often involving not just individual but also dyadic and group practices.

Leading with the Heart

Some of us lead more with our hearts. Our awareness of our hearts' intentions grounds us in the present moment and brings ongoing mindfulness in the midst of our activities. In the Buddhist tradition, this approach is especially nourished through lovingkindness and related practices. In the Christian tradition, it appears as the constant "prayer of the heart" (the "Jesus Prayer"), developed in the Orthodox tradition to put into practice Paul's invocation "Pray unceasingly" (1 Thess. 5:17). This in turn echoes Jewish themes, particularly King David's account of how, while pursuing all the manifold activities of a king, he could still remain in a present-centered awareness of God: "I keep Yahweh before me always" (Psalms 16:8). We might also remember Gandhi's Hindu-based devotional practice of constant silent prayer of the name of God (Ram); the moment after Gandhi was shot by an assassin in 1948, he uttered only "Ram." Or we might be inspired by Julia Butterfly Hill, the contemporary environmental activist, who speaks of asking of every action, "Am I acting out of love?"

Lovingkindness practice, which we will explore in more depth in chapter 5, also employs a technique of constant internal repetition of phrases in order to open and activate the heart moment to moment. In such a practice, we repeat over and over again phrases like "May I (or another) be safe...be happy...be healthy...live with ease," in what my friend and colleague Sylvia Boorstein calls a kind of "fervent prayer." Ultimately, the phrases are secondary to the increased presence of the open heart, wishing well to oneself and to others.

If the heart is our main thread of presence, we may practice some variety of lovingkindness or work with repeated prayers, phrases, and intentions that keep the heart open. So, for example, one of my students does lovingkindness practice as much as possible during the day, particularly while driving. A friend works regularly during the day with *tonglen,* the Tibetan practice in which we take in pain and suffering and send out warmth and blessings.[9]

There are also a number of other basic heart techniques and practices. One is to keep attention centered in the center of the chest, in the so-called heart-center area, and to act out of this somatically grounded awareness. Another is to keep remembering the intention to act out of love, in all actions and interactions. A third practice is to find ways to center oneself in kindness and caring, perhaps using specific words or images.

Leading with the Mind

Some of us lead more with our minds, with reflection or with our understanding of the dynamics of experience and particularly of our own minds. Our mindfulness can become very active and attuned moment by moment as we become very interested in how our experience works. One way in which this can occur is by being especially attentive to moments of reactivity, suffering, or distress. My first meditation teacher, Joseph Goldstein, gave me a practice question that I have used frequently: "If there's suffering, where's the attachment?" I would be attentive to moments of suffering, and then ask myself whether some kind of attachment was present. My strong interest in understanding the roots of suffering helped me to inquire and look more deeply in the very midst of ordinary experience. Moments of difficulty and reactivity—a strong emotional reaction in an interaction with someone close, sustained physical pain and aversion to the pain, waking up in the middle of the night with anxiety, fear about finances—can thus be wake-up calls for practice, reminders to be mindful, starting points for seeing more clearly (and ultimately acting skillfully). When we have such interest and intentions, the development of mindfulness can accelerate wonderfully.

Cultivating mindfulness while leading with our minds can occur in a number of other ways as well. For example, we can use various teachings as lenses through which to examine our experience, in the spirit of the fourth way of attending mindfully, much as we do throughout this book. We may study, for example, how impermanence arises in our experience and how we tend to want or assume permanence of a relationship, the state of our bodies, or an external situation. We may examine how the structures of self manifest moment to moment in self-image, habits, preferences, and so on. We may inquire into how we might more fully see interdependence in our experience. We may reflect on the causes and conditions leading to a particular situation.

Toward an Integrated Mindfulness of Body, Heart, and Mind

Mindfulness in action ultimately calls for the ability to be aware of each of the three fundamental aspects of ourselves, body, heart, and mind, even as we may lead with one of them. Indeed, these three aspects complement each other and help us avoid imbalances. We can become very grounded and present in our bodies, yet we may be without the warmth of an open heart or the mind's insight. We may lead with our open hearts, yet without adequate grounding in our bodies, or without wise perspective, we can easily become emotionally overwhelmed. And we can, perhaps most obviously in a more cerebral culture, lead with our minds and generate a rather mental or intellectual spirituality in which our thinking and inquiry are not well integrated with our hearts and with our concrete embodied being and actions. For many of us who are initially more oriented to thinking, in fact, it can be highly useful to focus on developing body-based or heart-based awareness, suspending the typical rule of mind over experience and exploring the autonomous intelligence of these other aspects of ourselves.

How might we experience a mature mindfulness in action? We would be able to be grounded in our bodies, with our hearts open and accessible to ourselves and others, and our minds clear and able to discern both more individual and more universal patterns of experience, both inside and outside. We would, as it were, honor the "multiple intelligences" of our being, respecting the relative autonomy and integrity of their different voices and inviting these voices into our lives and actions.

EXERCISE: Finding the Thread of Awareness in Daily Life

Which "thread of awareness" feels most accessible or most developed to you? How developed are the other two threads? How might they be developed? Where do you feel drawn to lead with your mindfulness (recognizing that often it can be helpful to learn to lead where we are less developed)? What kind of supports, both individual and communal, help to develop your chosen thread of mindfulness in your daily life?

Being aware of where you intend to lead with your mindfulness, you might set an intention in the morning, or before a specific activity, to have that aspect of mindfulness be present. So we might set an intention before a particular meeting, such as "Let me be aware of my body as much as possible," or "Let me interact with others from my heart," or "Let me track my mind carefully, being especially attentive to when I am reactive."

MINDFULNESS IN SPEECH

As I suggested in the last chapter, working with our speech is vital to our engaged lives. Cultivating mindfulness in speech provides a foundational practice for our relational and collective lives, whether we are with one person or acting within the context of a group, organization, community, or the larger society. Such a practice is a basis for wise, skillful, and compassionate action.

Yet being mindful in speech is difficult. Speech, whether in conversations or at meetings, is often fast-paced, linked with an action orientation in which we seek some immediate outcome and in which we often forget about the *process* leading to that outcome. Task-oriented speech is often cognitively oriented and typically disconnected from an awareness of the heart or body or even the mind; thus it rarely occurs with mindfulness or reflection. Being mindful in speech is also challenging because of the complexity of our relationships and the wide range of emotions and thoughts that arise. At other times, others' speech seems to us hostile or harmful, and it is difficult to be mindful when we feel threatened. Furthermore, attention to mindful and wise speech may not have been much of a focus in our lives. Many of us, through most of our lives, have probably approached speech without much consciousness or intention, perhaps assuming that we don't need to think about how we speak.

My own interest in wise speech was catalyzed more than twenty years ago, when after several years of meditation practice, a close friend told me rather bluntly, "You're not very mindful when you speak! Everything just comes out quickly and automatically." Although I felt shocked, something about what she said sank in. I had to admit that she was right, that I wanted to develop more mindfulness when speaking. I wanted to find a way to cultivate mindfulness in speech as a practice.

So what are the elements of such a practice? A starting point, of course, is training in the fundamentals of mindfulness practice, a necessary basis for cultivating mindfulness in the more complex activity of speech. On that basis, we can begin to follow the four guidelines for wise speech: truthfulness, helpfulness, kindness and goodwill, and appropriateness. As we have seen, implementing such guidelines invites us to be mindful particularly when we find ourselves violating the guidelines or entering gray areas. We begin to notice more clearly the intentions, motivations, and self-images that are present when we don't quite tell the truth, are not helpful or kind, or are somewhat lost or distracted. We become attentive to the exaggerations, the omissions, the sarcasm, and the judgments, as well as the somatic, emotional, and mental patterns connected with these speech acts. We see more clearly how much of unwise speech comes out of our reactivity, when we grasp some real or imagined pleasant experience or push away something we don't like. We can also be mindful of when we are truthful, helpful, kind, or appropriate in our speech. What does that feel like?

But what helps us to be mindful *in the midst of speaking and listening?*

Developing "50-50" Attention

A basic capacity demanded by mindfulness in speech, as well as more generally by mindfulness in action, is *the ability to sustain both "internal" and "external" attention simultaneously in the midst of a particular activity.*

John Travis introduced this perspective to me, pointing out that in our culture our attention is usually almost entirely directed to what is "outside"—not surprising in a culture in which "inner work" and the inner dimension of religion have largely been forgotten or marginalized for many centuries. When we meditate, we often give close to 100 percent attention to the "inner." John asked: "What does mindfulness in action look like when we have 50 percent inner attention and 50 percent outer attention? And what makes this '50-50' awareness possible in our active lives?"

To carry out such a practice in our speech, we need to have developed one of the threads of awareness of body, heart, or mind sufficiently so that it can ground our inner mindfulness without a great deal of effort, at the same time that we attend to the outside world. Some people attend to the breath, others to the contact with a chair, still others to the whole body. One friend finds that awareness of his feet on the floor is central to his maintaining mindfulness in speech. Others keep attentive to both the bodily sensations around the heart and the intention to "speak from the heart."

When such threads of inner awareness are present, we can more readily attend not just to the threads but to the general flow of inner experience, more easily noticing any bodily reactions or responses, as well as emotions and thoughts catalyzed by the verbal interaction. With practice, we can notice particularly when there is reactivity in relation to something that has been said by another, as evident in our commentaries, judgments, and tendencies to speak back reactively—perhaps in sarcasm, a quick comeback, a passive-aggressive joke, or a judgmental comment.

The continual setting of the *intention* to be mindful in speech is also a crucial element of this practice. Although learning to be mindful in speech is not easy and usually requires that we first develop general mindfulness, the fact remains that it is more difficult to *remember* to be mindful than to be mindful itself. Hence, setting an intention before any verbal interaction and finding ways to renew this intention periodically are crucial.

We can also train and practice. The following dyad practice can be carried out in group workshop or retreat settings, as well as with a friend or partner (much as we might practice a martial art), as a "mindfulness in action" practice.

EXERCISE: A Dyad Practice to Cultivate Mindfulness in Speech

1. First reflect on how you would like to grow or learn in terms of cultivating mindfulness in action. What are you already good at? Where do you have difficulties? What is your current practice of wise speech? What for you is the most important area in which to learn? (Responses to these questions can furnish the content for a conversation in this exercise.)

2. Work with a partner. Each person will have a chance to be both a speaker and a listener. The first person will speak for five minutes, with the second person as listener; then the second person will be the speaker for five minutes, with the first person as listener.

a. Here are the instructions for the role of the speaker: First bear in mind the four guidelines for wise speech, and consider what each of them might mean concretely in the upcoming interaction. Attempt to stay somewhat grounded in the body, at least 20 percent or so (being aware of the body while speaking is generally harder than while listening), and, if possible, be aware of any significant inner experiences that occur while you're speaking. The content of your communication can be an exploration of the questions mentioned in 1.

b. Here are the instructions for the role of the listener: Also bear in mind the four guidelines and consider their concrete meanings for the interaction, particularly in terms of listening. Try to cultivate a 50-50 differentiation of attention, with 50 percent inner attention, grounded especially in the body, and 50 percent outward attention to the speaker and his or her words. In this outward attention, you usually stay more or less silent. You thus gives 50 percent of your attention to listening inwardly, being present for your own process of commentary, reactions, distractions, and so on. In other words, there is an absorption not only in the words and being of the speaker. This may feel difficult. Sometimes we think we can't function if we are attending inwardly, that we need all of our attention to manage; hence we often need to experiment with attending inwardly in this kind of "training" situation.

3. Use a clock or alarm or another person to time the five-minute periods.

4. Before beginning each role, the two participants can take half a minute to set intentions.

5. If you are feeling distracted as a speaker, stop for a moment, coming back to an awareness of your body and/or heart, and renew your intentions. Attend to your self and the other much as you would attend to the breath. When your mind wanders, simply return to the focus of attention.

6. After each person has completed both roles, take another five minutes to debrief, talking informally. As much as possible main-

tain the 50-50 differentiation of attention during this interaction. Explore what you experienced in each role. What did you notice or learn? How are you drawn to developing further the practice of wise speech? What will support you? Before beginning this informal debriefing, again take half a minute to set intentions.

7. To end the exercise, you might bow or otherwise signify your appreciation for your partner's helping you to practice and learn!

Maintaining mindfulness in speech is hard for most of us, requiring considerable practice and a retraining of attention so as to monitor closely both the inner *and* the outer while in the midst of activity. Support from others to remind us of our intention to be mindful in speech is also crucial. In any case, experiment with what works—enjoy your explorations of mindfulness in speech!

MINDFULNESS IN RELATIONAL AND COLLECTIVE SETTINGS

Mindfulness practice as taught by the Buddha has historically been interpreted primarily as a personal and inner practice. Despite comments in the *Satipatthana Sutta* about contemplating the four ways of attending "both internally and externally," there has been little emphasis in the Theravada tradition on mindfulness of the outer world—of the qualities of the natural world, of other human beings, of groups and communities, or of larger systems.

In the Mahayana tradition, there has been more of an emphasis on bringing mindfulness into the world, through a focus on interdependence, nonduality, and attending to outer as well as inner phenomena. Still, the basic mindfulness practices have remained mostly directed toward inner experience.

In our time, there is considerable interest in extending the notion of mindfulness into these other settings, based on understanding mindfulness most generally as a kind of *open presence to what is.* At least two kinds of questions naturally arise: (1) How might we be mindful or aware in groups, organizations, communities, and societies or in the natural world? (2) How do we keep both an inner- and an outer-directed attention when mindful of these phenomena, similar to the practice of mindful speech suggested earlier?

A number of socially engaged Buddhists have helped to respond to these questions. Alan Senauke, Zen teacher and former director of the Buddhist Peace Fellowship, for example, speaks of cultivating mindfulness of relational dynamics in a way that combines inner and outer attention:

> A practice that I often do is to read the energy in a situation. To be mindful in this way is an important tool for me in interpersonal or social settings. First, I read my own energy. Am I anxious? Am I wired? Am I depressive? Am I angry? Am I joyful? Am I tired? I read whatever is there. Then I begin to tune into the energy of the situation, the energy of the people, the energy in the space, sometimes in an evaluative way. Of course, I have to be careful not to fool myself into believing that I'm actually reading someone's mind, even if I am mindful of the person's or group's energy.[10]

For Thich Nhat Hanh, even the most basic mindfulness, whether of our inner experience or of an outer object like an orange or a tree, tells us about larger relational and collective patterns. Through mindfulness, we begin to explore the reality of interdependence, of what he calls "interbeing." Writing about responding to the suffering during the war in Vietnam, Thich Nhat Hanh maintains more generally that mindfulness must also focus on the outer events in the world:

> When I was in Vietnam, so many of our villages were being bombed. Along with my monastic brothers and sisters, I had to decide what to do. Should we continue to practice in our monasteries, or should we leave the meditation halls in order to help the people who were suffering under the bombs? After careful reflection, we decided to do both—to go out and help people and to do so in mindfulness. We called it engaged Buddhism. Mindfulness must be engaged. Once there is seeing, there must be acting....We must be aware of the real problems of the world. Then, with mindfulness, we will know what to do and what not to do to be of help.[11]

Another related way that mindfulness can be brought into the world is through "bearing witness," deliberately attending to difficult or problematic relational and collective realities. For example, Bernie Glassman, a Zen teacher who has developed several communities linking Zen practice, everyday life, and social action, has conducted an annual retreat at Auschwitz and regular "street retreats" in which participants live on urban streets, typically for five days, with minimal money and no shelter or beds. At such retreats, mindfulness practice helps the participants to open to an awareness of a broad range of inner and outer phenomena, including the experiences and stories of the other participants, awakening a "desire to learn":

> It happens a lot to me when I encounter a situation I don't understand. It generally involves suffering. . . . When I enter a situation that is too much for me and I don't understand—I have a desire to sit there, to stay a while. . . . The people and situations I'm talking about are a metaphor for our whole society. . . . The human condition is laid more bare.[12]

Others have also chosen to conduct retreats or to meditate in settings where awareness of social problems is inescapable, rather than at protected retreat centers. For over twenty-five years, there have been silent meditations as part of protests against the continued construction and testing of nuclear weapons. These meditations have occurred, for example, at the Nevada Test Site, Rocky Flats in Colorado, Livermore Laboratory in California, and Los Alamos National Laboratory in New Mexico. Some have carried out mindfulness practice regularly for many hours preceding planned executions, for example, at San Quentin Prison near San Francisco or at political demonstrations. Daniel Doane, a friend, has often organized days of mindfulness in Oakland, California, involving periods of walking meditation through the city, with attentiveness both to inner and to outer phenomena.

The point of practicing mindfulness in these settings is not simply to bring more calm and kindness to places that often need such qualities, although that certainly can be significant. These practices are also based on the intuition that it is meaningful to talk about and explore mindfulness of relational and collective realities. In my own experience—for example, at Los Alamos, at San Quentin, at various antiwar demonstrations, or while walking the streets of Oakland—what has been most powerful is the sustained, focused nonjudgmental attention to a particular social phenomenon, such as nuclear weapons, executions, war and foreign policy, or contemporary urban life. Such attention generates a form of mindfulness significantly different from mindfulness exclusively directed to our inner experience. It also suggests a way of knowing that is quite different from the conventional, more externally focused knowledge of social problems. Yet in this sense, mindfulness of relational and collective realities can complement as well as bridge both mindfulness of inner experience and social analysis.

Joining Inner and Outer Attention

One of the hallmarks of such an extension of mindfulness into the social realm is thus that we, as in the practice of mindful speech, simultaneously attend to both inner and outer phenomena. *This blend of inner and outer attention is the basis for "mindfulness in action."*

Awareness born of such mindfulness is transformative, in large part because in such awareness we learn to and allow the social realities to touch our whole being, rather than protect a kind of inner peace either by avoiding the social realities or relating to social phenomena only with a (typically more mental) part of ourselves, in either case avoiding being deeply touched. For it is when we let these realities reach and move us that we access more fully the energies of wisdom, love, and compassion in our social change work.

We also see more clearly the interconnection of inner and outer transformation, how we ourselves are implicated in social problems, and how social problems manifest in our consciousness and behavior. Michele Mc-Donald, a friend and meditation teacher, spoke with me following the 2003 invasion of Iraq. In talking of her own experiences, she chose to emphasize such parallels: "Today, reporting from Baghdad, my mind. A lot of sniping going on and an explosion on the edge of town."

For Taigen Dan Leighton, a Zen teacher, scholar of Mahayana Buddhism, and activist, mindful awareness is the meeting point of inner and outer transformation.

> Awareness is transformative. It happens on the level of working out the conflicts in our own hearts and minds, as well as in the culture. In meditation, we become aware of our own inner processes and the primal separation of self and other. We come to see the interdependence of self and other, how our identity is dependent on so many things, including what's going on in society. Once we have some sense of any particular problem in society, then we can also look at it in terms of our own involvement. No one is pure and not part of the problem; we are in a web of connections. Even though I worked to oppose to invasion of Iraq, I am still connected to the murder of Iraqi civilians.[13]

To be mindful of social phenomena is thus to identify more clearly *hatred, greed, and delusion* as well as the *seeds of wisdom and compassion* both around us and in us. We can discern, for example, the extent to which many or most conflicts, such as the conflict between those advocating the "war on terror" and those supporting the jihad of Al-Qaeda, or the conflict between the Israeli government and the Palestinians, are in part expressions of vicious circles of tit-for-tat that go on and on; such vicious circles are familiar to most of us from our personal experience. Enmeshed in *collective hatred and anger,* each side proclaims the crimes of the other and its own righteousness, is unable to listen to the other's suffering, and cannot look at the deeper roots of the conflict and how we often need our enemies in order to maintain our rigid identities.

We can also understand how our economic institutions are increasingly rooted in *collective greed* and notice its basis, in society as well as in ourselves, in self-centeredness, a relative lack of sense of connection to others, and an inattention to long-term consequences. Similarly, we can identify and clarify the structures of *collective delusion,* evident, for example, in the workings of the mass media, educational institutions, and our self-congratulatory political ideologies and rooted in our self-ignorance.

Mindfulness of social realities, seeing through such "wisdom eyes," also helps us to locate the positive seeds for transformation. In American culture, this would be to become aware of the storehouse of wisdom and compassion embodied in American stories and traditions (and in us)— such as the (relative) freedom of information and expression; the great legacies of movements for social justice; the spiritual and creative gifts of those whom we have most oppressed, particularly those of Native American and African descent; the beauty and power of the land; the rainbow vision of harmonious living together with those from all over the earth; the spiritual resources of democratic traditions articulated from the Founders through Walt Whitman and Rosa Parks; and the moral richness of long-standing practices of hard work, plain speech, openness, community, and grass-roots activism.

BEING PEACE

To cultivate mindfulness in action is not just to connect inner experience to action and to an awareness of outer events. To bring attention to the qualities of our experience in the midst of things to do, deadlines, important outcomes, and long-range goals is also to join a focus on *process* to the emphasis on *tasks,* and to connect our *being* with our *doing.* It is one way of ensuring that we avoid being so unbalanced in the interest of achieving future goals that we somehow justify means contrary to our own ends.

Hence, Thich Nhat Hanh talks about the need to "be peace" and questions whether there is peace in the peace movement, pointing to the importance of manifesting that which we are trying to bring about in the world. The crucial link is mindfulness practice, through which we can more readily know whether there is a consonance of inner qualities and outer intentions and actions. Without such mindfulness, we are much more likely to be reactive, to "pass on the pain," all the while thinking that we are solving the problem. Peace, Thich Nhat Hanh tells us, "is every step":

> Without being peace, we cannot do anything for peace.... If we are not peaceful, then we cannot contribute to the peace movement.... The peace movement is filled with anger and hatred. It cannot fulfill the path we expect from them. A fresh way of being peace, of doing peace is needed. That is why it is so important for us to practice meditation, to acquire the capacity to look, to see, and to understand. Peace work means, first of all, being peace. Meditation is meditation for all of us.[14]

Chapter Three

CLARIFYING AND
SETTING INTENTIONS

Several years ago, the Dalai Lama participated in a number of days of dialogue with Western Buddhist teachers. At one point, one person asked him, "How do you respond to all the criticisms that you get?" He answered simply, "I have been called many things for many years, a 'wolf in sheep's clothing,' a 'counterrevolutionary,' and so on. When I hear such criticisms, I look carefully at my intentions. If my intentions are good and I know them clearly as such, then ultimately I just don't care about these criticisms." A second person asked, "How do you work with fear?" The Dalai Lama responded, "I look carefully at my intentions. If my intentions are good, then I am not afraid."

Exploring and working with our intentions is vital in transforming ourselves and our world. Clarifying intentions is another natural starting point for our spiritual practice as well as for our actions. Yet we also need to return continually to our intentions to help keep us aligned with our deeper values and aspirations. Such a practice is also, as the Dalai Lama suggests, ultimately a great protection, for ourselves and for others, a way of ensuring integrity.

We could simplify all of our spiritual practice and say that there are three phases. We first try to be mindful of what is happening in the present moment. On the basis of such awareness, we set our wisest and most compassionate intention. Then we act, as skillfully as possible, to implement that intention. In this sense, intentions are at the center of our spiritual lives, both moment to moment and in terms of our long-term actions.

In this chapter, I will focus on this fundamental practice of clarifying and setting intentions, as individuals, in relationships, and collectively, offering a number of concrete techniques and exercises for our ongoing "intention practice."

THE IMPORTANCE OF INTENTIONS

In the teachings of the Buddha and in mindfulness practice, working with intentions plays a very special role. In this context, it is only through our work with intentions in the present moment that we find our freedom, our ability to act with wisdom and compassion, rather than repeat the conditioned and habitual patterns of the past. Indeed, as we shall see, according to the Buddha it is only through acting on intentions, whether wise or unwise, that karma is set in motion.

We begin our work with intentions simply by starting to become aware of the prevalence of intentions. Every action, whether sitting down to read or going to the bathroom or planning a protest, is accompanied by intention. Indeed, when we examine our experience closely, we can begin to notice the continual flow of intentions moment to moment.

The focus on intention is important for two further reasons as well. First, many, if not most, of our intentions are beneath the threshold of awareness, carried by dispositions, tendencies, habits, and unconscious compulsions. We are always acting, and intentions accompany every action. Yet we are not necessarily aware of our intentions, and often we are even unaware of our actions.

This may not seem to be a problem in the case of lifting an arm to drink a glass of water. But many of our intentions are not so morally and spiritually neutral. When our intentions are linked with greed, hatred, or delusion, then our actions will tend to "habitualize" and even strengthen these qualities. Such actions will tend, in the short or long run, to produce suffering, whether our own or that of others. On the other hand, actions that follow intentions that reflect generosity, goodwill, lovingkindness, or wisdom will support and augment the continued presence of those qualities over time. These actions will tend in the long haul to produce happiness and liberation, even in difficult conditions. The Buddha, in a famous passage from one of the most beloved collections of his teachings, the *Dhammapada* (Steps of the Way), points out these tendencies, distinguishing between the two kinds of intentions and identifying the first as "impure" and the second as "pure":

> We are what we think.
> All that we are arises with our thoughts.
> With our thoughts we make the world.
> Speak or act with an impure mind
> And trouble will follow you
> As the wheel follows the ox that draws the cart.
>
> We are what we think.
> All that we are arises with our thoughts.
> With our thoughts we make the world.
> Speak or act with a pure mind
> And happiness will follow you
> As your shadow, unshakable.[1]

The main aim of mindfulness practice follows from this observation. It is to disclose the myriad patterns of our experience. As we begin to see our conditioned, habitual reactions and tendencies, we gradually start to discern the intention(s) that fuel each pattern. *With awareness of intentions, we are in a position to choose wisely which intentions to follow and which intentions to restrain or abandon.* This is it! This is the heart of our practice, whether for an individual, a group or organization, or a larger collectivity.

Yet in individual practice, coming to self-knowledge brings, as the Tibetan teacher Chögyam Trungpa Rinpoche once remarked, a certain amount of "bad news." In my own first years of daily practice and retreats starting in my twenties, for example, I was struck, as are many beginning meditators, by how "out of control" my mind and attention were, despite my educational achievements. I was also surprised by how much I didn't really know many of the most central patterns and intentions of my experience. During meditation retreats, I would notice, with some embarrassment, how much I was concerned with others' seeing me as a "good" meditator.

When I brought mindfulness practice to my conversations and encounters with others in daily life, I could see how much I was motivated by self-image, gaining something from the other, trying to feel safer, or wanting to be liked. In other words, I came to see how some of my intentions emerged out of a sense of unworthiness. I also came to notice more clearly when I was guided by motivations that I saw as more edifying, when I wanted to be helpful and kind or to connect emotionally.

We can carry out the same kind of inquiry in regard to our service in the world or our activism. We can see how our work to help others may similarly be motivated to a large extent by our needs to be liked or recognized or appreciated. We can start to distinguish these kinds of intentions from the intentions truly to help, to care, to bring about justice, to act so as to make possible a greater happiness and well-being.

Yet whatever the short-term "bad news" and the discouragement that we might experience initially in noticing accurately the intentions that motivate us, there can be a long-term and deep optimism that guides us in meditation and in action. It is the optimism and growing faith, we might say, in the link between coming to know what is present, however difficult, and coming to freedom. Unlike those spiritual teachers, philosophers, and psychologists who have proclaimed that we are somehow trapped by our past experience, that we inhabit a deterministic universe in which we simply live out the personal, familial, or cultural conditioning of the past, the Buddha teaches (as do others, both spiritual and secular) the possibility of freedom from such conditioning. It is in mindfulness, in our awareness of the contents of experience in the present moment in a nonreactive, nonjudgmental manner, whether in formal meditation or in the midst of action, that we establish a kind of open space, a "free zone" in which the past no longer rules us. We may be very aware of patterns and tendencies that have formerly bound us, but now there is a freedom, an energy, and a wisdom to not give in, as it were, to the intentions associated with the past, but rather to follow another intention, one that reflects wisdom and compassion. Working with intentions in this way is at the heart of both personal and social change.

I have long been very moved and inspired by those who, despite a very difficult and painful past, have had the strength to follow intentions that moved them toward healing, that expressed wisdom. One friend, now in middle age, for example, told me of the years and years that she had worked with the residues of a very traumatic childhood—particularly in therapy and in spiritual practices. A person with great gifts of vision, intellect, and communicative ability, she reflected that without such a difficult past, she might well have become a professor at a prestigious school and perhaps an author. She spoke candidly of her periods of loneliness. She also spoke of how often she had to reject a powerful voice in her that said, "I have had so much pain in this life. Nothing is going to be good. My life is too hard and things will not work out. I'm doomed. I give up." She spoke of how in those moments, she had, time and again, cultivated the strength, clarity, and faith to affirm her intention to open to and transform her grief and pain. A starting point had often been her mindful and open awareness of the critical voice and the ability to access kindness for herself, for her own predicament. Before she could even begin to open to the pain, she found that she could cultivate the intention to be kind, knowing that she would later open to the pain. In time, this intention ripened, and little by little she was able to grieve.

In a similar way, I have been inspired by seeing, in films of the civil rights movement from the 1950s and 1960s, how the strong intentions of elderly African American men and women sustained them—at demonstrations and marches, at talks, at gatherings in churches. In most cases, they had known injustice and oppression quite directly their whole lives. And yet they seemed able to avoid the extremes both of giving up and of reacting in hatred. Maintaining a profound dignity and humanity despite their years of pain, they followed the intention to love, heal, stand up, and act in strong and firm ways. It was as if they had the resources to touch something deeper in human life than pain, deeper than the long centuries of being devalued, "buked and scorned" (as the old spiritual tells us). It was as if, in the intentions that they followed, they were already free in the most profound sense. The political freedoms that ensued, albeit imperfectly, were in large part made possible, we might say, by the already present spiritual freedom, manifested in their intentions.

KARMA: CORE TEACHINGS

It is in the context of the possibility of such freedom, in the midst of the sometimes intense pains and pleasures of this life, that the Buddha discusses karma. As I mentioned earlier, the Buddha explains the dynamics of karma particularly through an account of the role of *intention* in moving either toward continued bondage or toward freedom.

Karma (*kamma* in Pali) literally means "action." *Karma* is the ordinary word that would be used, just like the English word *action,* in sentences like, "What action will you take with the snails in your garden?" or "His action to cultivate justice was very skillful."

Yet the Buddha's use of the term *karma,* as was common in the spiritual traditions of India, goes beyond being purely descriptive. Rather, it suggests the spiritual drama, we might say, of every moment. At every moment, we are acting, and through our actions, we set in motion, support, or undermine tendencies and habits. (This is one reason that the Buddha says that every moment of mindfulness, spiritual practice, and careful action truly matters; every moment has effects.) The Buddha speaks of finding in his own experience, during his time of intensive spiritual practice before he was enlightened, a basic distinction between two types of actions (or types of karma). One kind of action, which he termed *kusala* (usually translated as "skillful" or "wholesome"), increases our wisdom, compassion, generosity, and so forth. The other kind of action, *akusala* ("unskillful" or "unwholesome"), increases our greed, hatred, and delusion.

Yet for the Buddha, an action is deemed skillful or unskillful because of the *intention* linked with it: "Intention, I tell you, is kamma. Having intended, one performs an action through body, speech, or mind."[2] A given outward action can be linked with a number of different intentions and meanings, so we cannot simply look at the apparent behavior to determine the nature of an action.

Think of a team of people working to develop a trail system in a state park and of how their intentions might differ. One person may primarily have the intention to make money (and this might be to support a family or to pay for a drug habit). Another person may be most interested in being part of a working group and feel that he or she belongs. A third might be looking for meaningful work, perhaps any meaningful work. Another may want to meet interesting people, another perhaps to get into better shape through a few months of physical work. Another may be primarily motivated by the intention of helping the larger community, and yet another may be devoted to the glory of God through service to others.

At every moment, we are following (and sometimes choosing) intentions just like those of the people working on the trail system. Such intentions have profound effects. We tend to strengthen both the intentions themselves and their related states—of generosity or greed, love or hatred, wisdom or delusion. The Buddha tells us that, in this sense, we are constantly the heirs of our actions: "Beings are owners of their actions, heirs of their actions; they originate from their actions, are bound to their actions, have their actions as their refuge."[3]

KARMA: COMMON DISTORTIONS

This focus on intention helps us to avoid a number of different misunderstandings and distortions of the teaching on karma, many of which have been quite prevalent, both in Buddhist cultures and in the West, and are not compatible with our intentions to transform ourselves and our world. For anyone developing a socially engaged practice, it is crucial to be aware of these misinterpretations of karma.

We often hear the term *karma* used as a synonym for *fate,* with connotations of a kind of mystical calculus of retributive justice for each individual. According to such a calculus, we are each rewarded for good actions and punished for bad actions. If I step on an ant in the morning, I may be stung by a wasp in the evening. The unkind words I said to my partner are "punished" shortly thereafter by someone yelling at me at work. Or, just this morning, my houseguest decided that her karma caused the toilet to be blocked.

A related interpretation of karma is that *whatever* we are experiencing in the moment is the result of our past actions. A person is born into the pain (and challenge) of poverty or racism, according to this interpretation, because of that person's unwholesome actions in a past life. Presumably, the young child who died in the Holocaust had acted unskillfully in a previous life. A current form of this thinking surfaces in the assertion that a person who is ill, say, with cancer, is somehow "responsible" for the disease because of actions taken in the past, in this life or a previous life.

Yet such deterministic, fatalistic, and individualistic interpretations of karma are questionable. They can justify and perpetuate conditions of oppression and unnecessary suffering. My friend Jonathan Watts, a socially engaged Buddhist who lives in Japan and who worked in Thailand for many years with the International Network of Engaged Buddhists, told me about such fatalistic uses of the teaching of karma. He helped to organize a conference held in Thailand in the winter of 2003 called "Buddhist Responses to Violence." At the conference, Ouyporn Khuankaew, a Thai Buddhist activist with the International Women's Partnership who has led workshops on women's leadership, empowerment, and nonviolence throughout Southeast Asia and South Asia, reported that it is not uncommon for monks to counsel a woman abused by her husband to cultivate the important Buddhist virtue of equanimity. The wife typically is told to "be patient and kind to her husband so that one day the karmic force will cease and everything will be fine."[4]

Similarly, among adherents of the caste system in India, the teaching of karma often serves to justify and legitimize higher caste members' positions of power and dominance—the lower-caste members supposedly deserve their suffering because of past lives. Lower-caste people who share such beliefs submit of their own accord. These interpretations of karma thus tend to legitimize the social order and blame the victims; the moral and spiritual burden is on those who are suffering rather than on those who oppress. They tend to undermine efforts to bring about social change, partly because of the sense that "things are as they need to be," and partly because the main moral and spiritual focus is on the individual rather than the larger social systems.

These kinds of interpretations of karma go against the Buddha's central teachings. The Buddha, in his account of karma as intention, does not emphasize the external consequences of actions. Rather, the main emphasis in the teaching about karma is on how our intentions tend to condition similar intentions in the future, and how skillful intentions tend to produce liberation and happiness, whereas unskillful intentions tend to produce bondage and unhappiness.

The Buddha is also clear that it is not appropriate simply to say that any negative or unpleasant experiences are necessarily the results of karma from past actions. He speaks of karma as one among eight types of causes of events and experiences, alongside physical, biological, and environmental causes.[5] At times, furthermore, he mentions someone dying of a disease without attributing this to karma.

INTENTION PRACTICE: INDIVIDUAL, RELATIONAL, COLLECTIVE

What, then, strengthens our intention practice? What helps us to clarify and set skillful intentions, and to be aware of and abandon unskillful ones? How do we do this, first as individuals and then in our relationships, groups, organizations, and, further, in the larger society?

Just as individuals' intentions may be either conscious or unconscious, so are those in relational and collective contexts. We may find explicit intentions expressed in interpersonal agreements, marriage vows, group norms, organizational vision and mission statements, government constitutions, and judicial precedents. And yet in each setting, we also find unconscious and compulsive intentions crystallized in dispositions and personalities, individual and institutional practices, and repetitive behaviors, all of which may conflict with the more conscious intentions. Clearly we need relational and collective as well as individual intention practices.

I suggest four general guidelines for our intention practice in each of these domains:

1. Cultivating mindfulness of intentions.
2. Touching deeper intentions.
3. Setting clear intentions for particular activities.
4. Working with intentions in times of difficulty.

Cultivating Mindfulness of Intentions

First, we need to *practice mindfulness of intentions in general,* to become more aware of intentions in the present moment, without necessarily changing the intentions that we find. We can periodically "check in" with our intentions, in daily meditation or at different times during the day. In more intensive contemplative practice, we can give attention to the ongoing flow of intentions, becoming more mindful of the simple intentions necessary to take a walk, as well as intentions with a more moral, emotional, and spiritual scope. As we develop further in our ability to be mindful of intentions, we become better able to discern which intentions are skillful and helpful and which are connected with furthering suffering, for ourselves and others.

How can we be mindful of existing intentions in our *relational and collective* lives? We can point first to several group tools that support intention practice in these settings. For example, inviting attention to the sometimes diverse intentions of participants at the beginning of meetings or activities can bring our intentions to light, often remind us of our deeper intentions, and suggest whether it is important to align further the varied intentions of those present. Another tool is Thich Nhat Hanh's "mindfulness bell." In this practice, a bell is rung regularly, sometimes every twenty minutes, during a meeting or gathering; after the bell is heard, participants are invited to be aware of their breathing for three breaths. When the mindfulness bell is rung in the midst of interaction, people often become aware of both their prevailing intentions at the moment of the bell and, sometimes, their deeper, often submerged intentions. I have frequently seen conflicts at a meeting lessen or dissipate when the bell is rung; those in conflict realize that they have somewhat gotten lost in reactions and often come back to wiser or more helpful intentions.

Another way of becoming aware of our intentions in social settings is to notice the disparity between what we think are our primary intentions and the intentions our actions actually suggest. As a group or organization (and even as a whole society), we can conduct an *audit* of our actions, asking ourselves which intentions seem expressed through them, whatever we declare our mission statements to be. What qualities of mind and heart does my group or organization regularly bring into the world, in addition to its products, statements, or actions?

For example, many groups and organizations dedicated to social or spiritual transformation intend to be inclusive of and welcoming to all people, and yet they have to examine the disparity between their intention and the perception, often coming from the outside, that they are not so inclusive of and welcoming to certain people. I have been part of several organizations in which such disparities have been noted, particularly in terms of ethnicity and class, leading the group to considerable soul-searching, a deeper intention to be inclusive, and concrete actions to actualize this intention.

· Touching Our Deeper Intentions

A second dimension of intention practice is to *find ways to know and be regularly in touch with our deeper intentions, motivations, and aspirations*— in our lives in general as well as in particular situations. In the midst of the busy lives that many of us lead, we commonly forget such deeper intentions in the glut of the everyday details and routines of our habitual behaviors. Setting aside a time dedicated to our deepest values—whether in daily spiritual practice or study, a weekly sabbath, or periodic retreats— reminds us of and lets us establish more firmly our general intentions to realize and express these values in our lives.

At the end of a morning contemplative period, for example, we can set our general intentions for the day, perhaps focusing on qualities we would like to manifest, such as compassion or generosity, or on what we hope to learn. I may set the intention, for example, to keep my heart open in my interactions or to practice mindful speech. I may intend to look out for self-judgments and judgments of others. I may establish an intention to be aware of others' perspectives. We may not necessarily keep the intention in mind all day long or even through much of the day, but the intention may still exert considerable power, especially if it becomes a regular morning practice. One friend, for example, found it very helpful to remind herself of her intention to help all beings move toward freedom, before her daily work at a homeless shelter. Focusing on such an intention helped her to be less preoccupied with her ongoing personal issues or her emotional reactions while at the shelter.

Similarly, sabbath days and retreats can bring us "back to ourselves." I remember how, when I was a young teacher, I would get very busy with the new challenges of developing curricula and working with students. Even though I meditated daily and participated in a number of day-long and weekend retreats, I needed the depth and intensity of longer retreats at the end of each semester to remind me of my most fundamental aspirations.

We can think of ceremonies in which we take vows or forcefully state our deeper intentions as serving a very similar function. We may, for example, regularly take the three traditional Buddhist "refuges": in the Buddha (the possibility of awakening as a human), the dharma (the teachings of the causes of suffering and awakening), and the sangha (the community of fellow spiritual practitioners). The public expression of intentions, whether through vows and ceremonies or in a statement before a group at the end of a retreat or workshop, has a special power. Declaring one's own sacred intentions publicly can often grant a sense of reality and legitimacy that supports the realization of the intention.

We may also develop more specific and personal vows with friends or with a particular group. I once was helped greatly by taking a vow with a close friend and fellow practitioner that read, "I vow that all my actions arise from presence and kindness." I would bring a copy of the vow, written on a small sheet of paper, with me in my pocket, sometimes holding it before me at meetings. Others couldn't really see what was written on it, but *I* knew what was there.

We can also explore the wisdom of our major decisions by returning to our deeper intentions. During times when I considered changing my job or making another important transition, I often conducted a short, one- or two-day, retreat for myself so that I could consider the decision in the light of my deepest values. At other times, I entered longer retreats knowing that a given question or issue was unresolved. But rather than let myself be preoccupied with the question, I learned the discipline of waiting until the end of the retreat, and then contemplating the question in the light of the clarity gained in the days of silence and focus. In this kind of "going into the wilderness" for soul-searching, we follow the ancient practice of using silence, stillness, places of beauty and power, easing our everyday habits, and cultivating vision—in order to act with wisdom and to remember what our lives are about.

Identifying our fundamental intentions is also vital in our relational and collective lives. My mother, for example, tells the story of how she and my father sat down on a bench before they were married and drew up a list of their most basic intentions and values, to be used as a support and guide for their marriage and to make sure that they were well aligned. Similarly, wedding vows bring the power of intentions to public expression.

Ongoing groups and organizations (and societies) often engage, of course, in an attempt to identify core intentions by developing norms, mission and vision statements, strategic-planning documents, and so forth. At their worst, such statements of intentions can be superficial, vague, rhetorical, and highly politicized and bear little relation to actual practice. But at their best, they can serve to guide everyday work, remind us of what most deeply motivates us, and even be a powerful force in resolving conflicts.

One expression of deeper intentions in groups and organizations is the identification of "group norms" for how the group members intend to interact with each other, somewhat independently from the more "external" group tasks. Most groups do not have such explicit norms, and it is therefore not surprising that unconscious intentions often predominate.

In the Buddhist Peace Fellowship BASE (Buddhist Alliance for Social Engagement) program, founded by Diana Winston in 1995 to help integrate Buddhist practices with engagement in the world (typically social service or social change work), which I have helped to guide, we often focus, in the initial weekend retreat that starts a six-month training period, on developing such norms. One way to do this with a group of 8–12 people is to design a several hours' long process in which participants first talk in small groups of 3 or 4 about their positive and negative experiences in groups, and then name a number of guidelines or norms that provide them with relative safety, energy, and inspiration in groups and help them see the group as a place for opening, growth, and transformation. A small group might be instructed to choose four guidelines about which there is consensus, and then all the small groups can come together to reach consensus about the larger group's norms. These preliminary norms would be subject to revision and further exploration in the course of the six months of the program. One group, for example, came up with this set of norms, which were divided into several categories:

Helping to create a space of trust and safety
Maintain confidentiality.
Make a clear commitment to be in the group and attend meetings.
Use "I" statements and speak from the heart as much as possible.
Intend to appreciate and respect the others in the group.

Being explicit about aspects of group process
Identify group values.
Clarify the role of the facilitator.
Be aware of group dynamics, including conflict.
Agree to air and attempt to resolve difficult feelings with another
person, in the spirit of love and wisdom.

Developing communication and interaction skills
Cultivate active listening.
Make a commitment to learn from others.

Give some space after a person has spoken, not jumping in immediately.
Be willing to experience different group roles and sometimes roles that are new to you.
Generally give advice only when another has asked for it.
Share informal, unscheduled time together.

Being in groups as spiritual practice
Intend to integrate our work in the group with our spiritual practice.
Keep in mind our most basic intentions.
Commit to practicing mindfulness in the context of the group.
Be aware of and look deeply into one's own feelings and thoughts.
Look deeply into our true nature.
Be aware of the effects of one's words and actions on others.
Be willing to detach from fear.
Cultivate qualities of tolerance, gentleness, acceptance, generosity, and forgiveness in relation to others in the group.
Cultivate patience in relation to others and the group as a whole.
Cultivate qualities of being humorous and playful.
Develop rituals and ceremonies ... for beginnings and endings of gatherings.[6]

Some groups return periodically to a review of their norms, even reciting them publicly on a regular basis, much as, among Buddhist monks and nuns, the Vinaya, a collection of guidelines for conduct (well over two hundred norms), is traditionally renewed in a public ceremony every full moon.

Setting Intentions for Specific Activities

Being regularly in touch with our deeper intentions is crucial. Yet also needed is a way of connecting these more general intentions with the details of daily life. How do we keep such intentions from becoming abstract, overly intellectual, stale, or unreal? A third form of intention practice *establishes our own clear intentions for specific activities.*

As we have seen, we can set various kinds of intentions *before* activities, reminding ourselves to be mindful, to cultivate wise speech, to remember our deeper intentions, and so on. We can also recall intentions *following* activities—a traditional Buddhist practice called the "dedication of merit" often closes gatherings or periods of meditation with the intention that the fruits of the activity be shared widely, for the benefit of all beings.

Working with intentions is particularly useful in social action, especially in helping guide us when things become chaotic, when we become reactive, or when many other groups and individuals are involved, sometimes with quite different intentions. At the 1999 World Trade Organization protests in Seattle, for example, a Buddhist group stayed together for several days. Diana Winston reported on the group's work with intentions.

> Our group continually worked to clarify our motivation. We dedicated our actions to the liberation of all beings. On the morning of the large direct action, about 15 of us came together for sitting and intention setting. After the sit, we went around the group and spoke about our intentions for the day: "To be as present as I can," "To hold this all within the space of equanimity," "To benefit the countless suffering beings around the planet whom we are representing."[7]

Other Buddhist groups have made similar use of intention practice at demonstrations. In the fall and winter of 2002–2003, as large protests took place worldwide against the invasion of Iraq, the Buddhist Peace Fellowship (BPF) played a prominent role in some locales. In the San Francisco Bay Area, prior to the demonstrations, which at their height involved several hundred thousand demonstrators, several hundred people typically were present at premarch gatherings organized by BPF. There they meditated for up to several hours, and then, prior to the start of the demonstration, they were invited to break into small groups to clarify and set intentions, and then share these intentions with others. A number of the participants later reflected that they felt able to join in the demonstrations only after these conscious intention-setting practices.

A highly developed form of intention practice was evident at times in the civil rights movement. In the Birmingham campaign of 1963, for example, every volunteer was required to sign a commitment card that read:

I HEREBY PLEDGE MYSELF—MY PERSON AND BODY —TO THE NON-VIOLENT MOVEMENT. THEREFORE I WILL KEEP THE FOLLOWING TEN COMMAND-MENTS:

1. MEDITATE daily on the teachings and life of Jesus.
2. REMEMBER always that the nonviolent movement in Birmingham seeks justice and reconciliation—not victory.
3. WALK and TALK in the manner of love, for God is love.
4. PRAY daily to be used by God in order that all men might be free.
5. SACRIFICE personal wishes in order that all men might be free.
6. OBSERVE with both friend and foe the ordinary rule of courtesy.

7. SEEK to perform regular service for others and for the world.
8. REFRAIN from the violence of fist, tongue, or heart.
9. STRIVE to be in good spiritual and bodily health.
10. FOLLOW the directions of the movement and of the captain on a demonstration.[8]

Working with Intentions in Times of Difficulty

A fourth way to work with intentions is *to clarify intentions in moments of distress and difficulty.* Sometimes, when we find ourselves having acted or spoken in unskillful or harmful ways, we may be quite troubled. We can use such experiences as wake-up calls to help us clarify our intentions, sometimes right in the moment. We can practice a kind of contemplative inquiry: What *was* my intention when I was harsh with my friend? What is present when I follow, consciously or unconsciously, unskillful intentions? Such inquiry demands an ability not just to notice one's thoughts and to analyze, but also to listen with a relatively still mind to our hearts and bodies, to listen for motivations that may not always be accessible to the busy mind.

At difficult moments, sometimes, as in the stories I mentioned earlier, our deeper intentions somehow *are* present. At other times, we may not be very conscious of such intentions. I may be very confused about a course of action, a relationship, a way of communicating, and so forth. At those times, I can remember to invite my deeper intentions to be present. This is not always so easy if there is a substantial amount of pain, fear, anger, and confusion and a busy, even frantic, mind.

Norms and precepts may play an especially vital role when there are conflicts or difficulties. Of course, sometimes conflicts within a given community reflect ambiguities or tensions *between* norms or precepts, but most conflicts typically reflect a temporary forgetting of our deeper intentions and/or following more unconscious, compulsively driven, and self-centered intentions.

Martine Batchelor, a teacher, writer, and former Buddhist nun, once told me the story of a major difficulty that arose in her Buddhist-based Sharpham community in southwest England, a small rural community of about a dozen people near Totnes, in Devon. It seems that at one point, there were, in the opinion of some, "too many" visitors coming and going, and some community members wanted to change their policy about welcoming visitors. Discussion went back and forth, with various proposals proffered, all suggesting various adjustments that would make things more comfortable, until one person asked, "What about compassion?" Suddenly, the mood shifted dramatically, as if the difficulty had seemingly been resolved—through reference to a fundamental value. It was as if the group as a whole simultaneously thought, "We've forgotten about compassion and been preoccupied with our comfort! We *can* stretch our capacities to be with others, guided by our intention to be compassionate, because we really want to offer a temporary refuge for people in need. And we can keep our usual safeguards."

THE CHALLENGES AND PERILS
OF INTENTION PRACTICE

A lack of shared intentions with others and social support for our intention practice may be a major difficulty for most of us working to strengthen our intention practice. Until spiritual principles and practices are so deeply and powerfully internalized that support is not so necessary, our intention practice will continue to be a challenge.

Yet a number of other challenges also commonly surface in our work with intentions. I will mention a few, some of which I have already suggested.

First, it is important to remember that *we typically follow "mixed" motivations.* I may want to "save all beings," but I also may like to advertise myself as a compassionate spiritual activist. We might sometimes selfishly seek to serve selflessly so that we can carry the *self-image of being selfless.* We may be deeply concerned about ecological degradation and work for an activist organization while also hoping, especially as we get older, that it might offer a stable career.

I used to be much more troubled by the presence of mixed motivations than I am now. Like many, whenever I found evidence of significant egotism in my friends and especially my teachers—actions seemingly taken to enhance their self-image and status or signs of other flaws of character or ethics—I tended to write them off.

I have come to see that what is important is that we have an intention *practice* and that we see more clearly our various intentions. My own dismissal of those with sullied motivations, whatever their gifts and positive motivations, depended in part—I can reflect now—on my inability to admit and see my own mixed motivations. As I could acknowledge more of my "shadow," including my concerns about self-image, recognition, and security, I judged others (and implicitly myself) less harshly.

More recently I have appreciated how the Buddha essentially teaches that mixed motivations are both to be expected and entirely workable. Without noticing *both* aspects, the shadow and the noble intentions, we might become overly idealistic, like I was. Or we might become cynical, looking *only* for self-centeredness or corruption in endeavors related to spirituality or social justice, and then, finding such qualities, use this discovery as a reason to withdraw or give up in despair.

A second danger of intention practice develops when *we put too much emphasis on intentions and not enough on the link between intentions and actions in the world.* Especially in our society, in which spirituality is frequently framed subjectively and individualistically, we may be overly preoccupied with our focus on our inner process and the purity of our intentions. We may cultivate, as it were, our own private garden, in which we feel wise and equanimous in large part because we are not in touch with the suffering of the world. Furthermore, we may not pay much attention to actions and consequences in any of the domains of our lives, thinking that good intentions are all that matters. We my not study very much the consequences of our actions, either in our own immediate experience or in our relational lives.

This danger sometimes appears among spiritual activists who may not have given much attention to *systemic* (social, political, ecological, or economic) issues. The result can be a certain naïveté about such systems, coupled with a typically *moral* critique of a given problem and a focus on a relative personal purity in relation to the problem. We sometimes find such naïveté among those who are much more concerned about the purity and morality of nonviolent action than about the efficacy of action; the latter often rests on a clear analysis of systems. Although such a moral critique—for example, of war or greed—may be vital and an important starting point, it may also be incomplete and of limited effectiveness without any connection to an understanding of the roots of problems in institutions and systems and the development of effective transformative strategies. We need both. A focus on intentions, personal integrity, and ethics needs to be linked with an awareness of the dynamics of large systems.

EXERCISE: Setting Intentions for an Activity

Sit quietly, at least for a short time. Let your bodily sensations, emotions, and thoughts come and go, and let them settle as much as possible. Then invite to presence your intention for a given period and activity. Stay with the intention, letting it fill your awareness, your body and mind. If you have a way of giving physical manifestation (perhaps writing, speaking, or associating your intention with an object that might remind you of the intention), do that. Think of ways to return periodically to a renewal of your intention during an activity, during the day, or over a period of time.

———————————————

Chapter Four

OPENING TO SUFFERING, OPENING TO COMPASSION

The idea of opening to suffering is deeply embedded both in Western social justice movements and in Buddhist practice. A starting point for the former is often the publicizing and analysis of suffering related to injustice and oppression in order to help change the causes and conditions that lead to such suffering. Similarly, the Buddha's Four Noble Truths, the heart of his teachings, emphasize that we need to know the reality of suffering *(dukkha)* and its cause, as a starting point for the path that leads, we are told, to the overcoming of suffering. In both approaches, opening to suffering is pivotal to finding freedom.

Yet what does it mean to open to suffering? As a twelve-year-old, I was transfixed by the story of the Holocaust in William Shirer's *The Rise and Fall of the Third Reich,* hardly able to fathom the horrors described in the book. I also remember being both deeply curious about and somewhat fearful of the African American shantytown across the "rickety rackety" bridge, not far from where we lived in Maryland. As a teenager in the late 1960s, I was shocked and saddened to observe the conditions in Harlem and Bedford-Stuyvesant in New York City and angry to see on television the 1968 "police riot" at the Democratic Convention in Chicago. I also read about and saw on television the great pain of the Vietnam War. Several times, I witnessed firsthand the brutal police beatings of antiwar demonstrators.

I also observed how encountering such suffering, both in person and in reports, although often important in energizing action, often led to anger, blame, the demonization of the "enemy," and actions and behaviors that seemed unkind and hateful, creating further suffering. Yet these actions were carried out in the name of morality, peace, and justice. A natural question arose: How can we be in touch with suffering and work to transform it, but not react in ways that lead to further suffering?

WHAT IS SUFFERING?

One of the most powerful images in the teachings of the Buddha—the image of the "two arrows"—helps us to clarify the nature of suffering and how we might learn to open to suffering without creating further suffering. It also suggests an important and precise distinction between what we might call *pain* and *suffering*.

We can imagine, the Buddha says, that when we experience pain, it is as if we were shot by an arrow.[1] Each of us is sometimes shot by this *arrow of pain*. We each have a certain allotment of painful experiences, some of us more, others less. To be human is to be vulnerable to pain and at times to be in pain. Our soft bodies are easily injured and tend to break down over time. We are frequently startled and shocked—physically, emotionally, and mentally. We want meaning and connection, kindness and love, fairness and justice, yet we often find them lacking in our lives.

Typically, because of this first arrow of pain, we react in various ways. According to the Buddha, our reaction is equivalent to being shot by a second arrow. We can call this second arrow *suffering*. Suffering arises because when we experience pain—when we are injured or startled, or lack meaning and love, or are treated unjustly—we typically react by lashing out, at ourselves and others. We believe somehow that this will dispel or mitigate the pain. We act in such a way that a second arrow is shot, at us or others, on account of the pain of the first arrow. When we act so that the second arrow is shot, we *"pass on" the original pain*.

Suffering can thus be seen in large part as *a kind of resistance or reactivity to the pain of the present moment*. We tend to react physically, emotionally, and/or mentally when we have unpleasant or painful physical sensations, emotions, or thoughts. When we experience physical pain, we tend to tense and contract around the pain, as if this will somehow assuage it. Some doctors say that perhaps 80 percent of what patients experience as physical pain is not the result of the original stimulus but rather ongoing resistance to this stimulus.

Similarly, when there is emotional pain (think of the pain that may follow from a perceived slight by someone close to us or the breakup of an intimate relationship), we tend to comment at great length, produce a flow of emotions, and react physically as well, all on the basis of the original stimulus. We may generate anger and harsh judgments of self or others or rationalize continually, sulk in depression, find a scapegoat, or attempt to escape the pain through food, shopping, sex, or television. We do this individually and interpersonally, as well as in our groups, communities, and nations.

For the Buddha, however, the task of spiritual practice is not to rid ourselves of all pain, to prevent being shot by the first arrow. Rather, *our core intention is to not shoot this second arrow*. It is to learn how to *open to pain and suffering* when they appear in ourselves and others, so that *we can increasingly be present with the pain, but without suffering and without compounding the suffering.*

PAIN AND SUFFERING: APPARENT AND HIDDEN

Much of our pain and suffering is readily apparent and unavoidable, whether in our own lives or in the larger society. We may be very aware when we or those close to us experience pain and suffering stemming from physical causes (such as an illness, an injury, old age, and dying) or certain emotional and mental states (such as fear, hatred, grief, self-judgment, confusion, or psychological imbalance).

Similarly, there is much reported pain and suffering in our communities, societies, and in the larger world. The daily newspapers and television news shows give us regular accounts of natural disasters, wars and other armed conflicts, major accidents, local murders and crimes, and other situations of sometimes intense pain and suffering. Indeed, we might think of our mass media as largely presenting "Reports of Yesterday's Pain and Suffering, Brought to You by Our Corporate Sponsors."

Yet some of our pain and suffering is often hidden and even unconscious. Afraid of certain kinds of pain, and often not knowing how to approach such pain, we often segregate, marginalize, minimize, deny, avoid, repress, or hide the pain, when we are not simply ignorant. We do this as individuals, couples, families, communities, organizations, and societies. It is a vital part of our individual, relational, and collective practices to uncover this hidden pain and suffering so that we can open to and transform them. Hence, it is useful here to give an inventory of these more hidden types of pain and suffering.

As *individuals,* for example, we generally carry many residues of unresolved pain, pain that we either don't want to face or are unable to face. The work of contemporary psychotherapy rests in large part on a general understanding of how unresolved pain generates neurotic behavior. According to this understanding, certain experiences, often early in a person's life, were very difficult and even overwhelming. Such experiences may have been connected with feeling abandoned by one's parents, deprived of love because of one's behavior, or feeling deeply hurt physically or emotionally by particular interactions.

In order not to experience this pain again, we develop defense mechanisms—usually stored beneath the threshold of awareness—that keep us away from the painful areas. Through these mechanisms, our unconscious is constantly on the lookout, as it were, for anything that might touch or even remind us of the original pain, the original wound. With great creativity and attentiveness, we develop a vast array of ways to avoid facing such pain. We may *"space out"* and *distract* ourselves (perhaps finding refuge in fantasies, drugs, or television). We may develop complex *rationalizations* of our situation (with the result, for example, that we *minimize* or even *deny* the pain). We may studiously *avoid* the pain. We may *resign* ourselves to the pain grimly and resentfully, without really coming close to it. We may *cover over* the pain with the elements of a good life (work and career, family, worthwhile activities, and so on).

Around the place of pain we create a proliferating and increasingly rigid mass of thoughts, emotions, mental constructions, stories, and somatic manifestations, which tends to obscure and hinder our aliveness and authenticity. As individuals, we develop body armor, emotional numbness, and rigidity of thought. The poet Rilke writes: "We come of age as masks."[2]

These tendencies to avoid pain are evident in the *relational* dimension of our lives. In our *interpersonal relationships,* for example, we often avoid areas or subjects linked with past pain, sometimes to the point of having little about which to communicate. In our families, we may learn to avoid mentioning Father's alcoholism, the suicide some years ago of our aunt, the "black sheep" of the family, or that very painful discussion last weekend. We may steer clear of certain subjects that might lead to fresh reminders of the pain or to new painful experiences.

We are also largely driven to avoid pain in our *organizations and workplaces.* A friend tells the story of a university department in the Midwest where she once taught. She began to see, over a number of years, how there were a series of painful issues among the faculty members: distrust between particular persons, harsh judgments about others' competence, endemic misunderstandings, widespread feelings of not being "seen" and "heard" by others, and painful residues—with unhealed scars—from interactions in the past. These issues were almost never directly and publicly faced in meetings or between individuals. When concerns came up that had some link, even if small, to the unresolved issues, highly repetitive and quasi-ritualistic discussions arose, echoing the words of many years past, with surprisingly intense emotions. These discussions rarely came close to the basic concerns and often led to outcomes that left few feeling satisfied.

Such a situation of "normal" functioning amid general, chronic, and often unacknowledged but somehow tolerable pain may be more widespread than we like to admit. A cartoon shows a somewhat extreme version of this situation. A man sits at a desk, his head at a forty-five-degree angle, shaped like a triangle; his body, also shaped like a triangle, is inclined in the other direction. A sign sits on top of the desk: "Neurotic as hell, but still functional."

In the *collective* domain as well, our societies follow this general pattern of avoiding and hiding pain to a large extent. In modern Western societies, for example, we often segregate places of pain, particularly those related to poverty, illness, and death, away from the general population: in ghettos, poorer parts of cities, and hospitals. Often, we store or dump dangerous environmental toxins, in a sense the "pain" of our industrial processes, in marginalized communities (or in poorer countries), away from the mainstream population centers.

The everyday workings of our social, political, and economic institutions also generate a great deal of pain. Johan Galtung, the Norwegian founder of Peace Studies, invented the term *structural violence,* which is linked with this type of pain. Structural violence, Galtung believes, is distinct from, although related to, both the more obvious *direct violence* of physical attacks on people and the less obvious *cultural violence* of racism, sexism, homophobia, and the devaluation of particular groups and cultures. There is structural violence, for example, when African American women die of breast cancer at twice the rate of European American women because of inferior medical care and later detection of the cancer. Poor people have significantly higher rates of cancer, heart disease, AIDS, depression, environmentally related illnesses and accident, and premature death. Similarly, every year some fifty thousand people die in automobile accidents, and hundreds of thousands die prematurely from the effects of alcohol and cigarette consumption.

A third kind of typically hidden pain is the pain of our "enemies" and our "victims," often caused by our own authorities, friends, or allies. We can contrast the exceedingly poignant accounts in the *New York Times* of those killed in the World Trade Center with media directives *not* to cover in any detail or with sympathy the lives of the far greater number of civilians killed by the United States in Afghanistan and Iraq. The U.S. military, of course, has made reporting about casualties very difficult, and it has even adopted an official policy of refusing to account for the number of dead foreign civilians (and often foreign soldiers).

A last type of hidden pain is linked to the *collective shadow*—the legacies and lingering effects of violence in the past, such as the enslavement of Africans, the near-genocide of Native Americans, wars and civil conflicts, the Holocaust, and periods of great injustice. The hallmark of pain related to the collective shadow is that it is rarely approached or even acknowledged in public, yet, like the original wound of the individual, it may be driving the behavior of a given society to a large degree.

FACING AND WORKING
WITH PAIN AND SUFFERING

One of the reasons that pain and suffering are not commonly faced is that we generally lack both the understanding and the effective tools for working directly and consciously with the pain and suffering that surface, whether individually, relationally, or collectively. We also have little skill in bringing our hidden pain and suffering to awareness and transforming them.

The liberating message of the Buddha (and many others) is that we can respond skillfully and compassionately to our pain, no matter what its source, and not be driven endlessly by our reactions to it. In other words, although we cannot necessarily eliminate much of the present *pain* (the first arrow) from our lives, we can work through and eventually overcome our *suffering* (the second arrow). In other words, *suffering is workable. Suffering can be transformed.*

It is as if every moment of pain, for an individual, relationship or group, or society, opens up two possibilities and ultimately a choice between two options. The first possibility is to react to pain compulsively. It is to suffer, to shoot the second arrow. In this way, we pass on the pain, either to ourselves or to others, or to both.

The second possibility is to end the repetition of reactivity, of pain that leads to further pain and to suffering, to the shooting of the second arrow.

It is to learn how *not* to pass on the pain to self and others and to transform many of the conditions that lead to pain and suffering.

In our times, teachers of the second approach have often been members of oppressed groups who have counseled nonviolent transformative action rather than revenge. In the remarkable messages of such leaders as Mohandas Gandhi, Martin Luther King Jr., Desmond Tutu, and the Dalai Lama, we are guided to respond to pain and oppression with neither hatred nor passivity, but rather with compassion, love, forgiveness, and the intention of reconciliation, as well as firm commitment and dedicated action.

How do we learn to respond to pain and suffering in this second way?

OPENING TO AND TRANSFORMING PAIN AND SUFFERING: INDIVIDUAL PRACTICE

One way to understand mindfulness practice is as a basic *individual* training to face pain and suffering, to learn the difference between them, and to transform our suffering. In many ways, the cultivation of mindfulness offers a simple and direct way to learn fundamental principles and practices for working skillfully with pain and suffering, principles and practices that can then be extended creatively to our relationships and participation in larger systems.

Such training can be seen as resting on *six guidelines,* which we will explore here in the *individual* domain, but which apply as well to the relational and collective domains.

1. We first learn to open to the bare and direct experience of what is painful, distinguishing such experience from the proliferation of reactions that typically follow.
2. We train by opening to our smaller pains.
3. Sometimes it is wise to experience pain directly, and at other times it is wise to apply an "antidote" to the pain.
4. We learn by repeatedly noticing our reactive patterns in relation to pain.
5. In the long run and often in the short run, there is paradoxically less pain when we open up to pain and suffering than if we remain closed and resistant to the pain. This is a great secret!
6. Openly and directly facing our pain often brings wonderful and surprising gifts, both for ourselves and for the world—particularly the gifts of compassion, wisdom, and safety.

Opening to What Is Painful

With mindfulness practice, we learn how to be present to what is painful as it occurs. When painful physical sensations arise, say, in the knees or back while we are sitting in meditation (and we are sure that the short-term pain is not harmful in the long term), we may first use the technique of *naming* the unpleasant sensation. We then ground ourselves in the *direct experience* of the sensations. We may say very quietly to ourselves, "Sensation" and "Unpleasant," directing almost all of our attention to the sensations. We examine with "bare attention" the texture of the sensations as if we are naturalists exploring an unknown terrain or the qualities of a new species. We stay attentive for sustained periods as long as the pain is present, maintaining the discipline of returning to the "meditation object" (in this case, the painful sensations). We also notice and stay aware of the thoughts and emotions that the physical sensations may trigger.

Similarly, we learn to name and explore emotions and thoughts that are painful, such as fear, grief, anger, and confusion. We learn, for example, about our sadness as if for the first time, studying with great care the rhythms of our heart and the ensuing reverberations in body and mind. With sustained study, we become, as it were, experts on our own difficult emotions and patterns of thought.

Starting with Our Smaller Pains

The work of opening to pain is not at all easy, and at times it may be too difficult to face directly what we are given. We may need to face major pain and suffering indirectly, or at times only in small increments.

However, we can train with lighter material so as to develop the capacity to act wisely and compassionately with heavier material. We mostly train in the discomfort zone, we might say, rather than the comfort zone or the panic zone in which we are overwhelmed. Over time, two remarkable shifts typically occur. What was once an area of panic or of being overwhelmed may later become an area of workable discomfort. Second, we become in a sense more comfortable with being uncomfortable.

And so we learn better how to open up and remain present to a cold, a disappointment at work, a painful shoulder, the fear of public speaking at an event, the anger at a friend who hasn't come to our party, or the irritation with our partner.

Direct and Indirect Approaches

While there is a time for direct attention to, deep listening to, and inquiry into pain and suffering, there is also a time for a more indirect approach, particularly when defense mechanisms are quite strong or a given pain or suffering is very intense. As we become more proficient in opening to pain, we become better able to discern wisely what is appropriate at a given time.

The Buddha, for example, speaks of the practice of lovingkindness meditation as an antidote to fear. It was originally designed for a group of monks who had been overwhelmed by their fear of living in a forest filled, they believed, with malevolent spirits. Cultivating lovingkindness or joy, deepening self-understanding, or studying wisdom teachings may provide a grounding, stability, and indirect healing that strengthen us and later help us face what is painful when the time is right (or when we have no choice but to face the pain).

Noticing Our Reactive Patterns Over and Over Again

In continued mindfulness practice, we learn to distinguish pain from suffering and to discern varied patterns of reactivity to pain (as well as to pleasant experiences). We examine these patterns over and over again. The first insight into our patterns, no matter how stunning, is only the beginning. Eventually, repeated mindfulness weakens the hold that our habits have on us, and we strengthen the ability to not push away what is painful to the point at which this ability becomes stronger than our reactive tendencies. In doing so, we stabilize the relative peacefulness of experiencing *pain without suffering* and gradually learn how to bring this way of being into all the domains of our lives. We become much more sensitized both to how extensive the suffering is in our lives and to the insight that such suffering is unnecessary.

The Relief of Opening to Pain

To the extent that we are afraid of pain, we tend to believe that there is *less* pain in remaining closed, in large part because we are fixated on the short term. We choose to avoid focusing on a particular area of pain and believe that we are thereby choosing a less painful life in general. But we may be unaware of the long-term nature of the chronic pain related to anxiety, the fear of pain, illness due to stress, frozen relationships, or unconsciously driven behavior. We may be unaware of how our fear of pain dominates us, tending to diminish our ability to be vulnerable, honest, or authentic.

Even in the short run, it is often far easier and less painful than we imagine to open to pain and suffering because we lessen or eliminate the influence of a key component in our suffering—our fear of pain.

Here is a story that may serve as an illustration. At a three-month meditation retreat in England, I stayed in a small hut near the main dormitory of the meditation center and received guidance from my two teachers, Christina Feldman and Christopher Titmuss, talking with one of them every few days. After two weeks, I deepened my solitude by bringing my meals back to the hut rather than eating silently in the communal dining area. Over the next few days, I noticed my body getting very heavy and tight and my mood increasingly grim. As I would begin a meal in my hut, waves of nausea would wash over me, and some nausea would persist through most of the day.

After a few days of this, I spoke with Christopher. He asked about my balance of the Seven Factors of Awakening, referring to a teaching in which the Buddha outlines seven aspects of an awakened mind—mindfulness, inquiry, joy or rapture, effort or energy, calm, concentration, and equanimity. I noted that not much joy was present in me, and he asked how I might find a better balance. I responded that I could go back to eating with the group and spend my days cultivating joy, in the presence of the trees, the sun, spiderwebs, and birds, rather than staying inside so much. I knew that eating with the group was key, that I had crossed an inner boundary of the heart, that the extra degree of solitude was somehow linked to a deep fear, which then manifested itself in my body and heart.

In the next few days, I felt much more joy, moving from heaviness and grimness to lightness and happiness. A few days later, Christina came in the morning to see me in my hut, and I told her what had happened. She responded: "That sounds good. *But what about that fear?* Perhaps it's time to look into that fear again." With some resignation, I admitted that her suggestion was a good one. I set an intention to return to taking my meals alone in the hut, believing that this would lead me back into the difficult territory of fear. (I also decided that it was better not to begin right away with the upcoming lunch but to wait until dinnertime.) During the afternoon, I gave pep talks to myself and convinced myself that when the nausea would start, I would be a great spiritual warrior and face it directly, with confidence and determination.

For hours, I prepared myself by reading spiritual books, gaining inspiration, and garnering support for my moment of truth. Then came dinnertime. I walked slowly to the main building and brought back my meal. I sat down to eat, as if ready for the battle, ready for my body to tighten and the nausea to commence. I ate slowly. I waited. I continued to eat. I waited. But nothing happened. Time went on, and still nothing happened. There was no nausea, no heaviness, no grimness. Not that evening and not for the remaining ten weeks of the retreat.

It was as if the nausea and other bodily reactions had manifested my fear of deepened solitude. When I was willing to face that fear, the fear left. According to Jung, when we do not face our inner difficulties with consciousness, they are projected outward and manifest themselves as demons or "fate"; but when we face our inner demons, we take back, as it were, our projections. We diminish the stock of objects and situations in the world that would cause us to feel fear, discovering that many of them are quite imaginary.

When we face our pain directly, much of it is actually removed or transformed. This is because so much of our pain is based on a proliferation of resistance to the original stimulus, the original painful experience. When we face the pain, we begin to stop the resistance, and there can be a great relief from the tremendous effort involved in such resistance.

The Gifts of Transformed Suffering

Working with our suffering in these ways grants us three great gifts—the gift of compassion, the gift of understanding, and the gift of safety, of not passing on our pain to ourselves and to others. These gifts, as we shall see, are central to our skillful action in the world.

First is the gift of *compassion*. When I can work through my resistance and extended commentary related to the pain, and instead actually feel the pain, I am more likely to experience compassion—for myself, for other humans who are vulnerable, and for those who become unbalanced by pain and hence suffer. I may also develop forgiveness for others' reactivity to their own pain and fear and for their ensuing actions.

The second gift is deepened *wisdom.* We can look at our lives and at the world and know better the causes of suffering, both in ourselves and in others, and the causes of liberation.

Third is the gift of *peace and safety for ourselves and for those around us.* As we continue to learn how not to pass on pain to ourselves and others, as we end the cycles of pain and violence, we become, as we saw in chapter 1, "safety zones." Others know they have little to fear from us, and our homes and communities increasingly become sanctuaries.

Rachel Naomi Remen, a physician and healer, tells the story of a young man in his twenties who had lost a leg to cancer; the story points to how these gifts emerge from the process of being with what is painful. At the beginning of their work together, Remen asked the young man to make a drawing of his body. The man drew an outline of a vase with a deep crack running through the center marked over and over again in black, as if the vase were utterly broken, the loss final. However, as they continued working together over many months, he moved gradually from rage, harsh judgment, and self-destructive behavior toward an active concern for those in the hospital with similar losses. At their final meeting, Remen brought back the original drawing. He said that it wasn't finished; he took a yellow crayon and drew thick lines radiating out from the crack to the edges of the paper. He then put his finger on the crack, looked at Remen, and said: "This is where the light comes through."[3]

OPENING TO AND TRANSFORMING PAIN AND SUFFERING IN RELATIONAL AND COLLECTIVE CONTEXTS

The genius of teachers and activists such as Gandhi, King, Thich Nhat Hanh, and Joanna Macy has been to demonstrate that the *same core spiritual principles for working individually with pain and suffering apply in the relational and collective domains.*

As we saw earlier, for Gandhi the heart of nonviolence was the ability to respond with love to pain, including pain linked to hatred and oppression. He spoke of how "an eye for an eye leaves the whole world blind," how "counterhatred" only increases hatred. Furthermore, those engaged in Gandhi's nonviolent movement for an independent India often took on further pain—from beatings, arrests, and prison sentences. They needed, Gandhi believed, to train strenuously in what he called "self-purification," to be able to feel pain without hatred, anger, and fear. Indeed, he spoke of the ability to endure pain without retaliation as the "immovable force" of his movement.[4]

Thich Nhat Hanh also focuses on the importance of opening to suffering in one's community and in the world. He dedicates one of the fourteen precepts of the Tiep Hien Order to this theme, recognizing that much suffering is hidden:

> Do not avoid contact with suffering or close your eyes before suffering. Do not lose awareness of the existence of suffering in the life of the world. Find ways to be with those who are suffering by all means, including personal contact and visits, images, sound. By such means, awaken yourself and others to the reality of suffering in the world.[5]

In 1969, summarizing the Buddhist nonviolent response to the war in Vietnam, he wrote: "Nonviolent action, born of the awareness of suffering and nurtured by love, is the most effective way to confront adversity."[6]

In the following pages, I discuss three *concrete* examples of facing and working with the relational and collective dimensions of pain and suffering. All of them involve methods that are suitable for communities and organizations in transforming their own pain, as well as in working with more collective pain.

Opening to Organizational Suffering: The Work of Joanna Macy

In 2004 a small, spiritually based nonprofit social change organization located on the East Coast of the United States was facing considerable turmoil. There had been a financial downturn, a common occurrence among nonprofits, linked to the aftereffects of the September 11, 2001, attacks, as well as a number of interpersonal conflicts within the organization. Several staff members had been fired. Tension, mistrust, and difficulties in communication were common—between many of the staff members and the director, between some of the staff members and some of the board members, and between some of the organization's supporters and some board members. Many members of the unpaid board felt overworked, beleaguered, misunderstood or unappreciated, and ready to quit. This was particularly poignant and sobering for an organization intent on bringing about nonviolent change and peace in the world.

After some weeks, the board invited Joanna Macy—a teacher and writer grounded in Buddhist practice who for several decades had pioneered methods of transforming pain in group contexts—to consult with the organization. The intent was to ask her to help bring some of the difficulties to the surface as the starting point of a longer process to heal and transform the organization. About thirty people, including the organization's supporters, board members, the director, and staff members, among them those who had been fired, gathered in the home of one of the organization's benefactors one spring afternoon.

Joanna first invited the group to consider with gratitude the work of the organization, reflecting on what was important to each person. With considerable emotion, person after person spoke about his or her warm feelings and appreciation for the organization and its work.

Then Joanna invited those present to explore the recent problems through a practice she called the "Truth Mandala."[7] The group formed a circle, with the inner area constituting four quadrants, each a space of pain and each symbolized by an object: a stone, a cluster of dead leaves, a thick stick, an empty bowl. The stone symbolized fear, the hard and contracted heart; the cluster of dry leaves, sadness and grief; the stick, anger; the empty bowl, confusion and emptiness. After an initial blessing, the participants were instructed to move when ready, one at a time, inside the circle and to let the four symbols invoke some of the personal experiences and emotions of the last few months. By holding the stone, one might talk of one's fear; by holding the bowl, one might speak of one's numbness and confusion. Or one might stay in the center of the circle and speak of something that needed to be said that didn't fit in one of the four quadrants. People were instructed to talk directly from their own experiences, rather than focusing on analyses or reports or responding to what others had said, and to keep what was said confidential. They were instructed to say together "I hear you" after each person spoke and to pause briefly at that point. This would indicate not agreement or approval, but rather that the person speaking had been respectfully received and heard.

Slowly at first, individuals stepped into the inner circle one at a time and spoke movingly, often with tears in their eyes, in ways they had not yet done publicly. They spoke of their fears for the organization, their confusion at how good intentions had led to such difficulties and about what to do, their sense of betrayal about some of the firings, their sadness at witnessing the considerable pain of people dear to them, their anger at some of the actions taken, their sense of not being appreciated or heard, their exhaustion and sense of having reached their limits, as well as their respect for other individuals and the sincerity of their intentions. In perhaps an hour and a half, a great body of pain became apparent. At that point, the ritual ended. There was a short period of sharing what had happened in dyads, followed by a break. The afternoon concluded with an hour for brainstorming key questions and issues for the organization —financial, organizational, interpersonal, philosophical—and the formation of a small group that would be in charge of following up on the process of healing and transformation.

In the initial opening to the pain and suffering of the organization that afternoon, the ice was broken. Conversations began among some of those who were in painful relationships. About five weeks later, at a weekend gathering, the group again took up—this time more extensively—the tender process of truth-telling about what was painful within a protected and carefully facilitated environment. By the end of the weekend, some staff and board members had decided to leave their positions. An interim leadership team arose, with a vote of confidence from all the stakeholders, albeit with some difficult issues with which to deal. Within a short time, however, the focus in discussions was no longer on what was painful but once again on the mission of the organization, as well as organizational and financial questions.

Although the Truth Mandala was used in the above example to help focus on specific difficulties in a specific community, such work, usually carried out in retreat or workshop settings, generally opens us up, in very similar ways, to our pain about the world—related to war, poverty, oppression, and ecological degradation. Having faced pain and suffering more directly, participants in these practices are then ready to enter the second and third phases of Joanna's work: the "turning" to a broader and deeper sense of interdependence and awareness, and the practical "going forth" into the world and one's life, informed by wisdom and compassion.

Opening to Oppression: Mindfulness-based Diversity Work

A second application of working with pain and suffering is in bringing mindfulness to racism and other forms of oppression. Like Joanna Macy's work, this is similar to the work of "bearing witness" mentioned in chapter 2. Larry Yang, a leader in the development of Buddhism-based approaches to diversity issues, uses mindfulness practice to open to the pain of oppression, to touch rather than flee such pain. His intention is to do so without immediately going into the stance of being a victim and blaming oneself or others, even if assessing responsibility is important at a later time. Larry speaks of counteracting such tendencies by facilitating a more direct awareness of pain:

> One of the keys of this work is to be able to feel the intensity of this pain related to oppression and not personalize it, to not quickly move into cementing into place a victim role and the focusing of pain into blame. When we talk about institutional oppression, we're talking about the pain that has come down to us from lifetimes, pain that is washing through our culture right now, without being aimed at any particular life.
>
> When the pain arises in an individual in a circle or group doing this work, the facilitator can use mindfulness practice as a vehicle by which the individual can contact the pain, feel it in his or her body, and explore how he or she is desperately trying to escape the present moment. We try very simply to meet that moment, not by changing it or pushing it away, but by being as spacious as possible, allowing the pain, the anger, the injury, into the room.
>
> When we focus on one person, this looks at times like individual one-on-one work. But I think that we're actually working both in-

dividually and collectively at the same time. The experience of one person may be a trigger, but the whole group is going through the pain, even people who are in denial.

As the participants in his group stay with the pain, the pain "moves through" them, so that it does not stay "stuck" in them in ways that lead to reactivity and suffering:

> When the energy of pain goes into us and gets stuck, we become traumatized. Trauma can be conceptualized as a disturbing or pain-ful experience that intrusively reoccurs in someone's consciousness. If we can feel the pain fully, including how devastating it is, it tends to move through us, because we're allowing it to be present. In this act of being fully present, there is an inherent letting go of what has happened to us in the past, and a letting go of how we would like the future to be—simply being with what is in the present mo-ment. The ego doesn't get in the way, and the painful energy doesn't stay lodged with the ego.

As the group participants touch the pain, they may also become clearer about the need for social action and/or inner work:

> In bringing mindfulness to the pain or to the denial, we don't actu-ally resolve the racism, but we do fully experience what's present. From that moment on, though, people have a choice. Do I want to help change the circumstances which were the causes of this oppres-sion? Do I need to do my own inner work as a precursor to being engaged? Part of the contribution that mindfulness can bring to social transformation is that our response is based in experiential knowledge.[8]

Opening Collectively to Past Oppression: The Truth and Reconciliation Commission of South Africa

A third way of facing collective pain and suffering is through govern-mental inquiries and commissions. Timothy Ash, after having surveyed a number of ways of responding to the horrors of past atrocities, concluded: "What is somewhat biblically called 'truth-telling' is both the most desir-able and the most feasible way to grapple with a difficult past."[9] Led by Archbishop Desmond Tutu, the Truth and Reconciliation Commission (TRC) of South Africa, which completed its work in 2001, represents perhaps the most far-reaching attempt yet in human history to "tell the truth" about past pain and suffering. Its intentions were to set the collective record straight and to bring closure and healing to individuals who have had a chance to tell their painful stories before the whole nation.

Several years ago, I spent a number of days with Bongani Blessing Finca, one of the fifteen commissioners of the TRC. Finca, a veteran of the anti-apartheid struggle, is a minister and regional leader of the Uniting Presbyterian Church and has also served in political positions. He spoke to me of the work of the commission:

> The Truth Commission . . . did a lot of good for the victims, through its process. . . . They had been suffering in silence; it was all bottled up inside. A number of people would come before the commission and say, "I have not spoken about this ever in my life. I'm speaking about it for the first time and opening up." At the end of the day, they would stretch and give a sigh of relief and say, "For the first time, I've got this out of my system."
>
> The commission attempted to create the conditions whereby the victims were accorded respect, were made to feel as if they were the most important persons in the meeting room. A great deal of personal healing took place. There was a lot of bitter crying. Through that process, it seemed that the people had unloaded great burdens from their shoulders. They had each released a heavy spiritual load.
>
> We heard continually of the atrocities that had been committed. There were gruesome, gruesome stories, like that of the murder of the four United Democratic Front activists from Cradock who in 1985 were abducted, tortured, and killed, and whose bodies were burned. As the perpetrators from the security forces were burning these bodies on one side, on another side they were having what we call *braai,* which is a barbecue, and drinking beer. . . .
>
> The kind of cruelty that went with the system of apartheid was just unbelievable. But in all of it, people came forth and gave testimonies and said, "We want to forgive." I remember hearing the testimony of the daughter of one of the four gentlemen from Cradock, a girl who was 16 years old. She said, "I want to forgive. But I do not know whom to forgive. If only I could know who did what to my father, I would like to forgive." This was such a moving testimony by a young person who, at that age, we would expect to be so bitter. But there was no bitterness. So often the attitudes and responses of the victims to the Truth Commission were just amazing. It was an indication of the fact that the people who have suffered most become so generous in spirit, for some strange reason.[10]

In Finca's account we can hear echoes of many of the earlier themes—the importance of a "container" of care, respect, and safety for opening to pain and suffering; the transformative power of such opening; the possibility of ending the reactive cycles of passing on the pain; and the powerful and mysterious way in which gifts such as compassion and forgiveness arise from the process.

THE DANGERS OF OPENING
TO PAIN AND SUFFERING

Not surprisingly, a number of dangers can arise when we open ourselves to pain and suffering in any of the three domains. Here I mention a main area of concern, beyond those I have already discussed.

Perhaps the major danger is the obvious one, that of being overwhelmed physically, emotionally, and/or spiritually when we face pain and suffering more directly. This can occur in opening more fully to the pain, including the hidden pain, of our own lives, of others, or of the collective. The danger is well known from the short-term and long-term effects of those who have participated in or witnessed war and massive violence. Also pervasive is the phenomenon of burnout, particularly of those working in the helping professions and in social change.

The intensity of opening to pain may tend to unbalance us in several ways. We may lose easy access to joy, wonder, and a sense of beauty—becoming depressed, overly grim, or serious. We may tend to glorify our own pain, overemphasizing our sacrifices, becoming morally self-righteous in demanding similar sacrifices of others.

The question of how to take care of oneself while taking care of others and opening to pain is so central to the focus of this book—the connection between individual and social transformation—that I will devote the entire next chapter to the issue.

EXERCISE: A Guided Reflection on
Opening to and Transforming Suffering

After a short period of meditation, bring to mind an area of pain and suffering in your personal life, preferably not your most difficult area. It might involve a physical difficulty, an interpersonal tension or conflict, or personal challenges related to work, finances, or relationships. As you consider this area, be aware of what is happening in your body, heart, and mind. Then reflect on your responses to these questions:

How have you typically experienced this difficult area? Can you sense what has been helpful in your responses? How have you been reactive?

Is this area of pain readily apparent to you, or is it more hidden?

Can you distinguish between the pain that has surfaced and your suffering in reaction to that pain? Can you identify some of the reactive patterns associated with your suffering?

To what extent is the pain unavoidable?

Can you imagine the gifts that you might receive if you skillfully opened further to and worked with the pain and suffering of the situation?

How might you, at the right time, open further to your pain and suffering in a wise, compassionate, and relatively balanced way?

What tools, resources, and supports that you presently have would help you to open to and transform your suffering in this area? What further tools, resources, and supports do you need?

Continue this meditation and reflection over a week (or longer), bearing in mind that the transformation of suffering is commonly a long-term process.

At another time, carry out a similar meditation and reflection in regard to an area of pain and suffering in your relational or collective life, particularly with your family, community, or organization, or with the larger society. In reflecting on the above questions, rephrase them in ways appropriate to the situation, considering also that your response probably will be developed with others, as well as involving an individual component.

Chapter Five

BY TAKING CARE OF MYSELF,
I TAKE CARE OF THE WORLD

Myles Horton, the remarkable cofounder and longtime director of the Highlander School in Tennessee, entitled his autobiography *The Long Haul.* Highlander opened in 1932 and soon became one of the vital centers of the labor, civil rights, and environmental movements in the United States. Rosa Parks attended a two-week workshop at the school a half year before the moment in 1955 when she refused to step out of the "whites only" section in the front of the bus in Montgomery, Alabama. Martin Luther King Jr. went to Highlander regularly.

Horton, originally from the south Tennessee hills, was a powerful guiding force both for the school and for these movements for more than fifty years. Near the end of his life, he reflected on the factors important to keeping active for the long haul, including how long-term goals have to be connected with caring and attention to process:

> It's important to understand that the quality of the process you use to get to a place determines the ends, so when you want to build a democratic society, you have to act democratically in every way. If you want love and brotherhood, you've got to incorporate them as you go along, because you can't just expect them to occur in the future without experiencing them before you get there....A long range goal to me is a direction that grows out of loving people, and caring for people.[1]

Cultivating this understanding of the long haul, and learning what sustains ourselves and our communities, especially when we open regularly to pain and suffering, is crucial both for our spiritual practice and for our action in the world. In this chapter, I suggest perspectives and resources that support such sustained work. Perhaps most fundamental, as we shall see, is clarifying the relationship between self-care and self-love, on the one hand, and taking care of the world, on the other.

REPORT FROM THE FRONTLINES

Those of us who aim to transform both ourselves and the world come under heavy pressure, both from outside and inside, that make it very challenging to take care of ourselves and the world over the long haul. We know the outside problems well. There can be politically motivated repression and even violence directed against opponents and critics of local and national governments and policies. There are the difficulties of sustaining adequate funding for (usually nonprofit) social change organizations and the challenges of chronically low salaries and long hours if we work in such organizations, or of fitting in our spiritual and social change lives after regular hours if we don't. There may be criticisms and at times distortions from those in power and from the mass media and, perhaps worse and more likely, marginalization and lack of attention from the mainstream.

Yet the inner difficulties are perhaps more daunting than the outer difficulties, for they can paralyze and end our engagement. We must somehow sustain ourselves over a lifetime and work with and through such challenges as burnout, despair and hopelessness, fear, an often burning anger at injustice that can become destructive to ourselves and those around us, a sense of isolation, interpersonal differences and tensions within groups and organizations, cynicism, grief, and a sense of being overwhelmed by pain and suffering.

In early 2004 Diana Winston and I convened a gathering in the San Francisco Bay Area designed to provide Buddhist perspectives and resources for those following a life of service. Attending were activists, caregivers, teachers, and therapists, among others. We heard a powerful and sometimes overwhelming litany of wounds from those on the frontlines.

Susan, a teacher with tired eyes, confessed, "The kids suck me dry. I work so hard and sometimes I feel that I receive so little respect." Barbara, who cares for elders, spoke of how difficult it has been to work for such low pay while living in an expensive part of the country: "Money *is* an issue!" Heather, who also works with the elderly, glumly but matter-of-factly stated, "I'm in burnout. I've been sick for a month. I want to say, 'Please let me go!' I feel a lot of resentment, including tremendous frustration with the powers that be. I get really reactive. I feel like there's no space for me; I can't care for myself in this situation."

Jean, who has long worked with the disabled and with foster kids, spoke of being burned out and hopeless about the world. She felt a strong urge to recover her balance and hopefulness, but acknowledged how guilty she sometimes felt taking time off for a short meditation retreat: "I really want to take a year away from my work. That's too much, isn't it?"

Many people simply spoke of being stressed a great deal of the time, of there being always too much to do. For some of those in their forties or older, this meant juggling work, family, elderly parents, and home. A number of participants stated that regular spiritual practice and retreats seem distant possibilities—luxuries for people with other kinds of lives. Even trying to get help with all the tasks sometimes means adding another item to the "to do" list—an item that won't get done.

Others spoke of feeling isolated and of yearning for the support of a community. Stephanie slowly and softly added, "Something's missing for me. I think that I would call it the 'vessel' that might carry me."

Bill spoke of the difficulties he finds, even in his own organization, which is dedicated to social change: "I think that I'm not allowed to take care of myself. I even had pressure not to come here today, a Sunday, because of one of our deadlines!" Lynn said that what she is asked to do is too much: "There is no way that I can ever do what I'm supposed to do. But I try. And meditation and exercise come last. This activist work is so important. But now, I have to say, I feel a lot of disappointment. I feel dry." Ruth, a deeply committed spiritual activist who works long hours, has grappled regularly with despair and hopelessness: "Things just don't seem like they're getting better. We'll all die pretty soon, and what's the point?"

For those dedicated to social service and/or social transformation, these reports form a probably familiar catalog of the difficulties and dangers of such work. These problems can overwhelm us to the point of being unable to continue, to the point of burnout.

ORGANIZATIONAL AND SYSTEMIC ISSUES

As is clear from the testimonies of these caregivers and activists, burnout may be the result of a mix of individual, relational, and collective causes.

For those who were at our retreat, it seemed important particularly to point out how burnout is not simply the product of *individuals'* poor choices, confusions, neuroses, hyperidealism, lack of emotional balance, or spiritual immaturity. Rather, *relational and collective* factors contribute significantly to the difficulties of sustainable transformative work and need to be addressed along with our individual shortcomings.

Some causes of burnout may lie in the difficulties of being part of a particular organization. Christina Maslach and Michael Leiter, in *The Truth about Burnout: How Organizations Cause Personal Stress and What to Do about It,* identify six main *organizational causes* of burnout: overwork, a sense of powerlessness, insufficient rewards, a sense of unfairness, inadequate levels of community, and the presence of major value conflicts.[2]

Overwork, mentioned often by our retreatants, is a particularly prominent cause of burnout for those in organizations dedicated to service and social change because of the relative shortage of funds and the large amount of work that needs to get done. We may take on or be assigned too much work that is often difficult or stressful in itself. Focused on addressing suffering, helping others, or bringing about a new world, we may find it hard to say no to new requests or to limit our own activities. We may set aside insufficient time for our own enjoyment and renewal, even for taking care of our most basic needs. We may feel guilty about our pleasurable pursuits. After some time, the work itself, about which we were initially so enthusiastic, may seem to offer little nourishment. Some forty years ago, well before the recent speedup and expansion of the everyday work world in the United States, Thomas Merton noticed these tendencies with remarkable clarity:

> There is a pervasive form of contemporary violence to which the idealist...most easily succumbs...activism and overwork....To allow oneself to be carried away by a multitude of conflicting concerns, to surrender to too many demands, to commit oneself to too many people, to want to help everyone in everything, is to succumb to violence. The frenzy...kills the root of inner wisdom which makes work fruitful.[3]

Many groups or organizations also do not handle conflicts well, particularly interpersonal conflicts and conflicts concerning other areas mentioned by Maslach and Leiter: justice, power, and values. When individuals and organizations lack the tools and perspectives with which to work through such conflicts, problems may become chronic. When we experience continued frustration around key concerns for a sustained period, we tend to become demoralized and dispirited, and burnout may occur.

While skillful members of organizations may address to some extent the causes of burnout mentioned by Maslach and Leiter, Merton's comment suggests that some of these causes seem to be endemic in contemporary workplaces and in our larger culture. Juliet Schor, in *The Overworked American,* and others have documented that the average number of hours spent in the workplace in the United States has increased dramatically over the last few decades, despite "labor-saving" machines, particularly computers. American workers still have the lowest number of vacation days per year, about twelve, compared with the five or six weeks that are normal in Western Europe, even for entry-level workers. In our preoccupation with work, our main rivals are the Japanese, who recently added the term *karoshi* ("death by overwork") to their vocabulary.[4]

More than twenty years ago, the German philosopher and sociologist Jürgen Habermas pointed out another major trend.[5] He identified what he calls the "colonization of the lifeworld," the ways in which the imperatives of the profit-driven major corporations and the market have moved into domains, such as health and education, that formerly were mostly off-limits. This has occurred in most Western countries near the end of a long process of contraction and sometimes disintegration of the "public sphere," the sphere of public discussion of core issues. The decline of the public sphere makes it more likely that massive structural changes will occur *without* significant public discussion.

A deeper systemic cause of burnout may, however, be less apparent. Our culture focuses rather heavily on the external and relatively little on the inner life. It is not surprising, then, that most workplaces focus primarily on tasks, products, and efficiency and pay less or little (and sometimes no) attention to process, interpersonal relationships, and the inner lives and aspirations of the individuals. It is also not surprising that those who attend to the inner world and to relationships are usually women (still associated with what is inner and private, according to the codes of gender), that women form the large majority of those in the helping professions, and that those in these professions generally receive low salaries.

From this perspective, it is not surprising that these tendencies are present at times even in groups or organizations that are dedicated to social change or that are spiritually based. Unless explicit attention is given to these questions, and, in particular, unless there is a vision of the reciprocal relationship between individual and social transformation, social change organizations will tend to pay little attention to the care of individual change agents, and spiritual organizations will tend to have a difficult time doing other than reproducing the organizational and managerial strategies of the larger society.

For those in the helping professions and for activists, this combination of individual, institutional, and collective pressures can sometimes make it hard to imagine us sustaining ourselves for the "long haul." So who helps the helper? Who cares for the caregiver? Who is active for the activist? How can we both take care of ourselves and take care of others and the world?

THE BODHISATTVA: TAKING CARE OF SELF AND OTHERS

Two Buddhist teachings that resonate strongly with Western spiritual and social change perspectives can provide a powerful starting point. They may also inspire institutional and structural changes that help us take care of ourselves and others for the long haul. The first teaching concerns the vision and practices of the *bodhisattva,* one who is dedicated *both* to individual awakening *and* to responding to the suffering of others. The second concerns the practice of lovingkindness, the cultivation of caring attitudes and actions.

The bodhisattva, literally a "being" *(sattva)* oriented to "awakening" or "enlightenment" *(bodhi),* is a mythical and archetypal figure found particularly in Mahayana (Great Vehicle) Buddhism. The bodhisattva ideal has roots in the original teachings of the Buddha, who was himself described as a bodhisattva, understood at that time as one on the way to becoming a Buddha, a fully awakened one.

In the Mahayana traditions, there developed a pantheon of archetypal bodhisattvas, each of them suggesting and guiding a different kind of mature spiritual activity *in the world.* There is Avalokiteshvara, the male bodhisattva of compassion in India, who becomes Chenrezig in Tibet, and the female Kwan Yin in China (Kannon or Kanzeon in Japan), who is perhaps the most popular and well-known bodhisattva. Avalokiteshvara is sometimes depicted with a thousand hands, each with an eye— to see what is happening in the world and to respond, suggesting both the receptive and active dimensions of compassion. Kwan Yin is often described as the one who "hears the cries of the world." The Dalai Lama is regarded as an incarnation of this bodhisattva.

Manjushri is the bodhisattva of discriminating wisdom, one who sees deeply into the nature of things, and is typically shown wielding a sword said to cut through delusive thoughts and views. Samantabhadra appears as the bodhisattva of enlightening action in the world, particularly making more apparent the interconnection of all beings. Kshitigarbha (known as the very popular Jizo in Japan) is the bodhisattva who watches over the vulnerable, particularly travelers and children.

Such archetypal bodhisattva figures also manifest in ordinary human beings, who may not take particularly prominent social roles. They might appear as the radiant and kind grandmother or the generous and friendly owner of a town's general store, as well as better-known people such as Gandhi, Mother Teresa, Dorothy Day, and Martin Luther King Jr.

The ordinary bodhisattva follows a specific training, a series of disciplines. Such training begins with the orientation to awaken oneself, and to do so for the benefit of all. This intention is often expressed in the "four inconceivable vows":

Living beings are infinite, I vow to free them.
Delusions are inexhaustible, I vow to cut through them.
Dharma gates are boundless, I vow to enter them.
The Buddha Way is unsurpassable, I vow to realize it.[6]

The bodhisattva's training traditionally consists of following an expanded set of ethical precepts and developing in ten key areas, called *paramitas* in Sanskrit (*paramis* in Pali), usually translated as "perfections." The ten *paramitas* are *generosity, ethical conduct, patience, effort* or *energy, meditation, wisdom, skillful means, vow* or *commitment, powers,* and *knowledge.* The first six generally have to do with cultivating the qualities of a mature bodhisattva, and the last four are particularly connected with a bodhisattva's actions in the world.

Generosity (dana), the starting point in the training, has to do with developing the ability to give to others, to serve, which requires a transformation of our usual split between self and other, as well as an investigation of any sense of the superiority of the giver or helper. To develop in *ethical conduct (sila)* is initially to follow the core ethical precepts until they become the natural contours of one's being. *Patience (kshanti)* is particularly valuable in the face of difficulties, both inner and outer, and helps us to continue, no matter what happens. *Effort* or *energy (virya)* is not just the heroic ability to persist "when the going gets rough," but also the ability to act more and more with wisdom and compassion in each moment, rather than to give in to conditioning. *Meditation (dhyana)* concerns the development of both the concentration and the mindfulness practices that permit one to penetrate deeply into the nature of experience. And *wisdom (prajna)* is the deep seeing, the knowing of the nature of things, which is said to bring freedom.

Skillful means (upaya) have to do with the creativity, intuition, and large repertoire of tools that help us to intervene with a particular person or situation in such a way as to support freedom. *Vow* or *commitment (pranidhana)* reflects the focused and stabilized intention to work for the transformation of self and others in all circumstances. *Powers (bala)* refers traditionally to certain psychic powers that can be used in the bodhisattva's work; developing powers can also be seen as the cultivation to a high degree of our own strengths and gifts. Finally, *knowledge (jnana)* is an aspect of wisdom involving the maturation of the higher forms of spiritual understanding as well as the ability to act, guided by such understanding.

THE RESONANCE OF THE BODHISATTVA IDEAL WITH THE WESTERN PROPHETIC TRADITIONS OF SOCIALLY ENGAGED SPIRITUALITY

The vision and practices of the bodhisattva have sparked the imagination of many in the West, for a number of reasons. Perhaps foremost among them, as I suggested earlier, is the widespread attraction to how the bodhisattva connects both inner and outer transformation. But there are also profound resonances with Western cultural ideals, particularly with the prophetic commitment (Jewish, Christian, and Islamic) to spiritually grounded service and work for justice in the world. What seems to be added with the bodhisattva model is a clearer emphasis on inner training and transformation. Hence, as the bodhisattva meets the Western prophetic traditions (including the secularized progressive traditions of social change, heirs to much of the formerly religiously based prophetic energy), we may see a richer integration of inner and outer work than we have yet seen in either tradition alone. We may also find a powerful reimagination of the very meaning of the bodhisattva ideal.

The Jewish prophets of the Old Testament, appearing over some two centuries starting in the mid-eighth century BCE, pointed out with enormous fervor the problems of their times—including moral deterioration, hypocrisy, self-centeredness, and a lack of compassion for those in need. The moral and spiritual force of the prophets has left both Jews and Christians following in the prophetic tradition with a sense that acting to serve others and to bring about justice is a primary spiritual imperative, that the intention to "repair the world" *(tikkun olam)* should be a basic contour of our spiritual lives.

Jesus saw his own ministry as continuing the work of the prophets. Like them, he criticized religious hypocrisy among the scribes and Pharisees, throwing the money changers out of the temple. He spoke for the oppressed, the downtrodden, and the suffering. He was also particularly powerful in making clear the connection between inner states and outer action, emphasizing the centrality of love in responding to the suffering of the world. Such love is both of God and of oneself and one's neighbors.

In the contemporary setting of the United States, arguably the African American Christian tradition has most strongly continued the prophetic tradition and emphasized the role of love in social change. In that context, love is a way to answer hatred and violence and to work with the self-doubt, self-hatred, frustration, and conflict that racism tends to engender in its targets. From A. Philip Randolph and Howard Thurman, to Martin Luther King Jr. and James Baldwin, to Cornel West and bell hooks, love has been understood as central to social transformation.

Love becomes a primary means to work through the effects of oppression, including tendencies to hate the oppressor, and becomes a force for justice. Social critic and spiritual activist Cornel West describes the powerful response of Mamie Till to the murder of Emmett Till, her fourteen-year-old African American son, lynched and mutilated in Mississippi by two white men for whistling at a white woman at a rural grocery store in 1955. Before a packed church in Chicago, after 125,000 people had walked by the open coffin with her child inside, his head five times its normal size, she announced, "I don't have a minute to hate. I'll pursue justice for the rest of my life."[7] Yet to come to love is not so easy; one who is hated and oppressed must also counter an internalized self-hatred and often needs to begin with love of self, as Malcolm X particularly emphasized. Cornel West summarizes: "For the oppressed to love themselves is subversive; to love themselves *and* others is miraculous."[8]

LOVINGKINDNESS PRACTICE: THE CULTIVATION OF SELF-LOVE AND LOVE OF OTHERS

If love is central to taking care of both oneself and others, then the natural question is: How do we develop both self-love and the love of others?

Another great resource of Buddhist tradition is the practice of lovingkindness (*metta* in Pali, *maitri* in Sanskrit), in which caring for oneself is explicitly connected with caring for others. The word *metta* is etymologically connected with words connoting friendliness and kindness and suggests a fundamental quality of warmth, caring, and openness. The term has some but not all of the connotations of *love* (and its cognates in other Western languages); there is no suggestion, for example, of romantic love.

Of particular value for those dedicated to inner and outer transformation is the fact that there are detailed instructions for cultivating this quality, instructions that can be applied both in solitary meditation and in the midst of activity. Interestingly, although love is clearly at the center of Christian spirituality, there do not seem to be comparably methodical Christian practices, although the Jesus Prayer and the contemporary Centering Prayer open up very similar territory.

Hence the practice of lovingkindness can be at the heart of a life of service and transformation. In the classical tradition, it is the first of the four *brahmavihara,* or "divine abodes," the four qualities of the open heart, and it expresses a basic warmth and friendliness. When it encounters suffering, it becomes compassion *(karuna),* the second of the divine abodes, understood as the quivering of the heart that is in contact with suffering. When lovingkindness meets beauty or happiness, particularly that of others, it becomes *mudita,* or joy, especially joy in the joy of others. Equanimity *(upekkha)* is the fourth of the brahmavihara and serves particularly to balance lovingkindness, compassion, and joy with wisdom.

EXERCISE: The Practice of Lovingkindness

The practice of lovingkindness works with short phrases that one repeats constantly, first in reference to oneself and then in reference to various others, gradually extending toward all beings. We choose phrases, either the traditional ones or those of our own creation, that seem best to open our hearts and resonate emotionally with us. The traditional phrases, as collected in the fifth-century text by Buddhaghosa, *The Path of Purification,* are the following, with alternative phrases added (the alternatives are indented further):

May I (or you) be free from danger.
    May I be safe and free from harm.
May I have mental happiness.
    May I be happy.
May I have physical happiness.
    May I be healthy (or as healthy as possible).
    May my body and mind support my awakening.
    May I accept my limitations with grace.
May I have ease of well-being.
    May I live with ease.

Other possible phrases include:

May I accept myself just as I am.
May I be free.
May I be loving.
May I be peaceful.

Typically, we use four phrases like the classical ones that express several nuances of well-being: safety, happiness, health, and ease.

Adopting a comfortable posture, repeat these phrases silently and internally, over and over again. Start with yourself, and move in a sequence of bringing lovingkindness to those in different relationships with you, following this general order:

Yourself.

A benefactor (a mentor, teacher, guide, or someone who has helped you).

A close friend (usually not initially a partner or someone with whom there is a complex relationship).

A neutral person (perhaps someone at work or in your neighborhood to whom you pay little attention).

A difficult person (traditionally identified as an "enemy," but initially a mildly or moderately difficult person for you).

All beings (you can either gradually expand your awareness outwardly in space in all directions—to the front, to the back, to either side, above, and below—or bring your lovingkindness to different classes of beings—all females and all males; all humans, all nonhumans; all beings known to you, all beings unknown to you; and so forth).

One helpful way to work with the phrases that I learned from my colleague Guy Armstrong is, for each phrase, to first develop an image of the being (human or nonhuman) toward whom you are directing metta, then to bring your attention to the center of your chest (sometimes called the "heart center"), then to say the phrase, and finally to listen for the resonance in your body, heart, and mind. You can just take a moment for each of these steps.

Do this practice initially for 10 minutes at a time, before or after your main contemplative practice. You can also do the practice for longer periods, for 30 or 45 minutes daily, or even for an extended retreat of a day, a week, or longer. You can bring lovingkindness practice into the world, practicing while driving, at meetings, or taking a walk.

One Who Loves Oneself
Will Never Harm Another

In his fifth-century discussion of the practice of lovingkindness, Buddha-ghosa quotes a remarkable passage that Guy Armstrong pointed out to me, said traditionally to be one of the "inspired utterances" *(udana)* of the Buddha:

> I visited all quarters with my mind
> Nor found I any dearer than myself;
> Self is likewise to every other dear;
> Who loves himself will never harm another.[9]

When I first heard this passage, in the midst of coteaching a week-long lovingkindness retreat several years ago, it had a powerful impact on me. It seemed to bring together, particularly in the last line, a number of interrelated insights crucial for understanding the balance between taking care of oneself and the world. It suggested that

> love of self is fundamental to spiritual life and social change;
> love of self and love of others are connected, that love of self must
> be present in order to love another; and
> the act of harming others often comes out of a lack of self-love.

Love of Self Is Fundamental to
Spiritual Life and Social Change

The importance of caring for oneself and loving oneself may sometimes seem obvious. Yet as we have seen, it is surprising how many reasons we may accumulate to justify *not* loving ourselves. Primary among them is the belief that to love oneself is to be *selfish,* and "I should *not* be selfish, narcissistic, and navel-gazing"—because "I am a spiritual person," because "I don't want to be *that* kind of selfish spiritual person, or because "Others have far greater needs than I do and suffer more than I do, and my role is to serve."

Justine Dawson, who has worked at a Catholic Worker home for women and children in transition from homelessness, poverty, and domestic violence and has been an activist as well as a long-term meditator, speaks of the difficulties of taking care of herself in direct-service work and activism:

> In my work, there is not a focus on self-care. It is really about serving others, and sometimes self-care has been looked down upon. It

has been seen as close to selfish, as self-centered and sometimes as "bourgeois," almost as a kind of threat to the work that we do. I found the same tendencies among many activists. The idea is that you should be out there serving, night and day.[10]

It is very true that spiritual practice as well as service and social change work can sometimes be used in a self-centered way. We may create self-serving images of ourselves. We may be motivated in large part by what we take to be others' positive perceptions of us. We may also, while furthering our spiritual pursuits, tend to ignore the immense suffering in the world, perhaps taking advantage of our social privileges to help distance ourselves from such suffering.

But the corrective in relation to tendencies toward selfishness is not, as it were, to go to the other extreme and avoid any concern for oneself. Rather, authentic spiritual practices tend, as we have seen, to reveal and undermine selfishness, to transform the separation of self and other, and to lead toward the care of others. Somewhat ironically, we could say that going to the depths of the self is not selfish. The great thirteenth-century Japanese Zen teacher Dogen articulated this insight in this way:

To study the Buddha Way is to study oneself.
To study oneself is to forget oneself.
To forget oneself is to be enlightened by the ten thousand dharmas.[11]

The fear of appearing selfish may also be linked with one or more states of mind that make self-love and self-care difficult or impossible—for example, guilt, negative self-judgment, and despair. Of course, such emotional complexes may be operative in part because of difficult personal and collective histories; therefore significant healing and transformation may take considerable time and effort. Identifying, exploring, and working through them can involve a number of tools and approaches, including personal reflection, meditation and other spiritual practices, psychotherapy, participation in support groups or communities, living in a family, and having intimate relationships. These kinds of supportive settings help make self-love possible.

On the other hand, difficult conditions, such as family conflicts and violence, poverty, racism, sexism, and other forms of oppression, make self-love much harder. An awareness of such relational and collective contexts is often extremely helpful, most obviously among those who bear the burden both of difficult external conditions and of "internalized oppression."

For example, African Americans and other people of color, gays and lesbians, women, Jews, Arab Americans, young people, poor and lower-class people, among others, can *internalize* and accept, often unconsciously, mainstream views and stereotypes (especially negative ones) about their groups. Furthermore, members of these groups are sometimes conditioned to be "selfless" in their service and discover internal resistance to taking care of themselves. This is why Malcolm X, Martin Luther King Jr., and others have particularly emphasized self-love, self-esteem, and healthy "pride" and why feminists have often focused on the conditioning of most women to serve others, often at the expense of their own well-being.

But even for those who seem relatively unoppressed, there may be strong conditioning that makes self-love difficult. Indeed metta practice, as well as some of the other ways of developing self-love mentioned earlier, can be seen as a sometimes slow purification practice, in which we notice and over time transform the many patterns that hinder self-love, nurturing the plant of self-love as it becomes larger and healthier.

Negative self-judgment is a particularly pervasive pattern in Western societies, even among relatively privileged people. Indeed, self-judgment (and the judgment of others) is one of two or three subjects that I hear most frequently mentioned in my meditation classes and retreats.

When the Dalai Lama first came to the United States, in 1979, he visited the Insight Meditation Society in Barre, Massachusetts, where I was staying for a number of months. During a question-and-answer session with those at a three-month retreat, one person told him, "I don't feel deserving of love," and asked what he should do. The normally kind, gentle, soft-spoken, and receptive monk was forthright, direct, and blunt: "You are wrong! You deserve love."

Love of Self and Love of Others Are Connected

As we carry out this transformative work on ourselves, knowing firsthand what obstructs self-love and cultivating love of self, we begin to see the links between self-love and love of others. Having worked through our self-judgment, self-images, guilt, fear, internalized oppression, and despair to a significant extent, we recognize the dynamics of these patterns more readily in others and can more easily serve them, motivated in large part by compassion for suffering, which we have known intimately ourselves.

In lovingkindness practice, love of self is the basis for loving others. To cultivate lovingkindness toward oneself or others is to cultivate a kind of *unconditional* caring and well-wishing. Such love is not dependent on our meeting certain criteria, our own, those of others, or those of the culture. In traditional practice, starting with oneself was commonly understood as the most skillful way to access this unconditional care and kindness. In teaching lovingkindness in the West, however, many teachers have found that it is sometimes more skillful to begin with caring for others, especially when self-judgment and self-hatred are extensive. Some teachers have even suggested stuffed animals or pets as appropriate initial recipients of lovingkindness; the intention is to find any being or even object toward which lovingkindness flows easily.

Having accessed lovingkindness for ourselves, we begin to cultivate it toward others, starting with those for whom lovingkindness comes most easily (mentors, benefactors, close and dear friends), and gradually extending it to all beings (first with a person toward whom we feel neutral, then with a difficult person, and finally to all beings). In time, we find that the energy of caring, kindness, and love is ultimately without boundaries, although our habits and cultural conditioning limit access to this wondrous source of energy. Finding lovingkindness first in relation to ourselves, we begin to access the "boundless heart" of which the Buddha speaks in the *Metta Sutta*:

> This is what should be done
> By those who are skilled in goodness,
> And who know the path of peace...
> Wishing: in gladness and in safety,
> May all beings be at ease.
> Whatever living beings there may be;
> Whether they are weak or strong, omitting none,
> The great or the mighty, medium, short or small,
> The seen and the unseen,
> Those living near and far away,
> Those born and to-be-born—
> May all beings be at ease![12]

Tempel Smith, who has trained as a monk in Asia, worked extensively with teenagers, including as a counselor at a teen crisis center and as a meditation teacher, and guided the Buddhist Peace Fellowship's BASE program, speaks of a pivotal moment after he returned to the San Francisco Bay Area following a three-month lovingkindness retreat, and of the effects of metta practice on his action in the world.

> I remember sitting in the Berkeley hills after the retreat; I could see all of Berkeley, Oakland, and San Francisco. In the past, I had seen

myself as a "nature lover"; urban settings typically got my mind going in negative directions. But this time, looking at this large urban
area, I had a different thought: "Oh my God, so many people to
love, so many people I can see." In the past, I would usually look at
cars and feel bad about pollution. Yet on this day I thought, "I can
see individual people going about their lives. It's not abstract. I can
really take in millions of people in this view and I really do wish the
best for every single one of them." I found that these thoughts didn't
just come and go. Rather, they stayed and grew. I felt energy coming
into my mind and body and felt a new way to be in the Bay Area and
relate to that many people.

To practice metta for three months was a strong and clear indica-
tor of the heart's potential. It changed so many of my views about
the world. Previously, I had a huge list about what was bad about
humanity, and my list of what was good was pretty short. After the
retreat, I could more readily see the beauty in people, being very
touched, for example, by watching a father lovingly hold his daughter while she slept on public transportation. To be relatively free of
aversion for this period of time changed my entire motivation for
activism, which previously had been fueled by anger, frustration,
and judgment. Metta changed all that.[13]

When we face the many obstacles to self-love, we also face that which
separates us from others. By our willingness to touch our own pain, we
make sure not to pass it on to others through often unconscious hatred,
aggression, blaming, scapegoating, and projection.

In this way, the practice of love of self is a gift of safety, both to oneself
and to others—one who loves oneself will not harm another. As the Buddha remarks, "Protecting oneself...one protects others; protecting others, one protects oneself."[14]

Harming Others Often Comes Out
of a Lack of Self-Love

If one who loves oneself will *never* harm another, then one without self-
love *may* harm another. Indeed, much of the harm done in the world can
be attributed to a lack of self-love. As the Buddha pointed out in the
Dhammapada (echoed later by Jesus, Gandhi, and King), the cycle of hatred and violence depends on a lack of love. These cycles end when there
is love; "hatred only ends with love," the Buddha tells us. If the practice of
metta helps to transform the roots in ourselves of the harm we cause oth-

ers, then it is plausible that a dearth of self-love may be among the roots of hatred and violence.

We can address these roots, and thus transform situations of violence, in part by developing self-love and the conditions for self-love. One way to begin is to identify conditions that make self-love and self-care difficult, including some that we have mentioned in this chapter, and to work to eliminate or mitigate them. Among these conditions are the cultural devaluation of members of certain groups (identified by race, ethnicity, gender, sexual orientation, and so on); the institutional discrimination and repression related to such devaluation; the lack of attention to healing from the legacies of past suffering and violence; systemic overwork; and the lack of resources that can support various kinds of self-love and self-care, including psychological, medical, community, and spiritual resources. Naming these conditions suggests as well some of the antidotes to these conditions, including cultural visions of equality amid diversity, complemented by institutional expressions of these visions; a dedication to working to transform the residues of past suffering and violence, including an emphasis on restorative justice; and adequate resources for, and helpful perspectives on, self-love and self-care.

This approach can, I believe, help to integrate aspects of the typical conservative and liberal responses to violence in the United States. For example, conservatives commonly label the violence of crime (as opposed to governmental violence) as immoral or evil, focusing on its individual causes. Liberals usually attempt to locate external causes and to transform the structural and institutional reasons for violence—for example, in poverty or oppression. Focusing on the need for self-love *and* the conditions that make it possible is to refer to both inner and outer factors.

Such a perspective has many implications for our engagement in the world. It suggests programs for those with tendencies toward violence, whether they are our leaders or those on the bottom of the social hierarchy. It points to how, as Cornel West suggests, self-love, particularly of those on the bottom, is subversive of oppression and works against violence. It also suggests that taking care of ourselves and avoiding burnout are far from selfish. They ensure not only our own sustainability, but also help us penetrate some of the roots of our major social problems. Justine Dawson speaks of the importance of self-care in her own spiritually grounded direct-service work:

For me, it feels radical to say that self-care is important. It makes it possible for me to act more fully. I think that it is also a part of social change for me to model such self-care. Caring for myself every day as I care for others helps to make things different in the world, because it protects me from being workaholic and reactive.[15]

TRANSFORMING THE ORGANIZATIONAL AND SOCIAL CONDITIONS THAT LEAD TO BURNOUT

When we asked the caregivers and activists who attended the gathering mentioned earlier, and who had so poignantly named the conditions leading to burnout, about what helped them to take care of themselves, they responded in considerable detail. They pointed to the importance of diet, exercise, rest, spiritual practices, other ways to renew themselves, and a number of helpful perspectives and principles. They were less clear, however, about how to respond to the *relational* and *collective* roots of burnout.

So how do we begin to implement the bodhisattva ideal and the practice of love and self-care and create norms, practices, and structures for groups, organizations, communities, and the larger society? Asking and taking these questions seriously are a significant beginning, although to do so may require considerable leadership, skill, and willingness to take risks.

There are also a number of helpful resources. Over the last forty years, there has been considerable development in the areas of group dynamics, organizational development, and conflict resolution, of skillful ways to incorporate more caring and more awareness of our subjective lives into groups and organizations. This kind of work has identified ways to address many of the key factors identified earlier as the organizational roots of burnout, such as perceptions of powerlessness and injustice, lack of adequate community, and unskillful ways of dealing with conflicts.

What seems to be called for is a kind of marriage of spiritual perspectives and the best wisdom about healthy organizations. It may mean, for example, having short, regular periods of meditation as part of the workday. It may mean having periodic group or organizational retreats to develop deeper bonds of caring based on knowing one's colleagues well, particularly their aspirations and sufferings. It may mean paying attention to exploring ways of communicating, clarifying decision-making procedures, transforming conflicts, and examining shadow material.

For those of us in groups, organizations, and workplaces that are not oriented spiritually, our approaches will usually be somewhat different. We may seek to find ways to translate our spiritual values into a more secular language or sometimes into general interfaith spiritual perspectives.

Of course, this can be quite challenging. Yet even in secular settings, these values may not be so hard to translate. There can be a shared appreciation of quiet reflection and contemplative periods, as well as an openness to retreats. And it may not be difficult to find nonspiritual ways of "operationalizing" the values of love, compassion, and balance in our inner and outer lives in the areas of communication, decision making, and conflict. In this context, the pragmatic and experiential emphases of Buddhist practice may help us to find bridges.

Yet such local relational work can go only so far. As we have seen, groups, organizations, and communities are part and parcel of the larger economic, political, and social systems and vulnerable to them in many ways. How, for example, might we come to work less in this society and have more free time? How might nonmarket values guide our work lives, and how might the impact of market values and the colonization of the lifeworld be limited? How might there be public discussion of these kinds of questions? How might alternative models and institutions be developed?

In posing these questions, we begin to see that the intention to transform the systemic roots of burnout links us with the larger contemporary aspirations of social transformation: the development of societies and a world that are more *democratic* (and in which these kinds of questions are more matters of public discussion), more *sustainable*, and *more grounded in nonmarket ethical and spiritual values*. For each of these broad aspirations, there are valuable resources: analyses of the problems, alternative models and experiments, and scenarios for change (see "Further Resources").

In this sense, attempts to respond individually to the problem of burnout and self-care are vital, but they are insufficient. In examining concerns about caring for oneself and others, we may see more clearly how the roots of suffering as well as the possible responses to such suffering are indeed personal, but also relational and collective. We may come to see, paradoxically, as David Brazier suggests, that "[t]he most effective way of helping others is to make spiritual progress oneself and the best way to make spiritual progress oneself is by helping others."[16] As I take care of myself, I take care of the world. As I take care of the world, I take care of myself.

Chapter Six

NOT KNOWING BUT
KEEPING GOING

It is the winter of 1929–1930 in India, and there is tension in the air. The independence movement is in some disarray. Among the leaders of the Congress Party, including Mohandas Gandhi, there is a lack of unity and clarity about tactics. There have been conflicts between Hindus and Muslims as well as terrorist attacks on British officials. Rabindranath Tagore, the great Bengali poet, visits Gandhi at his rural ashram on the Sabarmati River near India's west coast and asks him which direction should be followed. Gandhi replies, "I do not see any light coming out of the surrounding darkness.... There is a lot of violence in the air."

Gandhi stays at his ashram for weeks. He withdraws from most contact and is alone most of the time. He prays and meditates, and for hours sits on the veranda of his home. No one knows what he is thinking; he tells fellow ashram members, "I'm just waiting. I'm waiting for the call. I know that I will hear the inner voice."

At the end of some six weeks of such waiting, not knowing, and contemplation, he finally "knows." He will lead a "Salt March" from the ashram to the sea, about 250 miles away, and make salt, which is against the colonial laws guaranteeing a British monopoly on making salt (a commodity necessary for cooking and preserving food in a tropical climate). The march takes three weeks. Tens of thousands gather at different towns and cities along the route. It initiates months of civil disobedience and is met mostly by repression—beatings, jailings, seizures of property, banning of publications, and outlawing of many organizations—as well as some negotiations.

Although this campaign does not force out the British immediately, it is pivotal in ending the legitimacy of British rule. After so much repression, the British can no longer maintain their civilizing facade and its associated claims—that their rule is for the betterment of the native population economically, socially, and politically and that it will eventually lead to home rule.[1]

The understanding that "not knowing" is at times central to spiritually grounded action in the world, as this story suggests, should not be surprising when we consider that we find "not knowing" or "unknowing" emphasized in different ways in many spiritual and philosophical traditions. Such a "not knowing" paradoxically can often bring us to a kind of deeper "knowing" that is unlike our ordinary knowing.

In many indigenous traditions, for example, we find the practice of the vision quest in the wilderness—for initiating young persons, for spiritual renewal, for seeking deeper understanding. This cultivation requires a kind of "not knowing." The person on the vision quest must drop preoccupations with the familiar details of everyday life, leave the community, and go into the wilderness, staying continually open to what he or she seeks.

Jews remind us of the ultimate unknowing and mystery of the sacred when they refuse to spell out the name of God. Christian mystics speak of the "cloud of unknowing," of immersing themselves in a "cloud of forgetting" of what they ordinarily know, enduring the dark night of the soul in which all that they think that they know has no meaning. Socrates, one of the originators of Western philosophical traditions, claims that the deepest wisdom is only to know that one doesn't know, as a prelude to deep questioning and possible knowledge. Hindu sages, when asked about the sacred, say, *"Neti, neti"*: "Not this, not this." The Tao Te Ching, to give a final example, opens with these famous lines:

> The Tao that can be told of is not the eternal Tao;
> The name that can be named is not the eternal name;
> The Nameless is at the origin of Heaven and earth.[2]

But what does "not knowing" or "unknowing" mean concretely in terms of our spiritual practice, our everyday lives, and our action in the world? Why is it important as a core principle for those committed to compassionate action, justice, and social change? Aren't certain kinds of knowledge—such as social analyses, strategies, and policies—sometimes indispensable? And how is not knowing different from ignorance, which according to the Buddha is the root cause of suffering? Are there traps in not knowing, dangers that we invariably encounter when we cultivate this quality? How in particular might we see "not knowing" as balanced by an emphasis on "keeping going"?

In this chapter, I will explore the meaning and importance of not knowing in individual, relational, and collective contexts. I will first (1) examine its meaning in individual mindfulness practice and (2) at times when it is important to cultivate new vision by suspending our habitual assumptions. Then, I will (3) present two further aspects of not knowing, in which we cultivate non-attachment to views and deep listening. Finally, I will (4) identify three dangers of cultivating not knowing.

NOT KNOWING AND MINDFULNESS PRACTICE

Developing a capacity to let go of habitual, routinized forms of knowing is fundamental to mindfulness practice. In such meditation, we cultivate, as much as possible, a bare attention to moment-to-moment experience, a kind of open, present-centered, direct, and nonjudgmental awareness.

Paradoxically, this awareness reflects a kind of knowing that depends on unknowing: on noticing and releasing our usual tendencies to "know" our experience through repetitive thoughts. We see and let go, at least temporarily, of the ways in which we frame our experiences through familiar personal and cultural stories and concepts, interpretations of the past and future, and the seemingly nonstop series of highly repetitive comments on the details of these experiences.

Most beginning meditators learn how hard it is simply to feel the sensations of the breath, to see a tree or watch a sunset, or to listen to a friend without an ongoing mental commentary. We discover, often with some surprise, how much of our life seems organized, dominated, and driven by repetitive ideas. (A Stanford University study once showed that 93 percent of our daily thoughts have occurred previously.) At later stages of our mindfulness practice, we may begin to be aware of the emotional correlates and the deeper roots of such repetitive thoughts—a varied mix of fears and anxieties, longings and hopes, painful and pleasant memories (both conscious and unconscious).

I was amazed, in my own initial meditation practice as a student, to notice how much I was thinking—all the time! I was particularly surprised to see the extent to which I would rehearse or plan for an upcoming activity. If I needed to give a report in a few days, I would go over my plan numerous times in a meditation period of forty-five minutes, often duplicating exactly what I had thought a few minutes earlier. I would also notice such planning occurring outside of meditation, in my passing thoughts, 50 or 60 times (or more) in a day or two, in addition to my actual time of sitting down and planning the report. It seemed quite excessive to me, and I was able to tell myself, with blazing insight, "Well, perhaps 10 or 20 times is quite enough!"

I could also discern that much of the planning seemed spurred by a desire to control the outcome (and my experience in general). There seemed to be a fear of what might happen were I not to exert control in this way.

One important aspect of our mindfulness practice is thus the exploration of the ways in which our everyday knowing—personal, cultural, or institutional—commonly has a shadow, a "dark side," that our human quest to know is often fueled by fear, greed, hatred, and (ironically) delusion. Our knowing may of course also be guided by love, wonder and awe, compassion, caring, wisdom, a sense of justice, or the intention to meet an important need or solve a problem. Often we can come to know the difference only after we have learned to suspend our ordinary knowing.

When we have learned not to know so compulsively, we can return to knowing. We come to see that *the problem is actually not thinking or knowing, but rather our lack of wisdom about such thinking and knowledge.* Hence, our practice of not knowing initiates a journey of discovery, in which we first study our ordinary knowing, then suspend such knowing in a kind of "not knowing," only to return to a new and extraordinary knowing. In this sense, not knowing is not at all the same as ignorance; rather it makes it possible for us to move from ignorance to deeper knowledge, to wisdom.

The transformative power of entering into the often paradoxical process of "not knowing" is strongly emphasized in Zen practice. In his "Verses on the Faith Mind," Seng-tsan, living in eighth-century China, urged his students to know the truth by cultivating not knowing:

> If you wish to see the truth
> then hold no opinions for or against anything.
> To set up what you like against what you dislike is the disease of
>   the mind....
> Do not search for the truth;
> only cease to cherish opinions.[3]

The Korean teacher Seung Sahn exhorted his students, "Only keep 'don't know mind.'"

A TIME NOT TO KNOW

While we may often enter contemplative practice to learn such not knowing, there are also other special times to cultivate this quality. We may periodically go into the dark and unfamiliar territory of not knowing, following daily, weekly, seasonal, and cyclical rhythms. And so we may engage in mindfulness practice once a day or more often, returning to unknowing, emptying ourselves of our preoccupations and subtle agendas.

We may keep the wonderful practice of the sabbath, so that once a week we let go of newspapers, television, radio, e-mails, and telephones. In our speedy culture, such a practice has a great impact—slowing us down to listen, not just on the sabbath day but on the other six days, as we more readily remember to be present, as our bodies and minds remember the sabbath. Or, as in most cultures, we may follow the seasonal rhythms of death and rebirth in rituals and celebrations in which we let go of the old and welcome the new, in which we overcome temporarily what we might call the tyranny of daily life, or in which we remember our deeper intentions.

Spiritual retreats can also be understood as a time of entering into the unknown, of letting go not only of our ordinary concerns but also of our spiritual expectations. Such sustained periods of unknowing may bring us renewal and inspiration and permit new ways of living, understanding, and knowing to emerge. We may also regularly go into the wilderness, or even on vacations, in the spirit of not knowing.

We may, like Gandhi, go into a brief or longer retreat or a period of inactivity when we don't know what to do, when we are at a crossroads in our lives. Upon his return to India in 1915, after having spent more than twenty years in South Africa, Gandhi vowed to renew his acquaintance with India by dedicating one year to traveling and listening, "his ears open but his mouth shut."[4]

Sometimes there are longer and often difficult periods in our lives when we either choose or somehow are chosen by our life circumstances to enter a sustained time of not knowing—of inquiry, listening, exploring, and sometimes confusion. The Buddha himself went off on a six-year voyage of discovery after he left the palace and his former life. Carl Jung, following his break with Freud in 1912, dropped much of the outer structure of his life for several years, in a period that led to what he called a "confrontation with the unconscious." He later wrote: "After the parting of the ways with Freud, a period of inner uncertainty began for me. It would be no exaggeration to call it a state of disorientation. I felt totally suspended in mid-air, for I had not yet found my own footing."[5]

Similarly, Thich Nhat Hanh entered a five-year period of retreat from 1977 to 1982 after being forced, by the hostility of the governments of Thailand and Singapore, to stop helping the Vietnamese boat people. During that time, he was largely in seclusion, mostly meditating, writing, reading, and gardening. For the Buddha and Jung, and to some extent for Thich Nhat Hanh, such periods generated the core insights that animated their later work.

At several transitional periods in my life, I chose to enter a time of not knowing. Several years ago, for example, I entered a period of over a year in which I deliberately dropped many of the structures and much of the busyness of my life, with the explicit intention of making space for what was new and deeper, more authentic, more passionate. I knew in a more intellectual way that what would probably surface from that open time and space would be an expression of a deepened commitment to spiritual practice and spiritually grounded action in the world and would be more practical and committed, more grounded in meditation, and less academic. But I knew neither the forms that would emerge nor the precise steps to take in that direction. I only knew that I needed to let go, wait, and listen.

And so I first dropped, within the first few months, most of my obligations. At times it was quite scary (although also a great privilege) to have so little structure. Yet over time, particularly with the aid of the retreats, I came to feel my deeper intentions. As I suggested, I was not surprised by the outcomes of the year. Rather, I grounded my core intentions more firmly and deeply, through a kind of clearing away of some of the inner and outer debris that blocked or obscured the path of my life.

TWO FURTHER WAYS OF PRACTICING NOT KNOWING

Mindfulness practice discloses that we are commonly dominated by habitual thinking. Such a training in not knowing can be further refined in two basic ways that are of great importance to us as individuals, in our relationships, and in our action in the world. First, *we may work through our "attachments" to our views and positions,* especially by developing mindfulness of such views and positions and inquiring into their roots. Second, and more positively, *we may cultivate a quality of deep listening,* especially to others.

Deconstructing Our Attachments to Views: Holding Our Views More Lightly

Dogmatically held ideologies and positions, whether found among dictators, religious leaders, or indoctrinated populations, in many ways seem to run the world and have caused immense suffering. Yet activists for political change, justice, and social liberation have also at times been notorious for their rigidity and suppression of dissent. Outsiders note the sometimes furious doctrinal infighting between progressive groups. Indeed, the very term *politically correct* originally was an inside joke among progressives about the tendency to be rigid and authoritarian about views.

Hence, a vital area for those bringing spiritual approaches to community, social, and political life is to explore our attachments to positions, opinions, and political ideologies, to what collectively we might call our "views." As we do so, we may see more clearly the ways in which rigidly held views give us a sense of solidity and identity, as well as a sense of being right, by defining ourselves in opposition to our supposed opponents or enemies. On the basis of such an identity, we may close our minds and hearts, demean and persecute others, or wage war. By deconstructing our attachments to our views, we may be able to preserve the insights linked with such views while working through our dogmatism, self-righteousness, and animosity.

The Problems with Attachment to Views

But what are the problems with attachment to views? Don't we need such attachment in order to have the clarity and energy to act?

In the teachings of the Buddha, as in many of the spiritual traditions mentioned in which "not knowing" is valued, dogmatic attachment to views *is* considered a significant problem, a manifestation of ignorance that leads to much suffering. Attachment, according to the Buddha, is the compulsive force of clinging to or grasping *(upadana)* what is pleasant (and the corresponding force of pushing away what is unpleasant). The roots of the term, *upa* (intense or extreme) and *adana* (grasping or taking), suggest a driven or obsessive—often relatively unconscious—quality. I may become attached to a person, an experience, a particular food or drink, objects that I own, and so on. The Buddha generally teaches about four main types of attachments: to sensual pleasures, opinions and viewpoints *(ditthi)*, religious rules and observances, and the belief in self.

The views specifically challenged by the Buddha were connected with the main metaphysical perspectives of his time. Such views expressed beliefs asserted in response to a series of metaphysical questions—about whether the world is eternal or not eternal, infinite or finite, what happens after an enlightened being dies, and whether there is a self or not. Those who hold such metaphysical beliefs, according to the Buddha, are caught in "the thicket of views, the wilderness of views, the contortion of views, the vacillation of views, the fetter of views." Fixed and dogmatic views prevent awakening and lead to suffering: "Fettered by the fetter of views, the untaught ordinary person is...not free from suffering."[6]

In our own time, Thich Nhat Hanh has also focused on working through attachments to views, beginning his set of fourteen guiding precepts for the "Order of Interbeing" with these three precepts:

Do not be idolatrous about or bound to any doctrine, theory, or ideology, even Buddhist ones. All systems of thought are guiding means; they are not absolute truth.

Do not think the knowledge you presently possess is changeless, absolute truth. Avoid being narrow-minded and bound to present views. Learn and practice non-attachment from views in order to be open to receive others' viewpoints. . . .

Do not force others, including children, by any means whatsoever, to adopt your views, whether by authority, threat, money, propaganda or even education. However, through compassionate dialogue, help others renounce fanaticism and narrowness.[7]

There are at least three main problems with attachment to views. First, *such attachment is often unconscious, beneath the threshold of awareness.* We become attached to views often as part of our social and cultural conditioning, and often without any awareness of our attachment or clinging. Holding on to a view may give me a sense of identity, a sense of who I am, as an individual, a member of a group, or a member of a specific culture. Views may give me a sense of what is "real" and what is important. I may not be aware that I cling to this view unless it is somehow called into question, as when I meet those with other views, or when over time the views become less coherent and compelling, or when they seem to conflict with reality.

We are often uncomfortable without views or stories to help us organize our experience and commonly superimpose our views on our experience without reflection. Sylvia Boorstein remembers a time of insight into this pressure to produce meaning. She had called up the San Francisco Zen Center in order to book a place in a retreat but had been unable to reach William, who handled the reservations. So she left a message. The next day, William called Sylvia on the phone and Sylvia was not there, so then he left a message. The next day, Sylvia called the Zen Center again. She reached the receptionist, who told her that William was not there. Sylvia then reflected, "I guess that this means I'm not supposed to do the retreat." The receptionist responded, "No, I think that it means that William is not here."

A second problem is that *clinging to views typically requires that I oppose someone with a different view,* against whom aversion, anger, and even hatred may develop. There is also often a strong tendency to get into disputes about differences in views in order to assert and defend the truth of our own views. In such disputes, we may manifest arrogance, hatred, self-centeredness, and an inability to listen to the other. (Potentially, though, differences in views may also, when there is relative non-attachment to views, lead to dialogue, insight, and learning.) At best, this may result in wasted time, a sense of isolation or separation, or irritation. "Those who grasp after views," the Buddha says, "wander about in the world annoying people."[8] Of course, disputes about views may also trigger interpersonal conflicts as well as the kind of massive violence and suffering that we know all too well from wars catalyzed in part by religious and political ideologies.

Third and most radically, *attachment to views reflects a lack of understanding about the very nature of language and concepts.* When we are attached to views, we believe that a view could be "true" (and its opposite "false") and that our basic concepts can accurately reflect or mirror reality rather than merely be selective and partial. But the Buddha and the second-century Buddhist philosopher Nagarjuna point out, as would Kant and Hegel several thousand years later, that the very structure of everyday thinking and concepts does not permit one view simply to be true and another false. Rather, views are dualistically structured. They typically come as one of a set of opposed pairs. I either believe in God or I don't. I think that there is a separate self or I question this view. I believe that there is an absolute, permanent reality or I believe that ultimately nothing lasts.

When I hold a view dogmatically, when I am attached to a view, I don't see how it *has meaning only in reaction to the view of my opponent.* Since I define myself in implicit or explicit opposition to the other, without the other my view has no meaning.

In this context, we implicitly collaborate with our opponents, our enemies, for we each implicitly require the other. This makes some sense of why we often so desperately need "enemies." It suggests the curious symbiotic relationship that existed between the United States and the Soviet Union, and how since 1989 (the fall of the Berlin Wall) there has been an often urgent search for a "new enemy" (Manuel Noriega? Colombian drug barons?) in order to find meaning, to justify immense military expenditures and the maintenance of weapons systems. Only after a number of years has this quest seemingly been satisfied with the "War on Terror."

The Possibility of Non-attachment to Views

The Buddha often speaks of the spiritual path as following a "Middle Way" between or, perhaps more accurately, beyond two extreme views. The Buddha identifies these two views as "eternalism" and "annihilationism." The first is a metaphysical view of an absolute being, the second a view of there being ultimately nothing. In questioning and rejecting these two views, the Buddha opens up a Middle Way. Yet this Middle Way, the Buddha claims, is not itself a *further dogmatic view,* or somehow a compromise between the two polar views.

Rather, the Buddha points to the possibility of a way of being *free from all dogmatic views.* He speaks of "those wise ones who do not grasp at any views." For them, "there is no conflict with the views held by others."[9]

Both the Buddha and Nagarjuna declare that they do not take "views" or "positions." Their pragmatic intention is only to cut through any and all attachments to views, *leading to wisdom, not to a view.* Nagarjuna indeed warns of the subtle danger of clinging even to a spiritual view about freedom, non-attachment, or "emptiness":

> "I am free! I cling no more!
> Liberation is mine!"—
> The greatest clinging
> Is to cling like this.[10]

Dogmatic attachment to Buddhist (or other spiritual) views is, if anything, more pernicious than attachment to other kinds of views because in a way it is more subtle and harder to see. The worse thing is to turn the Middle Way into a fixed view. Nagarjuna writes: "Believers in emptiness/ Are incurable."[11]

Yet, as we will see more fully in chapter 10, *non-attachment is not the same as a lack of commitment or a lack of effort.* We do not require attachment to views in order to act. Rather, our motivation for action comes out of a deeper part of ourselves, out of our compassion, our love, our awareness, and our wisdom, none of which are linked with holding to rigid views.

Cultivating Mindfulness of Views

In our individual mindfulness practice, as well as in our relational and collective lives, we can begin to be alert to the appearance of dogmatic views, initially simply noting them as they appear. We can discern when attachment to views is present especially by the degree of repetition and the powerful emotional (and even somatic) charge that typically is connected with such views, especially when contrasted with the level of emotional charge linked with other views. We can look for the urgent sense of being right that typically accompanies such views, and the sense of aversion and negative judgment that we feel toward those with opposing views. We can notice when we feel a strong, even compulsive need for our views to prevail in discussions, or when we force our views on others. We can especially bring mindfulness to those times in which we find ourselves engaged in disputes, verbal conflicts, and other emotionally charged situations. What views are we defending? What views are we attacking?

We can also give individual labels to our various views to help us see them more easily. They may be views about the rightness or wrongness of this or that policy; about capitalism or racism or imperialism; about the Democrats, Republicans, or Greens; about a colleague's or friend's or family member's ideas; about this person's or this group's strategy. In conversations or meetings, as well as in communications and publications, we can be alert for such views, again initially just noting what we find.

Over time, we can develop an inventory, producing a sense of our framework of views through which we experience and interpret the world and our own role. If we have any difficulty in developing such an inventory, we might also ask those close to us about what they take to be our most dogmatic or fixed views. They will usually be able to respond with detail and precision!

EXERCISE: Developing an Inventory of Your Views

Over a period of a week in which you carry out daily mindfulness practice and bring mindfulness to your conversations, identify your "top five" views. You may locate them in the main themes that surface during meditation or in conversations in which you find yourselves attacking or defending particular views. The views may be quite personal, or they may concern your work situation or the larger society.

Attachment to Views as a Starting Point for Inquiry

A second basic way of working with attachment to views is more active. It is to use charged moments about beliefs or positions (or the simple presence of rigid views in less charged circumstances) as a point of departure for *inquiry,* looking more deeply into the complex of thoughts, emotions, and somatic experiences that support our dogmatic views.

I first learned this kind of practice more than fifteen years ago, when I was participating in a three-year national program called "Revisioning Philosophy," a wonderful gathering of philosophers both inside and outside of the universities who hoped to rescue the practice of philosophy from its overly narrow, intellectual, and professional contemporary fate. The intention was to bring back the original wisdom and spiritual dimensions of a discipline that in its original Greek meant "love of *(philo)* wisdom *(sophia)*" and to restore as well other aspects of philosophy that had been largely denied, excluded, forgotten, or prohibited—the connection with the lived experience of the body and emotions, with public life, and with moral and political practice.

Yet we found that in spite of such wonderful aspirations, there were some difficult moments when we all felt highly charged differences surface in the group. While many of us hoped that our sessions would not include the kind of self-centered and mean-spirited exchanges that we knew all too well from other settings, we seemed at times to mimic such discourses. In such warlike interactions, each of the protagonists seemed to claim absolute truth for his or her position, was unable to recognize much or anything of value in (or to listen much to) the opponent, and mustered all available verbal and nonverbal weaponry in order to "win." For many of us, it was rather dismaying to notice such sparks appearing amid the general camaraderie.

At a key moment early in our gatherings, one of our participants, Robert McDermott, now with the California Institute of Integral Studies, made an impassioned plea to develop a different way of working, and his suggestion has inspired me in my own practice and teaching. He invited us to notice our strong positions and to take this moment of noticing as the starting point for inquiry: Why is there such a strong view? Why do I have such a strong interest in "defeating" the other person? What emotions are present? What complex history of my own ideas and emotions has been touched? Might I learn something from this other person?

Since that gathering, I have integrated such an inquiry practice into my teaching and work with others, urging participants to connect their more "outer" participation with an "inner" listening and exploration when there is reactivity toward the views of others. When we do such a practice, we may find that our rigidity may cover over a broad range of experiences. I may be deeply angry about the government's foreign policy and discover, as I sit with the anger, that there is also sadness, love, and a passion for justice. I may find that my reaction to a given philosophy or ideology is closely linked with a long-forgotten pain or traumatic episode.

When there is sufficient mindfulness and concentration, we can take a moment of noticing an attachment to a view as an invitation, a point of departure, to explore more deeply, to see what emotions, thoughts, memories, and bodily experiences are present. We can do this kind of practice "on the cushion" or in the midst of action, training ourselves to listen to the views, and then "drop down" to other experiences, discerning what is present, without expectations of what *should* be there. We may find a mixture of unacknowledged pain linked with the view; some kind of insight, intelligence, or observation; and, when we go deeply enough, some kind of caring response.

As we touch the pain, note the intelligence, and become aware of the caring, we are transforming the reactivity to pain that often drives our dogmatic adherence to views. We are separating out the reactivity from the intelligence and the caring, thereby coming to preserve the latter as starting points for our action in the world.

This is why such transformative work, contrary to some "spiritual" perspectives, does not simply abandon the cognitive basis for all views, leaving ourselves in a kind of relativistic or mindless limbo. We abandon, rather, our *attachments* to views and dogmatically held positions, leaving, if we have done our work, the purified intelligence and the energy of compassion as the basis for a different approach to ideas and action. We learn how to use beliefs and concepts more lightly, as skillful means for compassionate action rather than as signposts of our fixed connection with truth and rightness. *We preserve discernment while abandoning the reactivity connected with dogmatic views.*

EXERCISE: Inquiring into Your Attachments to Views

For a period of a week, notice when you experience a significant charge in relation to your views. This charge may be emotional, somatic, or mental. You may want very much to defeat another person and refute that person's view. When you notice such a charge (or even later), begin inquiring into your view; take your noticing of the charge as a starting point for inquiry and reflection. What is my view here? What is the nature of the charge? What thoughts, emotions, and bodily experiences are connected with my strong view? Are there experiences, including painful experiences, that are linked with my view? What might I learn from the other and the other's view? Why is it so important to me to win? Do I really know with certainty that my view is correct? Do I tend to exaggerate the degree of support for my view in my own mind or when I speak to others? Why do I do this?

Cultivating Deep Listening

A second way of practicing not knowing, through deep listening, is illustrated by a famous Zen story. A Zen teacher receives a well-known Japanese professor and offers him tea. The teacher begins pouring the tea, fills the professor's cup, but then continues pouring as the tea flows out of the cup and onto the floor. The professor implores the teacher to stop: "My cup is already full!" The teacher replies, "Just as your cup is full, so is your mind already full of opinions and ideas. You must learn to empty it."

To listen fully and deeply to another, or to the wind or ocean, requires that we no longer be dominated by our thoughts, opinions, plans, or views. Listening is both a fundamental practice and one of the great metaphors for spiritual practice, lack of attachment to views, and compassion. The great Tibetan poet and meditator Milarepa is typically portrayed in woodblock prints and paintings with a hand cupped to his ear as he sits listening in the mountain wilds. Kwan Yin, the bodhisattva of compassion, is said to listen for the cries of the world.

Listening begins with general training in mindfulness, a training in which we become more aware of that which makes it hard to listen. On that basis, we can start to see the power of listening for both interpersonal relationships and social action. I came to be more aware of this power of listening in the two years that I was chair of our graduate school faculty. During that time, I was somewhat surprised that so much of my work involved simply listening carefully to another person. Typically, a faculty member would come to me with a story, usually linked with a grievance. I would listen to the complaint as best I could, usually without offering my opinions or taking sides. Most often, I would then simply say something like "It sounds as if you have a conflict with Charles. I suggest finding a good time to talk to Charles about this conflict."

A number of innovative approaches to dialogue depend on the capacity to listen carefully, to oneself and others, and to be able to identify and suspend temporarily one's core assumptions in the very act of communication with others. As in the scholarly discipline of hermeneutics, in order to be open to and learn from another, whether another person, another culture, or a work of art, we need to be able to know our own views and assumptions, which influence so much how we encounter the other, and be willing to question and temporarily suspend them.

In social conflicts and work for social change, listening is also an important resource. So often, conflicts, especially violent ones, reflect a state of affairs in which listening to the other has become almost impossible, in which ordinary communication has broken down. The peacemaker or mediator must often start with the act of listening. Indeed, listening is not only a starting point but a primary tool for healing, reconciliation, and the restoration of communication.

For many years Christopher Titmuss has both taught meditation retreats in Israel and facilitated workshops in the Palestinian territories. He speaks of the importance of listening:

> Listening is so central, particularly with the Palestinians. The one thing that is present in nearly every conversation is that they want people from outside the Palestinian areas actually to listen to them speak about their circumstances. That listening, without any particular intention to resolve the conflict, seems to bring its own insight. There is a great, great need to be heard and feel understood.[12]

Peacemakers thus need to be skillful not only in listening but in *knowing how to create the conditions that make listening possible.* For example, at the 1993 Oslo talks between Israelis and Palestinians, which led to a temporary breakthrough, the turning point was when the delegates, after several days, were able to drop their stances and rhetoric and begin to listen to their counterparts "on the other side" as human beings—to hear stories about their children and their lives. Such a breakthrough was made possible when the Israelis and Palestinians met for several days at the country home of the Norwegian foreign minister Johan Jørgen Holst and his wife, Marianne Heiberg, eating and living together, talking over meals, playing with the couple's four-year-old son, Edvard. Holst later wrote: "We tried to deal with one of the most complicated conflicts in modern human history by creating a human framework within which to deal with the issues."[13]

Over the last forty years, the renowned peacemaker and scholar Johan Galtung has developed a form of "conflict transformation" based on a very simple model. A "peaceworker" meets with each "side" (often there are more than two) and simply listens. Galtung stresses the centrality of open listening and recommends that the peaceworker not even read very much about the details of the conflict. His finding, borne out by years of practice, is that the ability to listen by an open, unbiased, and unopinionated person not only lets those on the different sides feel heard but also leads to highly creative ways of seeing and understanding the situation, breaking open the frozen, habitual conflictual patterns, and suggesting imaginative resolutions.

Yet such listening requires mindfulness training—to be able to know our own views, listen without our views dominating, and be present with and transform our own pain and anger. Without these trainings, "it will be difficult," says Thich Nhat Hanh, "to listen to another person's suffering, especially if the other person's speech is full of negative judgments, misperceptions, and blaming."[14]

"NOT KNOWING BUT KEEPING GOING": AVOIDING THE DANGERS OF NOT KNOWING

During a retreat with teenagers, my colleague Diana Winston was exploring the principle of "not knowing." Laura, one of the retreatants, immediately spoke up: "Not knowing is good enough. But it's not complete. You have to add, 'But keep going.' We're always acting and somehow we need to act and keep going even when we don't know."

Laura's comment points to some of the dangers or traps of what we might call our "not knowing practice." Here, I point out briefly three ways in which we may lose balance in not knowing. First, we may become fearful, paralyzed, or lost in not knowing and hence *not* keep going. Second, we may come to believe that "not knowing but keeping going" means that "anything goes." And last, we may become overly attached to not knowing, such that we ignore the value of knowing.

The first danger is perhaps the most obvious. When we enter a period of not knowing, or when we go for some time without knowing what to do—about a future action or about a problem—we usually encounter fear and confusion. Jung, for example, talks about the powerful "inner pressure" of his period of unknowing. While it is important periodically to take a break from the pressures of certain actions, we also need to be mindful of such fear and confusion, learning to "keep going" even when fear or confusion are present. We need to listen carefully, to know when it is time to return to action, much as Gandhi did prior to the Salt March.

What is required is to combine the openness of not knowing with commitment to and faith in our deeper intentions. We must, as the poet Rilke advises us, "live the questions" rather than let our despair about the unanswered questions remove us from life. In his *Letters to a Young Poet,* Rilke wrote to a young man in his early twenties:

Be patient toward all that is unsolved in your heart and try to love the *questions themselves* like locked rooms and like books that are written in a very foreign tongue. Do not now seek the answers, which cannot be given you because you would not be able to live them. And the point is, to live everything. *Live* the questions now. Perhaps you will then gradually, without noticing it, live along some distant day into the answer.[15]

The second and third dangers occur when we turn not knowing into a fixed view. We may, for example, believe that not knowing justifies not acting ethically. We may "keep going," but now "anything goes." Historically some Buddhists, as well as those in other spiritual traditions, have used teachings about not knowing as a reason to ignore or marginalize fundamental ethical precepts. Such examples may remind us that our not knowing is not an independent principle. Rather, it is held, as it were, by our wisdom and compassion. Our wisdom may lead us not to know, but it does not lead us not to care.

We may also become overly attached to not knowing, perhaps as a spiritual position, and ignore the value and place of knowing. But, as Nagarjuna suggests, to make a fixed view out of a potentially liberating practice is like holding a poisonous snake by the tail. Furthermore, as Rilke writes to the young poet, we may eventually come to knowledge; an answer to a question may well follow a period of unknowing.

Not knowing is a practice designed to clear away habitual knowing, attachment to views, and barriers to communication. When such barriers are no longer present, when we are no longer dominated by such knowing and such views, it is both possible to use ordinary knowledge in the service of wisdom and to open up to deeper knowing. As Sir Richard Francis Burton, the nineteenth-century English translator of the *Arabian Nights* once suggested, one "knows not how to know / who knows not how to unknow."[16]

Chapter Seven

INTERDEPENDENCE

I first met the Vietnamese teacher, activist, and poet Thich Nhat Hanh in 1987, at a retreat at the Insight Meditation Society (IMS). I had been attending retreats at IMS for some ten years and, like many of the re-treatants, was very familiar with the style of spiritual practice there. This involved almost complete silence for a week or more, alternating forty-five-minute periods of sitting meditation with slow walking meditation, and a sustained focus on the development of stillness, concentration, and moment-to-moment mindfulness.

For some of the retreatants and the IMS staff, Thich Nhat Hanh seemed to offer a lighter kind of spiritual fare. We typically meditated for only twenty minutes at a time, and there were often periods of informal conversation, with no attempt to keep silent, which would have been very difficult anyway because of the large number of children at the retreat. We would sometimes walk together outside or down the rural road in a large group, at a pace only slightly slower than normal. Thich Nhat Hanh would talk to us for two hours at a time, usually twice a day. I heard some IMS old-timers ask what was going on, implying that this was not a real retreat.

Yet clearly something else was going on. I emerged from the retreat deeply moved. When a friend later asked what I had learned, I found myself saying, "It wasn't about concentration. Rather, I learned about in-terdependence. I learned about the wisdom of coming to perceive the interconnection of things moment to moment. I learned more about how I separate myself from the world and from others, even in some ways *through* my meditation, stillness, and concentration."

Thich Nhat Hanh often would start a talk by inviting the children to sit near him at the front of the hall. He would hold up an orange and ask them, "Can you see the clouds where the oranges were growing?" "Yes," the children would readily answer. "Can you see the rain coming down?" "Yes." "Can you see the soil and the earthworms in the soil?" "Yes." "Can you see the farmer picking the oranges?" "Yes." After the children left, Thich Nhat Hanh would continue with the adults, talking about "interbeing," the way that "this exists because of that," that nothing and no one are totally separate from everything else, how an orange has "nonorange" elements in it.

Other dimensions of interdependence were more poignant and sometimes painful. They were catalyzed by the participation of about forty Vietnamese Americans (including many children), nearly half of those at the retreat. The Vietnam War had ended with the fall of Saigon some twelve years earlier. Yet the effects of the war seemed to reverberate in the hall—as Thich Nhat Hanh told stories, as we watched a film on his work which included footage from the war years, with B-52s raining bombs and children screaming, as many who had lived through those years sat as part of our group, as Vietnamese American children wandered among us. I could feel both my complex interconnections with those of Vietnamese descent and how powerful, unresolved traumatic events from the past cannot be somehow neatly segregated from the present, however we might wish to get on with our lives.

Cultivating a sense of interdependence and cutting through the rigid sense of a separate self are at the heart of the contemporary connection of spiritual practice and social transformation. Three interrelated areas of practice are particularly important. The first is to learn to see more clearly and gradually to deconstruct, at the level of individual experience, the images, beliefs, and ways of acting of the rigid, separate, distanced self.

The second has to do with learning to understand, perceive, and live interdependence more directly in our experience of the world—whether in washing the dishes, placing a young tomato plant in the soil in the spring, driving a car, purchasing a new shirt, being with a partner, attending a meeting, or watching the evening news. The third area of practice has to do with transforming our tendencies to form "enemies"—who typically are seen as "bad" and to whom we are diametrically opposed.

"I AND IT": THE SEPARATE SELF
AND ITS WORLD OF OBJECTS

The German Jewish philosopher Martin Buber is well known for identifying (in *I and Thou*, published in 1923) two ways of meeting the world. On the one hand, an "I" experiences an "It"; on the other, an "I" relates to a "Thou" (or a "You"). In the "I–It" mode, "I" have goals and interests, but the "It" does not. While in this mode, I, as the subject, experience the It, the object, through my senses and their technological extensions (like cameras or recording devices). I may have an image of the object, or feel its textures, or taste it. I may study its properties. I may even enjoy gaining detailed knowledge about a given object. Yet there remains a vast divide between the qualities of the I and the qualities of the It; the I is at the center of being, the It peripheral.

However, what becomes It for me is not just the inanimate object, like the floor or pot, that I use to meet my needs. I may also approach the rest of the world in this way, including trees and nonhuman animals, as well as the elements of the earth—the water, the minerals, and the air. As we know, this objectifying attitude has been increasingly influential in the West in the last few centuries, with the rise of science and the technological application of scientific knowledge, and has led to a great number of scientific and technological breakthroughs, bringing both numerous benefits and major problems. This objectifying attitude has also often been linked with a denial that the nonhuman natural world, including other animals, shares the most basic qualities of the human, of the I—particularly consciousness, intelligence, and purpose.

Such an attitude has often led to what we might call an *instrumental* everyday relationship to the objects, the Its, of the world. At one extreme, which is surprisingly prevalent in the contemporary Western world, I may give an object, such as my rug, my dinner plate, my shirt, or even my meal minimal or no attention, taking for granted that it will simply fulfill a function *for me*. I may notice these objects only when something is not working. In fact, I may have little knowledge about the basic objects in my life, not knowing where my water or food comes from, whether the effects of my use of objects are helpful or harmful, rarely or perhaps never at all giving any sustained attention to ordinary objects.

Everything becomes, as it were, generic and simply ready to consume, as in a scene from the film *Repo Man*. The teenage character of Emilio Estevez has come home to have dinner. But there is no freshly made meal because his parents are glued to the television set, smoking marijuana and watching a Christian evangelist. So he finds a blue and white can in the pantry marked "Food," opens the can, sticks a fork in it, and says, "Yum!"

We know all too well that I may also take an "I–It" approach to other human beings, seeing them only as objects in my calculations, significant only to the extent that they help or hinder me (or my organization or my nation) in reaching my goals. My human interactions may become entirely or primarily strategic.

I may even bring this objectifying and distancing attitude to myself, understanding and manipulating aspects of my experience, such as my body and emotions, from afar, as if they were objects. James Joyce, in his short story "A Painful Case," in *Dubliners,* describes a certain Mr. Duffy: "He lived at a little distance from his body, regarding his own acts with doubtful side-glances."[1]

THE BUDDHA ON THE SEPARATE SELF

The Buddha deeply questioned models of the separate self prevalent during his time. He saw these models as rooted in spiritual ignorance. Someone with these models, unaware of the impermanent nature of experience, tends to believe that happiness consists of gaining pleasant experiences and avoiding unpleasant experiences *for the self.* With such a view, one seeks to manipulate the world toward such ends. The result is a kind of compulsive and driven grasping of some aspects or objects of the outer and inner experience and a pushing away of others. According to the Buddha, such grasping (and pushing away), grounded in ignorance, is the proximate cause of suffering. The deepest happiness is not the result of accumulating pleasant experiences and avoiding unpleasant ones but rather of learning to let go of the urge to grasp, and touching a much deeper level of our being—at which we know peace and interdependence.

Thus at the heart of Buddhist practice is a sustained and alert watchfulness for different forms of grasping and the links to a fixed notion of self, self-image, and self-identity that might be defined in opposition to (fixed) others.

Although the Buddha strongly criticizes the view of a fixed, permanent, separate self because this view is closely connected with suffering, he never endorses the opposite view, that there is somehow "no self" (contrary to many interpretations of Buddhism). Either of these extreme interpretations would lead to a lack of understanding of interdependence. The first interpretation suggests an extreme *independence* and an overemphasis on autonomy and separation. It is characteristic both of the views of the self that the Buddha criticizes and of what the sociologist Robert Bellah calls contemporary Western "hyper-individualism."

The second interpretation suggests an extreme of *fusion* and an over-emphasis on communion. It is characteristic both of what the Buddha calls "nihilistic" views and of situations in which autonomy is stifled, often in the name of "being together." We find this in highly traditional or conformist relationships, communities, and societies. I remember the comment of one of my students from a small, close-knit community in the mountains of eastern Kentucky. As we were studying the nature of community, which for many was valued quite positively, she remarked, "Community! I want to get as far away from community as I can get!"

EXERCISE: Exploring the Fixed, Separate Self

In the protected space of your formal mindfulness practice, be attentive when a fixed sense of self appears in your experience. Notice when you either strongly grasp or push away particular bodily sensations, as when you strongly want ice cream or don't want to be too hot, and how there are thoughts about "me" and "mine," beyond the sensations themselves. Notice when you maintain, in your thoughts, "This is *my* view" or "*Her* view is wrong—*mine* is right." Notice when a kind of self-image is developing, as when you think, "That was a good meditation.I'm really a good meditator, aren't I?" Notice the other thoughts and emotions linked with self-image and ideas about self, as when you congratulate or judge yourself, or when there is a longing to be approved, loved, or confirmed.

One way of carrying out this investigation is, for a week, to devote the second half of your daily sitting to being alert for such patterns. Take notes after each sitting. At the end of the week, review the notes. You may be able to produce a comprehensive model of the current preoccupations, beliefs, images, and tendencies of your rigid, separate self.

VISIONS OF INTERDEPENDENCE

In our mindfulness practice, we study the construction of a rigid, separate self, opening ourselves to a more relational view of experience. We can also examine interdependence more directly. One way to do this is to explore how different traditions and approaches, both ancient and contemporary, point to the interdependent nature of reality. In North American indigenous traditions, for example, human lives are understood relationally, as essentially linked to animals, plants, spirits, the sun, the moon, and the earth and its elements, as in the common ritual invocation from the Lakota to "all my relations" *(mitak' oyas'in)*. Such interdependence has profound implications: maintaining care and respect in a wide web of relationships and everyday activities is seen as helping to keep the health and spiritual balance of an individual and a community.

In questioning the fixed, separate self, the Buddha and later Buddhist traditions also point to the relational and interdependent nature of experience and reality. At the center of the Buddha's experience on the night of his awakening, for example, is an understanding of what he called "dependent arising" (in Pali: *paticca samuppada*). Rather than posit a separate self, the Buddha finds that experience contains no such "self" but rather involves a dynamic process of interrelated factors, which open up, without rigid boundaries, to the world.

Later Buddhist traditions developed ways of understanding the interdependent quality not only of the elements of *individual* experience but also of *all phenomena and objects*, whether inner or outer. Neither the self nor phenomena have separate existences; they are all interdependent. The great second-century Indian philosopher-practitioner Nagarjuna concludes:

> You are not the same as or different from
> Conditions on which you depend;
> You are neither severed from
> Nor forever fused with them.[2]

Other traditions emphasize the *ethical* aspects of interdependence. Confucians see the interdependence of individual action, community life, the life of the nation, and the entire cosmos. The Jewish and Christian prophetic traditions, as we have seen, emphasize how the reality of human interdependence suggests our responsibility for each other, and particularly for the least well off. Martin Luther King Jr., in his 1963 "Letter from a Birmingham Jail," expresses this understanding in the context of responding to the issues of racism, injustice, and poverty:

> I am cognizant of the interrelatedness of all communities and states. I cannot sit idly by in Atlanta and not be concerned about what happens in Birmingham. Injustice anywhere is a threat to justice everywhere. We are caught in an inescapable network of mutuality, tied in a single garment of destiny. Whatever affects one directly, affects all indirectly.[3]

CULTIVATING A LIVED SENSE OF INTERDEPENDENCE: BEING WITH ORDINARY OBJECTS

From the study of spiritual traditions, as well as the contemporary sciences, such as ecology and physics, we may develop a general understanding of interdependence and question our tendency to consider ourselves separate selves, distanced from other beings and from the objects of the world. But how do we come to know the interdependence of phenomena *experientially,* in ways that influence our choices and actions, and our relational and collective lives? *How, in other words, do we cultivate a sense of interdependence as an ongoing practice?*

As a starting point, I suggest four basic practices that can help us shift from the stance of being separate, isolated selves toward being part of a web of interdependence, initially in relationship to objects, and later through relationships with humans and other beings. In other words, we begin to develop aspects of "I–Thou" relationships toward the objects in our world, and then toward other beings. These practices, developed initially with my colleague Julie Wester, a teacher at Spirit Rock Meditation Center in Northern California, involve cultivating (1) basic attention, (2) gratitude, (3) imagination of the particular web of interdependence in which a given object is embedded, and (4) the ability to "become" another object.

EXERCISE: Being with Ordinary Objects

Look around you at this time and choose an "ordinary object" that can be the focus of these four practices: for example, a piece of clothing, a pen, or a tree. It might even be the very book that you are reading.

Attending to the Object

In our usual way of being with objects, we do not give them much attention, except for more strategic reasons, for example, to fix or repair them, when there is a problem, or when an object reaches the exalted status of becoming the focus of aesthetic attention. Hence, it is a radical shift just to be attentive, even for a minute or two, to an ordinary object, with basic mindfulness. To do so is to be open to the presence of the object in the web of interdependence, to relearn, as it were, its claim to being, and to let go of our self-centeredness to some extent.

EXERCISE: Being Mindful of an Ordinary Object

Be present with the object that you have chosen for a few minutes or longer. Be mindful through your various senses—touching, smelling, seeing, and tasting, when appropriate, the object. Let this object be like the breath in meditation, the only object in the universe for these moments.

Developing Gratitude

A second way to move out of self-centeredness is to appreciate the object we usually take for granted. It is to be aware of how our lives are helped by the object, much as when Zen students bow to their cushions, as if to acknowledge that the cushion makes it possible to sit longer and hence supports us, both literally and in helping us to carry out our spiritual practice.

One of my favorite (and shortest) books is *St. Francis Preaches to the Birds,* by Peter Schumann. The founder and director of the legendary Bread and Puppet Theatre shows, through a series of twenty-six color woodblock-style prints, a day in the life of Saint Francis.[4] Saint Francis wakes up. He then "brushes his teeth & says: 'Thank you teeth!' He washes his toes & says: 'Thank you toes!' He gets milk, drinks his coffee & says: 'Thank you coffee!'" He then goes through the town, over the pasture, and up the hill, where the birds come flying to him, and where he preaches to the birds all day, until the sun sets. "Yes! Until the sun sets." This wonderful portrayal of a life radically open to ordinary objects and other beings, radiantly kind in an interdependent world, suggests a direction for our practice.

EXERCISE: Developing Gratitude for an Object

Be again with the object that you have chosen for at least a few minutes. Reflect on how this object supports your life and your activities. Reflect on how your life is fuller and richer because of this object, and express your appreciation in some way, verbally or nonverbally.

Exploring the Causal Web of an Object

A third practice is to imagine how the object is embedded in a vast network of causes and conditions, to be aware of the object much as Thich Nhat Hanh contemplated the orange with the children in the retreat.

EXERCISE: Exploring the Causal Web of an Object

Be present again for several minutes with the object that you have chosen. Using your imagination and perhaps some of the knowledge that you have about the object, consider the net of causes and conditions that made possible the object's being present to you at this moment. Reflect on the nonhuman and human materials and causes, and consider how other networks of causes and conditions ripple out from each part of the net.

Thich Nhat Hanh's exercise with the children, pointing to the causes and conditions of the orange in his hand, or perhaps our own exploration of a given object, may suggest us a fairly beneficent image of interdependence. Yet often when we have concrete knowledge of the reality of interdependence, we may also encounter a less pretty picture, in which we can see that to know the interdependent net in which we are involved is also to touch suffering.

Consider, for example, if we had chosen, in the above exercise, to explore the causes and conditions of a chocolate bar. In her consulting work, one of my students, Cecilia Garibay, in the context of a Chicago museum, developed what she calls the "chocolate chain exercise" to help people interactively explore the links in the chain leading to the afternoon snack of a chocolate bar. She started with cacao trees growing in tropical regions, including the fact that to increase the size of cacao yields, thousands of acres of rain forest have been cleared. In the Ivory Coast (the largest producer of cacao) 14 percent of the rain forest has been cleared solely for cacao production (some 90 percent of the West African rain forest is now gone because of this and other factors). Outside of its natural environment, however, the cacao tree is vulnerable to pests and disease, so pesticides are heavily utilized, with effects on the workers, the soil, the water, and other plants. The work is extremely labor intensive, sometimes dangerous, and has often involved children. The cacao soon makes it way to the futures market, the farmer receiving back one penny for a sixty-cent chocolate bar, and to the factory, where chocolate is manufactured and packaged, using plastic, film, aluminum foil, and paper products.[5]

Much of the important education in our time of increased globalization is to clarify what makes possible the objects of our everyday lives—the morning cup of coffee and the newspaper, the T-shirt and shoes, the computer, the hamburger and cola, the broccoli at the market, and so forth. Again, the picture is less a simple, inspiring account of the wonders of interdependence than an invitation to consider the complexities, ambiguities, and challenges of interdependence, and to ask how we might act.

"Becoming" the Object

A fourth practice is to "become," as best we can for a short time, the object. This may be to role-play the object, to imagine, enact, and express the object "from within." In some ways, this is to use imaginative, expressive, and even dramatic means to move out of our stance of being separate, isolated selves. Such approaches are still present in the ceremonies of many indigenous traditions, where participants often act not only as animals but also as plants.

Several years ago, I was part of a six-month training group in integrative spirituality, led by Marina Romero and Ramon Albareda of Barcelona, who over thirty years have developed a large repertoire of creative practices. In one practice, I joined a group of seven participants, in which we "became" trees, burying ourselves a foot or two in the ground and standing silently for several hours. After returning to the human world, I wrote a poem, which ended with these lines:

> The ground deepens.
> I forget my human concerns.
> The crow cries.
> Soil rich and cool—
> my home,
> Sky open and moving—
> my mind,
> Great forces going down,
> Great forces going up.

EXERCISE: "Becoming" an Object

This time, "become" the object that you have chosen for at least a few minutes. You might very simply role-play the object for a short time, placing your body in a position like that of the object, making sounds or moving if appropriate. Or you might become the object for a longer period.

INTERDEPENDENCE, COMPLICITY, AND THE "BAD GUYS"

Exploring interdependence helps us to understand why some of the most important contemporary ethical issues are sometimes so perplexing. When we look at the interdependent causes and conditions of a particular situation, as we did with the chocolate chain, we realize that it is not always easy to speak in comfortable moral terms of the "good guys" (usually "us") versus the "bad guys" (typically "them"). Rather, it is clear that in many ways it is almost impossible for those of us in the United States, for example, not to be *complicit* and significantly *responsible,* as ordinary citizens, for a number of ecological, social, and political problems and much human pain, even if we are not politicians and leaders.

We may, for example, be very concerned about ecological issues such as pollution, the extinction of animal and plant species, or the loss of the rain forests. Yet we also contribute in various ways to these problems through our use of automobiles, our investments in companies whose profits come at the expense of ecological degradation, or our government's support of policies that are linked with ecological problems at home and abroad. Of course, some people contribute to these problems more (some much more) than others, and it is possible and very important to make choices that add as little as possible to the problems, even if it is virtually impossible not to be complicit in some way.

We may also be very concerned about the poverty of several billion people in "underdeveloped" nations, yet we are also often happy to find good deals on clothes or chocolate, which are often possible only because of difficult conditions and very low wages for the workers producing such commodities. We may protest against imperial wars by our government, carried out in part to control oil and other resources in order to ensure the "American way of life," but we still drive our cars thousands of miles each year, use many other petroleum products, and, collectively, at least, elect the politicians who carry out these policies. Thus it is an important and radical question to ask, as did the Zen teacher Sasaki Roshi some twenty-five years ago in a talk, "*Who* pollutes?"[6] We might add other questions: *Who* is responsible for poverty? *Who* invades other countries?

Our participation and complicity in these larger systems is complemented by the ways in which we share in the inner roots of these problems. As we've seen, there is no easy and absolute separation between my greed in accumulating a large closetful of clothes and the greed of corporate heads in making money by stimulating the desire for more clothes. There is no easy separation between my hatred and harsh judgments toward those politicians I oppose and these politicians' similar acts of demonizing and often attacking *their* enemies, domestic and international, perhaps including me! There is no easy separation between my own self-centeredness, compulsive reactivity, and lack of knowledge of many of the details of how I am interdependent and similar tendencies manifesting in arrogance, self-righteousness, and ideology-driven delusion among those in power.

A number of implications for spiritually grounded action for social change follow from a consideration of interdependence. Here, I want particularly to point to the importance of a shift away from the strict dualism of "good guys" and "bad guys" and toward a nondualistic approach grounded in an understanding of interdependence.

It should also be said right away, however, that this approach has its dangers and may lead to confusions and distortions. It is important to point out, for example, that understanding interdependence and questioning an easy dualism of good and bad, or good and evil, need not lead to passivity, inaction, and the claim that we are somehow all equally responsible, and thus that no one is really responsible. Rather, interdependence and nonduality can provide a strong basis for assessing different degrees of responsibility and for compassionate action in the contemporary world.

DECONSTRUCTING OUR OPPONENTS AS RADICAL OTHERS: "OPPONENTS PRACTICE"

Much, if not most, of Western social and political discourse in the last few centuries, including that of most contemporary progressives and most radical and revolutionary movements since the French Revolution, shares a simple and basic dualistic moral framework. Such a framework typically rests on variants of the claim *We are good; they are bad. We* want to bring about a just world; the government is often unjust. *We* want to end oppression; *they* are oppressive. *We* (our country) want to bring about a free and democratic world, and *they* (our enemies) are dictatorial.

At the surprisingly common extreme, we dehumanize our purported enemies or render them bereft of *our* normal humanity, through ideology, rhetoric, propaganda, and stark images. And so the enemy becomes a monster or animal, a criminal or barbarian outside the guidelines of normal civilization, or an expression of evil. Sam Keen, in *Faces of the Enemy,* collects and analyzes a number of propaganda posters, largely from the twentieth century.[7] Among the images Keen collects are Jews as vermin, African Americans as gorillas, Soviets as bears, Japanese in World War II as rats, capitalists as "running dogs," police in the 1960s as pigs. We see Americans in Vietnam as criminal gangsters, Israelis as Nazis, Germans in World War I as barbarian "Huns," Muslims as terrorists. We see the Nazis, Islamic terrorists, the Americans in the Middle East, and Communists portrayed as evil, as demonic, as diametrically opposed to God.

Despite the apparent advantages of simplifying the moral, political, and spiritual situation, there are dangers to this dualistic approach. A main danger is that we may be unable to admit or even see our own shadow material because we believe ourselves or need to be totally "good," in opposition to the "bad" or "evil" enemy. This can be linked with a kind of unconscious hatred of part of ourselves, a part that is actually similar to that aspect of the enemy that we consciously hate. Thomas Merton points to the nature of such unconscious dynamics:

> It is not only our hatred of others that is dangerous but also and above all our hatred of ourselves: particularly that hatred of ourselves which is too deep and too powerful to be consciously faced. For it is this which makes us see our own evil in others and unable to see it in ourselves.[8]

Unaware of or unable to attend to such unconscious material, we may tend to become like our enemies, letting our identities be formed by them. Given how bad or evil the opponent is, and our own fears, we may justify aspects of our own behavior that subvert our deeper values or norms, as typically happens in wars and conflicts. Supposedly to safeguard our freedoms, for example, we curtail civil liberties, as has happened repeatedly in U.S. history. Without the ability to touch our own pain and transform our unconscious patterns, we tend to be caught in the kind of reactive patterns that we have examined in previous chapters. Yet in such reactivity, we tend to become like our enemies.

Unfortunately, such tendencies have pervaded progressive social change groups and organizations. Those who attempt to transform oppression or injustice, and who perhaps have been unjustly treated, often become oppressive or unjust themselves—in interpersonal relationships, in organizational structures and the uses of power. It has not escaped the notice of many people that many purported progressives at times seem to mirror exactly what they criticize in others.

Many of us who have been activists have felt uncomfortable with the level of internal conflict and external demonization we found in some progressive organizations. When I was in college, for example, I was drawn to the incisive critiques of American foreign and domestic policies that those in progressive campus groups made, but I was confused about and often questioned the way they treated their opponents—whether the opponent was a group member who questioned a strategy or idea, or whether the opponent was the government. To have different views in activist groups often seemed to bring down a furious, dogmatic, and self-righteous wrath, and it was evidently off the agenda to raise issues about how we treated each other. Justine Dawson speaks of similar experiences in activist groups in Canada in the 1990s:

> At the university, which was very progressive, I got really involved in several activist groups. These groups were very secular, with a strong non-spiritual bent—with no talk of personal growth or us as spiritual beings or of group process, which talk was seen as *so* "bourgeois." What was particularly hard for me was that there was always so much conflict in these groups, with bad communication and a lot of anger—"Kill the rich, they're terrible!"[9]

In the twentieth century, a clear exception to this dualistic approach to enemies, both external and internal, was the spiritually based nonviolent approach, particularly as we find it expressed by Gandhi and King. Gandhi and King both treated their opponents, British imperialists and American racist southerners respectively, *not so much as enemies to be defeated but as potential friends,* with whom they hoped eventually to reach reconciliation, even as they refused to cooperate with their opponents' injustice.

Gandhi writes about nonviolence as suggesting a radically different approach to "enemies":

> Acts of violence create bitterness in the survivors and brutality in the destroyers: Satyagraha [Holding to Truth—Gandhi's name for the nonviolent movement] aims to exalt both sides...a nonviolent

revolution is not a program of seizure of power. It is a program of transformation of relationships.... It is the acid test of nonviolence that in a nonviolent conflict there is no rancor left behind and, in the end, the enemies are converted into friends.[10]

King encouraged those in the civil rights movement to follow the example of Jesus and love their enemies: "We rise to the position of loving the person who does the evil deed while hating the deed that the person does...one seeks to defeat the unjust system, rather than individuals who are caught in the system."[11]

We can find similar intentions to transform how we relate to so-called enemies in Buddhist traditions, from the teachings of the Buddha to the Dalai Lama's approach to the Chinese. In famous lines from the *Dhammapada,* the Buddha speaks of shifting away from a repetitive and hateful brooding on the enemy's actions; such brooding will never end hatred.

More than a thousand years later, Shantideva, in his eighth-century *Guide to the Bodhisattva's Way of Life,* not only identifies the problems of taking another person as a fixed enemy but also points, in his chapter on the cultivation of patience, to the potential of learning spiritually from one's relationship with an enemy:

> Therefore, just like treasure appearing in my house
> Without any effort on my behalf to obtain it,
> I should be happy to have an enemy
> For he assists me in my conduct of Awakening.[12]

One of the great contributions of spiritual traditions to social transformation is thus helping to develop another way to relate to enemies and opponents. If we were to systematize this contribution, we might imagine a kind of *"opponents practice,"* grounded in mindfulness, lovingkindness practice, and an understanding of interdependence, in which we transform our relationships to opponents or enemies at the same time that we act in the world.

What might such opponents practice look like, in its individual, relational, and collective forms? I suggest and clarify the following six basic aspects of *individual and relational opponents practice*:

1. forming the intention to learn from the opponent;
2. reflecting in ways that ease the dualism with an opponent;
3. examining our actual experience with the opponent;
4. practicing *internally* with our reactivity in relation to the opponent;

5. practicing *internally* through lovingkindness and forgiveness practices; and

6. practicing *externally* (as well as simultaneously internally) through increasingly nonreactive actions and responses to a given situation.

In the remainder of this chapter, the emphasis will be mostly on our individual and relational inner practice (1–5), with relational and collective responsive action (6) explored briefly here and more fully in the next chapter, in the context of working with anger toward an opponent.

Intending to Learn from Our Opponents

We begin with the intention to take our encounters and relationships with opponents or enemies not simply as problems or curses, or somehow as crusades for the righteous against evil, but rather in significant part as opportunities to learn, to grow spiritually—as well as to respond to suffering and/or injustice.

With what kinds of opponents or enemies might we practice in this way? As the lives of Gandhi, King, and the Dalai Lama suggest, this practice is appropriate with any kind of opponent, including the extreme kind —brutal, violent, and seemingly unresponsive. Nonetheless, for most of us, our initial practice, *as a training,* will generally be with opponents who are not trying actively to harm us physically, that is, with our "ordinary" opponents.

And so we may practice with political opponents—those on the opposite side of the ideological spectrum—or with those whom we hold responsible for injustice or exploitation—persons we know directly or those we know only as national or international figures. We may conduct our opponents practice more intimately by examining conflicts with coworkers, colleagues, and fellow community members, even those with whom we are generally aligned politically or spiritually.

A number of years ago, I had a difficult relationship with a person with whom I was in regular contact in a social change organization, meeting for several hours every two weeks or so for nearly two years. After our first few meetings, I realized that in a sense this person, whom I will call Steve, was becoming an enemy. Our interactions brought out in me considerable reactivity—anger, moral and spiritual judgments, withdrawal, and at times a dualistic opposition between good (me) and bad (him).

And so I began to view my meetings with him as a potential learning experience. I, who sometimes complained about being overly busy, of not having enough time for formal spiritual practice, began to say: "Okay, to-day, the day of our meeting, is a day of practice with my difficult person!" I would meditate in the morning and set strong intentions, remember the ethical precepts, particularly the precept about speech, meditate while on the bus and sometimes cultivate lovingkindness toward all around me, and do walking meditation on the way to the meeting. Sometimes I would contemplate beforehand possible scenarios and ways in which I might respond in a nonreactive and helpful way. And I would make an effort to be mindful and in touch with my intentions during the meetings.

Reflecting on Our Relationships with Our Opponents

A number of reflections can help ease the dualism with our opponents. For example, we might be inspired to reflect on some of the perspectives on opponents given earlier—about the possibility of learning from the opponent, about the possibility of eventually becoming friends with the opponent, about how hatred never ends hatred, about how we can understand our problems as due to the "system" of antagonistic actions between ourselves and our opponent rather than simply as caused by the opponent himself or herself.

Here, I mention six further reflections and explore them in the context of interdependence. The first five are identified by Diana Winston in an essay about forming opponents or enemies entitled "Seven Reasons Why It's Better Not to Hate Them (even if they really are horrible, greedy, corrupt, and completely deserve it...).[13]

First, it is very helpful to reflect on the suffering of both parties. Such suffering may stem from hatred, fear, anger, grief, or depression. In the light of awareness of this suffering, we can open to compassion—for myself, for my opponent, for the difficult situation of being so painfully polarized.

A second reflection can be directed to the way that we tend to fixate on a particular quality of the opponent or enemy—say, greed, arrogance, or cruelty—and tend to believe both that this quality will always be present in the opponent and that there are no positive qualities in him or her. Yet we can reflect on how there are indeed other qualities present, or that the negative quality can change, or even that the opponent can become a friend.

Third, we may also reflect on how we share some of the negative qualities of our opponents. We can ask: How am I like my opponent in terms of what I most criticize? How am I greedy? Self-centered? Aggressive?

While this does not equate my actions with those of the opponent, it helps to bridge the apparent chasm between us.

A fourth reflection is that it is quite possible that I may not be totally "in the right," that I am not seeing something important, or that I am being overly rigid in my views. Such a reflection helps me both to ease my attachment to my views and to be open to learning from my encounter with the opponent.

A fifth reflection is particularly linked to an understanding of interdependence and is suggested by King's reflections on how southern racists are "caught in the system." Can I contemplate some of the web of causes and conditions that have led to the current conflict and polarization?

A sixth reflection may come from our understanding about the divine or sacred nature of all beings. Such principles are found in most spiritual traditions, as when Mahayana Buddhists talk about how all beings have "Buddha Nature" or when Jews, Christians, or Muslims speak about all human beings being made "in the image of God." One of the most difficult set of reflections can be about how opponents or enemies share this sacred quality. Etty Hillesum, a young Dutch Jewish woman writing during World War II, reflected with anguish on this principle while interned at a German transit camp:

> When I think of the faces of that squad of armed, green-uniformed guards—my God, those faces! I looked at them, each in turn, from behind the safety of a window, and I have never been so frightened of anything in my life as I was of those faces. I sank to my knees with the words that preside over human life: And God made man after His likeness. That passage spent a difficult morning with me.[14]

What Do We Actually Experience with Our Opponents?

Guided by our intentions and reflections, we are ready to explore our experience with our opponents. When we can look carefully at the nature of this experience, an important shift occurs. We realize, perhaps with some surprise, that what is difficult about our relationship with our opponents is that *we have difficult experiences* (as may others). We experience anger, fear, sadness, shame, and so forth, sometimes quite regularly. Such an understanding further eases our habitual polarized attitude, in which we simply assume that the problem is *external,* "out there" only because of the difficult person. We are convinced that we bear no responsibility for the problem and that were the opponent gone or behaving well, there would be no problem.

Looking more closely at my experience with my opponent, I can see in more depth how I become reactive. I can slow down the sequence of experiential events and notice the typical patterns. I particularly study my main forms of reactivity with this person. For example, there may be (1) a stimulus by the opponent (such as a comment or an action), which then (2) "triggers" a reaction in me. I soon find myself (3) in the midst of one or more of these difficult states, sometimes (4) feeling pain (although often not), and (5) reacting in various ways toward the opponent to "defend" myself. And so I attack, I judge, I withdraw, I strategize. I find myself in a stance whereby the opponent is the "other," the "bad" cause of all my problems.

At my meetings with Steve, I was on the lookout for my reactivity. When I became reactive, I tried to be mindful in the midst of my interaction with him. Over the months, I began to notice different patterns and discussed them with a mentor. I began to see the elements of my most basic reactive pattern with Steve, in which the stimulus was that I was thinking he was not listening to me or was distorting what I was saying. When that happened, I would notice myself starting to feel agitated, becoming judgmental toward him, and withdrawing emotionally from the meeting. It became exciting for me to examine these patterns closely. Sometimes I would be quite eager to be at the meeting, anticipating my discoveries.

Transforming Reactivity in Relation to Our Opponents

The heart of our inner practice with opponents is to examine our reactive patterns with mindfulness, compassion, and care, over and over again. Of course, this is not particularly easy. Not only are the states evoked by opponents or enemies difficult in themselves, but we often don't want to experience such states. I shouldn't be angry not only because I don't want anger to be present, but perhaps because I am not the kind of person who gets angry—but my opponent often triggers anger in me. It is, I think, all my opponent's fault.

And so, as I went to meeting after meeting with Steve, I sometimes felt like a martial artist, a warrior in training. Before the meeting, I would contemplate scenarios: "When he doesn't listen to me, I'll notice what's happening internally, and act in this way," or "When I perceive a lot of aggression coming from him, I'll try to be in touch with how it feels, rather than go to defensive reactivity right away." As I noticed the patterns more clearly, I also began to touch the pain involved—of anger and sadness at not being listened to being treated aggressively—and to notice similar pain outside of the meeting, seeing how the pain was linked to more general pain that I had held for years. To touch the pain with awareness, kindness, and some understanding, over and over again, seemed to set a kind of further healing in motion.

Developing Lovingkindness and Forgiveness in Relation to Our Opponents

A number of other individual internal practices can complement sustained mindfulness of reactive patterns and help us to work through the dualism of self and the opponent or enemy. In Buddhist tradition, lovingkindness and related practices, such as forgiveness and *tonglen* practices, are particularly helpful.

Lovingkindness practice can be very effective in softening this dualism in that it opens the heart generally, which usually shifts us away from an antagonistic posture. As we saw in chapter 5, lovingkindness practice in relation to a difficult person rests on having developed lovingkindness toward oneself, a benefactor, friend, and neutral person. If lovingkindness does not flow easily toward an opponent, it is sometimes useful to imagine that person as a more vulnerable being—as a child, as someone who suffers (even in relation to us), or as elderly—or to appreciate the opponent's positive qualities.

Forgiveness is often practiced as an adjunct to, and sometimes preparation for, lovingkindness with difficult people, in that it also tends to free our hearts from a fixed, polarized way of relating. In such practice, I extend forgiveness both to myself and to the other, first for any actions that I have committed, consciously or unconsciously, through word, thought, or deed, that may have led to the other's or my own pain and suffering. I then extend forgiveness similarly for another's actions that may have led to pain and suffering for myself.

Intending to forgive myself and the other, I do not necessarily condone either my own or the other's actions. Nor do I say that these actions were necessarily morally acceptable. Rather, I attempt to work through the effects of a painful past on my present experience, on my rigid, oppositional stance, on my continuing reactivity. My intention is to come closer to some degree of acceptance that the painful past actually happened (to move toward giving up "hope for a better past") and to being able to stay with the pain less reactively.

Developing Nonreactive Responses
in Relation to Our Opponents

As we train internally to transform our dualistic relation with the opponent or enemy, we also begin to act less reactively. As I was able to see much more closely, over and over again, the sequence of my reactivity with Steve, I was much more able to know, in the moment, "Oh, I'm in my reactive pattern," or "It feels like I'm shutting down and beginning to be reactive." I was increasingly able to feel the pain, for example, of not being listened to or ignored, of being misunderstood, rather than automatically finding myself being quite reactive following a short interaction with Steve.

Knowing that I was reactive or tending to become reactive gave me at times a choice about not being reactive. I could then act, keeping my "center" and "ground," to use the language of the martial arts, while addressing Steve relatively nonreactively: "I'm not sure that you understood what I said, but this is an important issue for me, and I want to continue to raise it." Or I might choose at some point to address the difficulty in the relationship in a nonreactive way: "When you changed the subject from what I had brought up, I felt a little frustrated, because this is a crucial concern for me. Would you be willing to look again at this issue?"

In such individual exploration of relatively nonreactive communication and action in relation to a difficult person, we receive training in how to respond to an opponent in ways that do not perpetuate the rigid dualism of self and enemy. Such practice provides an everyday laboratory for the work of peacemaking in more complex and/or difficult relationships, or with conflicts in groups, in communities, in organizations, in societies, and among nations. I will explore further how to respond more nondualistically in relational and collective domains in the next chapter, in the context of working with anger.

EXERCISE: Applying Opponents Practice

Choose someone from your everyday life who is a kind of opponent or enemy for you. Choose not the most difficult opponent you have but someone with whom there is a moderate amount of difficulty, and with whom you are in regular contact. In your relationship with this person, commit to carrying out opponents practice for a sustained period. Work with each of the six stages (see above) of such practice. Take notes on your experience over the days. If it is helpful and possible for you, work with a mentor.

Chapter Eight

TRANSFORMING ANGER

In March 2003, several days after the invasion of Iraq by the forces led by the United States, I joined with thousands of others in San Francisco to demonstrate against the invasion. Several hundred of us, gathered by the Buddhist Peace Fellowship, meditated together for one hour prior to the rally, and we continued in meditation as a set of speakers began to denounce the invasion. The anger and even rage of most of the speakers was palpable, with harsh denunciations of U.S. leaders, marked tones of righteousness, and impassioned calls to protest. The anger, agitation, and rapidly moving arms of the speakers contrasted powerfully with the stillness and the seeming lack of emotion of the meditating protesters. Some of the meditators no doubt felt that the speakers' words and gestures were aggressive and hateful, a kind of war-making—at a demonstration purportedly meant to contest war and promote peace. Some of the speakers and other demonstrators no doubt considered the meditators, if they even noticed them, as engaged in what seemed like passive inactivity, refusing to express a fully justified anger and being unable to join the larger group that was fueled by such anger and outrage—when supposedly they had come to be part of a unified demonstration!

A second vignette: At a landmark conference titled "Spiritual Activism," held in July 2005 in Berkeley, California, I led a workshop on the kind of training needed to become more mature "spiritual activists." I began by asking the participants what they thought they most needed to learn. While some spoke of the need to develop further in such qualities as compassion, patience, humility, and courage, the most common response centered on difficulties relating to anger, conflicts, and differences in viewpoints. "Anger is so hard for me," one person commented; "it sometimes tears apart our organization." Another person confided, "I get so angry when others don't believe as I do, on things that really matter, on life-and-death issues. How can I work with this anger spiritually?" A third person wanted to diminish her anger and increase her tolerance toward those in her organization who do less work. A fourth participant spoke of working with young campus activists who have a great deal of anger but little compassion, and how the anger was often directed to others in their group. Others spoke of how their anger toward political leaders often left them unable to act effectively.

These two vignettes point to the importance of working with *anger* in both spiritual practice and social change work. Yet understanding and transforming anger can be highly challenging and often quite confusing. At times we may feel as if we have internalized both the angry speaker and the quiet contemplative and don't quite know how they can coexist or whether we must somehow choose only one of them.

Developing a skillful approach to anger, one that preserves its energy and intelligence (evident in the best speakers at the demonstration) while transforming its potential reactivity and destructiveness, is central to spiritually grounded social action and builds on our exploration of interdependence. To understand first why we are often confused about anger, and then to identify concrete ways of transforming anger—individually, relationally, and collectively—is the theme of this chapter.[1]

SOURCES OF CONTEMPORARY
CONFUSION ABOUT ANGER

Our starting point in working with anger in the West is likely to be a state of confusion and ambivalence. That has certainly been my personal experience. We may, if drawn to spiritual practice, particularly Buddhist practice, hear that anger is simply destructive and negative. If we are also drawn to working for social change, we may receive the opposite message: anger at what is unjust and immoral is justified and necessary and is the basis for action. Some people, particularly members of oppressed groups, may be wary of Buddhism because of their perception that Buddhists consider anger inappropriate, even as a response to injustice.

We may hear some contemporary Western psychologists tell us that it is best to work through our anger without expressing it outwardly, while others tell us that expressing anger is imperative, for both emotional and physical health. Similarly, some of us may have been brought up in families, cultures, and subcultures in which the direct expression of anger was not acceptable, while others of us grew up in an atmosphere in which anger was readily expressed.

As if there wasn't enough confusion already, consider that the words from both Asian and Western languages that we translate into English as "anger" have a number of different connotations. Not only is it likely that the "anger" described in Buddhist texts is *not* typically the same experientially as the anger at injustice mentioned in Western traditions, but cross-culturally there seem to be *many kinds of anger*—some highly destructive, others leading to healing and justice. So one preliminary task is to be attentive to this range of connotations as we survey briefly the history of both Buddhist and Western conceptions of anger.

ANGER IN THE TEACHINGS OF THE BUDDHA

The understanding of anger in the teachings of the Buddha seems to be clear and simple: Anger is a problem! Anger is unambiguously destructive and negative, in terms both of the immediate experience and of the consequences of anger. In the *Dhammapada,* for example, the Buddha speaks about anger only negatively (here the word *anger* is a translation of *kodha*):

> Give up anger...
> Conquer anger with non-anger...
>   If one...is not angry...
> Then one comes into the presence of the gods.
> Guard against anger erupting in your body...
> Guard against anger erupting in your speech...
> Guard against anger erupting in your mind....[2]

Shantideva (eighth century) also sees anger (*krodha* in Sanskrit) as purely negative, "the source of hellish misery"[3]:

> Whatever wholesome deeds,
> Such as venerating the Buddhas, and generosity,
> That have been amassed over a thousand aeons
> Will all be destroyed in one moment of anger.[4]

In these teachings, what is translated as "anger" is seen unambiguously as an "unwholesome" *(akusala)* state. Anger is rooted solely in *dosa,* in ill will or hatred, and is linked with greed and spiritual ignorance. Such ignorance leads us to believe that happiness is dependent on an accumulation of pleasant experiences. Anger arises when we have unpleasant experiences, typically either getting what we don't want or not getting what we do want. When anger is taken as a basis for action, it generates suffering for oneself and for others. Hence it is labeled one of the "afflictive emotions" *(kilesa).* It should be uprooted through sustained mindfulness, lovingkindness, and spiritual reflection.

In Tibetan Buddhist tradition, we find somewhat different approaches to anger. There is, for example, a pantheon of "wrathful deities" said to manifest themselves in angry and fearful forms in order to confront greed, hatred, and delusion or to cut through an individual's deeply rooted habits. In some methods of working with anger, anger is actively evoked and embraced as a way of transforming it. We also find examples of great teachers seemingly acting angrily, even as they claim that their behavior is not the result of ordinary anger. Yet commonly the claim that anger is afflictive and a root of suffering remains.[5]

However, it is not clear that the Pali and Sanskrit terms that are translated as "anger" have the same connotations as *anger* in English. Broadly speaking, the Asian terms seem to reflect an understanding of anger as *only* negative, as linked with the intention to harm. These terms might be better translated as "ill will" or "hatred." The Western terms, as we shall see in the next section, point to the possibility of anger *at times* embodying wisdom, moral vision, and love. For this reason, the Dalai Lama recommends against translating the Tibetan term referring to afflictive emotions into English as "anger."[6]

A SHORT HISTORY OF WESTERN
AMBIVALENCE ABOUT ANGER

In the history of Western languages in the last three thousand years, we find that the word *anger* has *both* negative and positive connotations. Although sometimes anger has been understood as sinful, destructive, and dangerous, at other times it has been seen as morally and spiritually justified and linked with virtuous actions—such as questioning the violation of moral norms and contesting injustice—and positive qualities, such as wisdom, love, and compassion.

Among the ancient Jews, anger, expressed in its different nuances through a number of Hebrew words, is seen as a cause both of evil and of good. For example, at the beginning of Genesis we witness the murder of Abel by Cain, out of anger. In later Jewish literature, there are frequent admonitions never to be angry, for, as is sometimes said, "God loves one who never gets angry"; "Do not get angry and you will not sin."[7] Yet anger is also at times seen as an appropriate response. Both God and the human prophets who claim to speak for God express what the Jewish theologian and activist Abraham Joshua Heschel calls "divine rage" in response to immoral acts and injustice. The prophet Isaiah speaks of God's anger "burning" against his people because of their sins (Isaiah 5:25). However, such anger is always connected with love, mercy, care, and compassion, writes Heschel: "Anger, too, is a form of His presence in history. Anger, too, is an expression of His concern. This is the grandeur of God's compassion as proclaimed by the prophets. It is a love that transcends the most intense anger."[8]

For the ancient Greeks, anger is similarly seen sometimes as horribly and uncontrollably destructive and at other times as quite appropriate; several Greek words were linked with different types of anger. *The Iliad* opens with the line "Sing, goddess, the anger [*menis*] of Peleus' son Achilleus and its devastation, which put pains thousandfold upon the Achaians."[9] Yet anger is also valued as the "moral emotion" and understood as an appropriate response to what is socially inappropriate, immoral, or unjust. Aristotle summarizes this understanding of anger *(orge)* as sometimes wise, sometimes not:

> A man is praised for being angry under the right circumstances and with the right people, and also in the right manner, at the right time, and for the right length of time ... those who do not show anger at things that ought to arouse anger are regarded as fools.... [Yet] it is not easy to determine in what manner, with what person, on what occasion, and for how long a time one ought to be angry, and at what point right action ends and wrong action begins.[10]

The teachings of Jesus and many centuries of Christian theology also seem to show several ways of understanding anger. Jesus seems to question the appropriateness of anger under *any* circumstances in his teaching of turning the other cheek, proclaiming, "Everyone who is angry with his brother shall be liable to judgment" (Matthew 5:22). Yet he seems to manifest anger in brandishing a whip and throwing the money changers and vendors of cattle and sheep out of the temple in Jerusalem, criticizing the turning of a holy place into a market (John 2:14–16).

Early Christian theologians such as Augustine stress the negative side of anger, seeing it as simply sinful and unwholesome. Their reflections led to anger's classification, starting in fifth-century monasteries, as one of the Seven Deadly Sins. Yet in the Middle Ages, Aquinas, influenced by Aristotle, returned to a more nuanced understanding of anger. Sometimes he wrote of anger as a sin, following the teaching of Jesus, but at other times as quite appropriate and virtuous, particularly when there is injustice; God himself becomes angry, according to Aquinas, as "a judgment of justice."[11]

When we turn to the modern social and political movements for freedom, liberation, and justice starting with the American Revolution, we also find claims that there should be a "righteous" anger or indignation toward injustice and oppression. Anger becomes an important fuel for these movements, which many believe represent secularized expressions of the prophetic tradition. For example, in *Common Sense,* published in 1776, Thomas Paine gives perhaps the most influential argument for American independence, pointing to the vital, natural, and divinely sanctified place of emotions such as anger and indignation:

Hath your house been burnt? Hath your property been destroyed before your face? Are your wife and children destitute of a bed to lie on, or bread to live on? Have you lost a parent or a child by their hands, and yourself the ruined and wretched survivor?...I mean not to exhibit horror for the purpose of provoking revenge, but to awaken us from fatal and unmanly slumbers....

The Almighty hath implanted in us these unextinguishable feelings for good and wise purposes....The social compact would dissolve, and justice be extirpated from the earth, or have only a casual existence were we callous to the touches of affection. The robber, and the murderer, would often escape unpunished, did not the injuries which our tempers sustain, provoke us into justice.[12]

In the early 1840s, Karl Marx, as a young man, wrote of the need to criticize and overthrow "*all those conditions* in which man is a debased, enslaved, abandoned, contemptible being." Expressing a palpable anger, he pointed to the need for passionate "indignation" and "denunciation."[13]

The radical, reform, revolutionary, and anticolonial movements since Marx, whether they have called themselves democratic, socialist, Communist, or anarchist, typically channel a similar anger at injustice and oppression. For example, Gandhi speaks of how it is important for him to make use of the anger that he feels in everyday experiences for "fighting bigger battles"; "anger controlled can be transmuted into a power which can move the world."[14] Dorothy Day, in her autobiography, writes of how enraged she became after being arrested at a woman's suffrage demonstration, prior to her own sustained activism.[15] Martin Luther King Jr. points to the way that anger can be the starting point for social movements rather than lead to hatred: "The supreme task is to organize and unite people so that their anger becomes a transforming force."[16] Anger has commonly been an entry point for activists in recent years, whether in the peace, feminist, environmental, or gay and lesbian movements.

Indeed, anger is so often present in activist settings that Jim Forest, a longtime nonviolent organizer and writer connected with the Catholic Worker and the Fellowship of Reconciliation, once returned from a difficult meeting and humorously announced: "Now I know why the peace movement exists. The purpose is to take the angriest people in the world and keep them out of the military."[17]

Yet, as with the prophets, such anger at injustice is often linked with love, as in these reflections by the nineteenth-century French writer George Sand: "Humanity is outraged in me and with me. We must not dissimulate nor try to forget this indignation which is one of the most passionate forms of love."[18] Similarly, Cornel West speaks of Malcolm X as connecting anger, love, and work for justice, seeing him as "the prophet of black rage primarily because of his great love for black people."[19]

The general Western ambivalence toward anger can lead, as I suggested, to considerable confusion, particularly for those connecting Buddhist and Western approaches. So how do we make sense of these different views of anger in a way that can help us work with and transform anger?

One starting point, reflecting the spirit of both Buddhist mindfulness practice and Western science, is first to look directly and intimately at the nature of anger, to investigate anger in one's own experience, free, as much as possible, from any fixed views about anger. For me, such inquiry has been an essential starting point in my exploration of anger and ways of transforming it.

THE NATURE OF ANGER: A PERSONAL INVESTIGATION

A number of years ago, I was angry virtually all day long, for many days on end. Minute by minute, hour by hour, I was angry. Day by day, the anger continued, rising and falling in intensity.

What was particularly interesting about my experience was that at the time I was attending a ten-day meditation retreat, designed, we might think, to develop peacefulness and calm. Nonetheless, near the beginning of the retreat, I became angry, and I stayed angry for virtually the whole retreat.

I was angry initially at the meditation teachers. At the time, I had just moved to the San Francisco Bay Area after seven years of living in Kentucky and Ohio, where I had been interested in connecting meditation to the different parts of daily life. And yet this retreat, including the meditation instructions and the evening talks, seemed to have no *explicit* connection with daily life concerns. It was, I thought, as if we were supposed to be monks and nuns. But we were not!

Even though I had gone to many similar retreats in the past and had not experienced much, if any, anger in relation to this issue, for various reasons I was now very angry. I spoke to Jack Kornfield, one of the teachers, whom I had known for some time. He told me, "I have sympathy with your reasons for being angry. But you have basically two choices: You can leave the retreat, or you can stay and explore your anger."

I chose to stay. He then gave me instructions on how to work with my anger: "Be mindful of your anger, of how it is in your body, your mind, and your heart. Stay with your anger, and notice if it changes. At the end of each sitting or walking period, take notes on what has happened in the period. Come back and tell me what you've found."

And so, over the next ten days or so, I studied anger like I had never studied anger before. I had been raised to be a nice boy and hadn't been outwardly angry often in my life or for very long, certainly not for days on end, as I was now.

I explored anger in my body, feeling a variety of sensations: fire, excitement, and releases of energy; pain, dullness, and sometimes even chills and nausea. As the anger continued over the days, I noticed in my mind and heart many different states that seemed closely linked with my anger and often emerged when the anger shifted: irritation, frustration, resentment, judgment, despair, self-doubt, shyness, sadness, loneliness, grief, emotional fatigue, longing, acceptance, caring, and love. Grounding my awareness in my body and heart particularly helped me to open up to the wide variety of bodily states and emotions and not to stay predominantly at the level of thoughts.

After about four or five days, I looked at the notes I had taken. Going over them carefully, I saw that anger is a broad *concept* rather than a term that refers to one discrete experience. There is no one experience of anger.

Sometimes I found a narrow, petty, and reactive anger. I simply wasn't getting my way, and I didn't like it; I was quite irritated. With this more shallow anger, I often felt as if I wanted to see the targets of my anger suffer. There was no caring for them.

At other times, I could feel a frustration, which would sometimes shift to sadness, along, at times, with a sense of hurt or loss: "I feel lonely. My voice is not being heard. There's no way for me to communicate. I want to be heard. I've reflected on this a lot!" At times, other states followed, particularly grief about the lack of close communication, here and at other periods in my life, and self-assertion. My anger had clearly brought me in touch with other areas of pain and growth in my life.

Sometimes my anger was linked with issues of justice. I would become very judgmental about the power structure in the spiritual community, including at the retreat, which I thought didn't leave room for my voice. Or I would reflect: "Don't pathologize my anger! Or reduce it to *my* individual issue. This is about relationships in the community, and we need to see this and act!"

Sometimes the sadness and loneliness would shift further, to a warm sense of caring and even love: "I really care about this community and want it to be healthy! It's important to have these questions be aired more openly." I would feel warmth for those with whom I was angry. At times I felt gratitude for and even wonder about the whole process of looking more deeply, and for my mentors, with whom I was sometimes angry! I was often excited by the learning.

Sometimes the anger would move to fear, including a fear of not being able to control things, and a fear that I shouldn't have opened so much to anger; people wouldn't like me unless I was a nice person. I might be rejected simply for what I was feeling, and so maybe I should suppress my emotions. Occasionally, the fear would lead further into despair.

At other times, particularly when I reflected on injustice, I experienced a kind of Old Testament prophetic *rage* and even cosmic *wrath*: "They can do what they want, but if they don't act wisely, they will suffer! I proclaim it thus!" With this manifestation of anger, I felt at times other states as well: deep peace, happiness, acceptance, and compassion about the whole situation, linked with an intention to act.

BASIC GUIDELINES FOR TRANSFORMING ANGER

Such explorations, complemented by my own and others' further investigations of anger in contemplative practice, daily life, psychological work, and social change, suggest some basic guidelines to help navigate the contemporary confusions about anger and to develop ways of transforming anger. They reflect an integration of Buddhist and Western perspectives.

1. There are different types of anger, linked with different intentions; a core Western contribution to transforming anger is to observe that anger is sometimes connected with insight, caring, and love and with issues of morality and justice.
2. It is important to distinguish between the experience of anger and actions following from anger, and sometimes, when we are angry, to suspend action temporarily.
3. An important Buddhist contribution to transforming anger is to offer the tools of mindfulness, lovingkindness, and reflection with which to approach anger. Using such tools helps us as *individual* practitioners to separate out the intelligence and energy of anger from its reactivity and self-centeredness, leading to action based more in wisdom and compassion.
4. There are a number of similar skillful ways to interact *relationally* and *collectively* with both friends and opponents when anger arises.

WHAT WE CALL "ANGER" APPEARS IN DIFFERENT FORMS, LINKED WITH DIFFERENT INTENTIONS

One important way to make sense, both conceptually and experientially, of the great variety of views about anger, is to recognize the wide range of experiences that we bring together under the label of anger. Looking historically and cross-culturally, we can suggest several ways of making sense of the varieties of anger. We can notice that there is a spectrum of the level of anger's intensity, with mild irritation and annoyance at one end and fury, rage, and wrath at the other end. Some members of the anger family may carry other emotions; indignation may be linked with disgust, resentment with hatred. We can further ask whether the anger conveys hostility and aggression, or whether concerns about morality and justice are present.

We can also ask whether caring and love are linked to the anger. The psychologist and spiritual teacher Robert Masters speaks of "heart-anger" in order to name more explicitly anger that coexists with and is guided by love. Heart-anger is "wrathful love in the raw," "anger from the heart, openly expressed in a mindful context."[20] Masters understands such anger as a fairly rare expression of moral or spiritual maturity.

DISTINGUISHING THE EXPERIENCE OF ANGER FROM WHAT WE DO WITH OUR ANGER

Many of those who view anger as negative focus on the destructive *consequences* of anger and the ways in which it is linked with the intention to harm or with aggression or violence. However, they and many of those who see positive uses for anger stress the importance of distinguishing the *experience* of anger from our *reactions,* from what we "do" with anger.

This distinction may lead us, when we notice that we are angry, to *suspend all actions temporarily,* taking a "time-out." Shantideva counsels: "Whenever there is the desire to be angry, / I should not do anything nor say anything, / But remain like a piece of wood."[21] The Buddhist psychologist Harvey Aronson suggests that our initial response to anger be that of restraint—to avoid acting out our anger through violent behavior, threatening postures, or verbal shaming and blaming.[22]

Given such "breathing space," we may then find ways to work with the anger in a protected environment. Later, we may be able to transform anger more quickly or even in the very midst of action, but for most of us, creating a simplified situation separated from the demands of action is initially optimal.

SEPARATING THE INTELLIGENCE AND ENERGY OF ANGER FROM ITS BLINDNESS AND REACTIVITY

The heart of transformative work with anger is to separate out the intelligence and the energy of anger from its reactivity, permitting action based more in wisdom and compassion. Here, I outline one way to transform anger that both makes use of Buddhist tools and recognizes the predominantly Western insight that anger may be motivated by care, love, and deep commitment to personal integrity and justice.

In what follows in this section, I will explore in depth three tools— mindfulness, lovingkindness, and reflection—that particularly facilitate the transformation of anger.

Mindfulness of Anger

As in my explorations at my "anger retreat," with mindfulness practice we study the nature of anger as we find it in our direct experience. Given that anger typically arrives with alarm bells, strong energy, and powerful tendencies to act (or act out) rather than to pay attention, we may actually have never before examined the dynamics of our anger and the nature of anger in general. We may have rarely suspended the link of anger with immediate words and actions. So being mindful of our anger may be a very new experience. It is also not easy.

In holding anger in awareness, it is often helpful to use a mental label with which we periodically note "anger" lightly when it is present. We can also guide mindfulness with gentle inquiries, asking: What does anger feel like right now? What do I experience somatically, emotionally, and mentally? What are the different sensations in my body when I'm angry? What thoughts, particularly negative judgments, are associated with my anger? What insights are connected with my anger? When I stay with mindful awareness with my anger for a while, what changes, if any, occur? When I listen attentively (being careful not to project what I think "should" be there), what other emotions seem to exist "beneath," "beside," or "around" my anger?

We may at times notice that *painful experiences* such as hurt, sadness, memories of past pain, fear, or loneliness surface. When we can be mindful of these painful experiences, we can experience a healing and some relaxing of the tendencies of largely unconscious and unacknowledged pain to drive us. Mindful presence to pain, without the effort to get rid of it or somehow to "fix" the situation, can be powerfully and sometimes dramatically healing, both in a given moment and over time, individually and with others.

We may also hear voices that reflect important *needs,* both our own and those of others, as with some of the needs that surfaced in my own explorations: to be recognized and heard, to feel part of a community, to be treated respectfully, to set limits or establish boundaries, and so on. The anger may in part indicate that such needs are not being met. In his well-known method of "Nonviolent Communication," which I will explore later in the chapter, Marshall Rosenberg argues that the very meaning of anger is to lead us to "wake up" and acknowledge such unmet needs.

As we listen more deeply to anger without clinging or aversion, we may also touch the purer states of our heart—*love, caring, joy, compassion, and equanimity.* Our anger may—sometimes rather amazingly—be transformed into these states, as occurred for me.

As we work in these ways, we may be able to *act* much more skillfully. We will have some insight into the problem that presents itself and, to a significant extent, will have freed such insight from reactivity, from blame and the intention to harm. We will have preserved the energy of anger, yet transformed it, so that it appears more as clarity, moral force, strong presence, love, care, or compassion. To be sure, such a transforma-tion may sometimes take considerable time and energy, depending on a number of factors—the depth of the pain, our ability to be mindful, and the support and guidance we have in investigating anger.

As we work more with anger in protected environments, we become better able to extend mindfulness to the more complex and challenging situations of daily life. In the midst of interaction, we learn to carry out the same practices of mindfulness: naming what is happening; noticing what is occurring physically, emotionally, and mentally; and looking more deeply.

Lovingkindness Practice and Anger

A significant amount of care, gentleness, and kindness is required simply to carry out such mindful inquiry into anger. Thich Nhat Hanh speaks of being like a mother to one's anger, embracing it and holding it in mind-fulness. Carrying out a separate practice of lovingkindness can comple-ment mindfulness practice, helping to transform anger that one feels toward oneself or others.

At times, these practices have been used in the midst of social action. A Thai friend, Pracha Hutanawatr, an activist and later a monk under the great Thai teacher Ajahn Buddhadasa, used lovingkindness practice while in prison; he worked with his anger and avoided being trapped in bitterness and polarization.

EXERCISE: Reflecting on Your Anger

The practice of contemplative reflection, used both in Buddhist and Western settings for thousands of years, can offer further tools. In such reflection, we attempt to look more deeply, primarily with the intention of understanding our anger. Here are six reflections that can complement the reflections listed in chapter 7 for deepening our sense of interdependence in relation to an opponent. You may reflect

> on how you can learn and grow from this situation of being angry, and to that extent, be grateful for your opponent and for this learning opportunity;
> on your own contribution to a given conflict, rather than assigning blame only to the other;

on how your anger and the other's anger may be based on your
unmet needs or values;

on whether there is an underlying moral clarity linked with your
anger;

on nonreactive ways of responding creatively to the situation; and

on how someone you admire (for example, the Buddha, Kwan Yin,
the Dalai Lama, or your grandmother) might respond were he
or she in your situation.

SKILLFUL WAYS OF WORKING WITH ANGER IN RELATIONAL SETTINGS

How do we work in similar ways with the anger that arises in relationships, groups, communities, or organizations so that we can transform any reactivity and aggression contained in the anger while integrating whatever insight and caring energy are carried by the anger?

Transforming anger in these contexts in many ways follows the general orientation of how we open to suffering, as explored in chapter 4, and how we work individually with our anger. In this section, I add a further focus on how we use *speech and communication,* providing specific methods of transforming anger in the midst of verbal interactions and complementing the earlier discussions of wise speech.

A common strategy is to communicate the insights and energy of anger in ways that neither blame the other—which may put the other person on the defensive and make it more difficult for him or her to listen —nor suppress the anger. A key starting point is to frame the anger in terms of one's own immediate experience, without making assumptions about the other's intentions, and without immediately analyzing what is wrong about a given situation.

One of the best-known approaches to skillful communication is Nonviolent Communication (NVC). Marshall Rosenberg, the founder of NVC, sees this communication methodology as a kind of nonsectarian spiritual practice in which one comes ultimately to see the divinity of the other through methods that support respectful and compassionate communication. The basic technique is to learn to speak more skillfully by focusing, both in one's communications to others and in one's receptive and empathic listening, on four areas:

1. the (relatively) neutral observation of what has been said or done that catalyzes one's emotions;

2. the emotions that arise in relation to what has been noticed;
3. the underlying needs (or values, intentions, or desires) linked with the emotions; and
4. the actions requested in order to meet such needs.

This might lead to communicating to another in the following way: "[1] When you and the others made the decision without asking me for my views, [2] I was upset and angry [3] because it is important for me, as a member of this small organization, to be consulted on these kinds of issues. [4] Would you be willing to bring in my view on this matter, and to agree that I will be consulted in the future?"

In the context of anger, Rosenberg counsels several additional steps. First, he agrees that it's often important to stop for a moment and breathe. Then, knowing that we are angry (see 2, above) in relation to something that occurred (1), we can look specifically for the *judgments* associated with the anger. When we can identify such judgments, it can become much easier to identify our basic needs (3) in the situation and to communicate both the fact of having been angry and our requests to have our needs met (4). At times, however, a further step is needed; Rosenberg believes that often we also need to be empathic in relation to the other *before* expressing our requests in order to reduce the defensiveness of the other.

He gives a powerful example from his own experience. Once, he was being driven from the airport in a cab when a message came to the cabbie from the dispatcher to pick up a man at a synagogue. The man sitting next to him made a comment about Jews getting up early to "screw everybody out of their money." Rosenberg was intensely angry for a while but remembered to take several deep breaths, give empathy to himself for his own hurt, fear, and rage, and let his thoughts and emotions play out internally. This helped him to empathize with the man's pain and ask, "Are you feeling frustrated? It appears that you might have had some bad experiences with Jewish people." As the man said yes and went on to talk disparagingly of Jews (and, later, African Americans) through a series of negative judgments, Rosenberg listened to the emotions, pain, and needs behind the man's statements. Only after the man stopped talking did Rosenberg start to speak of his own experience, telling the man: "You know, when you first started to talk, I felt a lot of anger, a lot of frustration, sadness, and discouragement, because I've had very different experiences with Jews than you've had, and I was wanting you to have much more the kind of experiences I've had."[23]

Rosenberg continued to speak, slowing down the conversation whenever it seemed as if the man was interpreting Rosenberg's words as blaming so that he might more easily know Rosenberg's pain. With both of them listening to the other's pain, pain closely linked with anger, there was at least the possibility of communication rather than a continuing cycle of blaming and distancing (although admittedly, in many situations, there might be a limit to the degree of communication possible).

TRANSFORMATIVE WORK WITH ANGER IN COLLECTIVE CONTEXTS

The great challenge—in working with the anger that often surfaces strongly in relation to injustice, oppression, and ecological devastation— is to develop transformative collective processes that have similar general intentions and structures as those we have explored in individual and relational contexts. How do we channel, as King suggested, the anger of citizens into actions that are neither destructive of others nor self-destructive?

In social contexts, sometimes only anger, typically coming at first from the margins of our society and sometimes escalating into violence, is able to draw attention to the pain related to systemic problems that have been ignored in mainstream society. Sometimes it takes such anger, appearing much like the Tibetan wrathful deities, to break through collective ignorance, denial, and complacency.

Yet there are many dangers to such anger if the anger remains reactive and untransformed. It may easily turn inward and harm individuals and organizations. Outwardly, it may lead to polarization, destruction, and violence, in which case the original issues can easily be forgotten.

The spiritual activist and writer Starhawk speaks of anger that is sometimes directed toward like-minded individuals: "I see many progressive groups faltering or splintering not over deep political divisions but out of frustration with interpersonal conflicts."[24] Dennis Bernstein, a veteran journalist and activist with the Pacifica Radio network, reflects on how anger in relation to social realities can surface in many ways:

> Often, I'm so angry. I'm so angry with the people I work with, as well as with the people I resist. I feel so angry sometimes that I don't feel good. It darkens what may be a beautiful soul. I feel so angry that I'm not even likable. I think that we get on each other's nerves out of this anguish and this fury.[25]

Similarly, untransformed anger often leads to a *rigid polarization between angry, judgmental, self-righteous, and sometimes violent activists, on the one hand, and those in power and often the mass of the population, on the other.* It can be difficult or impossible for those in the latter group to hear the message of the activists if they feel harshly judged, blamed, and even attacked.

When anger is not transformed, furthermore, *awareness of the underlying pain and even love that fuel anger is obscured, both in the activist and in the general population.* It is, I believe, in large part the ability of the activist to be in touch with the pain and suffering—of injustice and oppression—and to communicate such pain and suffering skillfully to others that makes social transformation possible, leading to action that may open the heart of the listener. As Joanna Macy suggests, "Where anger goes sour is when it denies its source in the pain."[26]

The deep question that we need to ponder in the light of these reflections is this: *How do we work skillfully with our anger to communicate the pain and suffering linked with injustice and oppression in ways that help to break through what we might call our fellow citizens' "trance" of comfort, privilege, attachment, conformity, and denial, without, as much as possible, blaming and polarizing, without simply venting anger?* How we respond to this question in the coming years, and how creative and skillful we are in our responses, will, I believe, determine to a large extent the degree of social transformation possible.

We can point to several approaches to the transformation of anger in the collective context. For example, Thich Nhat Hanh often talks of working with his own *individual* anger at violence and war, using the tools of mindfulness and reflection, so that anger yields insight, particularly into interdependence, and compassionate action. In 1991, as he heard President George H. W. Bush give the order to attack Iraq, he became very angry, yet practiced mindfulness and reflection:

> I could not sleep. I was angry and overwhelmed. The next morning in the middle of my lecture, I suddenly paused and told my friends, "I don't think I will go to North America this Spring." The words just sprang out.... I practiced breathing, walking, and sitting, and a few days later, I decided to go. I saw that I was one with the American people, with George Bush, and with Saddam Hussein. I had been angry with President Bush, but after breathing consciously and looking deeply, I saw myself as President Bush.... The President acted the way he did because we acted the way we did.... Our society is filled with hatred and violence. Everything is like a bomb ready to explode, and we are all a part of that bomb; we are all co-responsible.[27]

Joanna Macy's work offers a way of transforming anger at the collective situation in *relational* contexts. In the practice of the Truth Mandala within a group, organization, or community, as we saw in chapter 4, the expression of anger in relation to a particular pain or the "pain of the world" is welcomed, along with the expression of fear, sadness, and confusion, as part of a larger transformative process.

With such practices, we can observe the shifting of emotions that we also witness in our individual practices, as a person in the group may move from anger to other emotions. In my own experience of this and similar practices, expressing such anger in a public way has often freed up, for me and others, the reactive and stuck qualities of anger. I found, for example, that in touching anger in a group ritual led by Macy just after the Gulf War started in 1991, I was able to release a kind of paralyzed, bitter anger toward the government, which had been present since the beginning of the war. Such anger shifted, releasing the earlier paralysis and leading directly to action with greater equanimity and compassion. More than ten years later, in leading groups in these practices both just before and just after the invasion of Iraq in 2003, I also noticed the powerful transformative effects of exploring and expressing anger in public groups, where such anger was at times directly heard but neither fed nor criticized. Participants seemed much more ready to act with clarity and compassion, and less reactivity, after engaging in these practices.

Zen teacher and activist Taigen Dan Leighton consciously channels *individual* anger arising in relation to governmental policies into the action of distributing information to a wide audience through daily e-mails. He speaks of transforming anger in this process.

> There are times when things happen to which one needs to respond, from the viewpoint of the ethical precepts, for example by preventing harm from being done. The point is to own one's anger in relation to these situations, not just to vent the anger reactively, from one's habits and conditioning. Rather, how do we respond directly and calmly? This sometimes means that we have to speak negatively about situations.
>
> The point isn't *not* to get angry. Rather, we follow the precept "The disciple of the Buddha does not harbor ill will." We don't hold on to anger. So how do you not turn anger into grudge? That's when anger becomes very corrosive, and one's anger against others hurts oneself more than others. How do you express your response to a situation that you find outrageous without holding on to some corrosive kind of anger or having it lead to hatred?

I have been channeling my anger particularly into sharing information. That hopefully helped to transform the anger. When anger
is transformed into just being present, I think it has the capacity to
help you see things more clearly.[28]

Transforming anger on the larger scale of *social movements* is naturally
much more difficult than working individually or in groups. Of course,
it helps for participants in such movements to make use of some of the
individual and group methods mentioned in this chapter. Yet there are
nonetheless examples of movements that parallel the individual and
group work in (1) offering a number of methods to transform the anger of
individuals, (2) effectively expressing the pain and suffering of injustice
and oppression, (3) communicating to those on the other side without intending to polarize them against us, and (4) pointing to principles that
might be shared by those on the other side and that can motivate change.

The nonviolent movements associated with Gandhi and King, for example, (1) provided concrete ways of transforming anger. For Gandhi's
movement, the methods of developing "purity of heart" included fasting,
prayer meetings, music, chanting, readings of scriptures, meditation, and
spiritual talks. Gandhi once said, "It is not that I am incapable of anger...
[but] there is always in me the conscious struggle for following the law of
non-violence deliberately and ceaselessly."[29] Similarly, participants in the
civil rights movement made use of such varied tools and resources as
Christian prayer and worship, reflection on scripture and the life of Jesus,
role-playing, and music. (2) Through the practice of civil disobedience
and the strategy of taking on "redemptive suffering" by being arrested,
activists made very public both the pain of those being arrested and the
pain of the situation that they were protesting. They took care, in King's
words, (3) to criticize the system of "sin," not the "sinner," (4) appealing to
what they took to be universal principles of democracy and human rights.

Such nonviolent action serves to break through the trance of ignorance, complacency, and denial by tending to open the heart of the ordinary citizen and even the opponent to the pain of the situation, often
leading to empathy and at times an emotional and moral crisis for the opponent, a kind of disorienting dilemma that often is a spur to learning.
Reactive anger, on the other hand, tends to close the heart of those who
are the target of such anger.

This is why, as Thich Nhat Hanh suggests, one role of the peacemaker
is to bring the pain of each side to the attention of the other side. It is why
breakthroughs often occur in conflicts when each side can hear the stories
of pain and suffering and recognize the humanity of the other, without

the political rhetoric and reactively angry judgments that typically block the possibility of being present to pain.

For example, in the 1970s and 1980s, the Mothers of the Disappeared in Argentina kept meeting and holding vigils every week in the Plaza del Mayo in Buenos Aires and in other cities and provided some of the impetus for major change—in large part by transmuting their anger into a public sharing of their grief, touching others in the process. We can also point to the catalytic protest of Cindy Sheehan in August 2005. Sheehan, the mother of a young solider slain in Iraq, went by herself outside President George W. Bush's Crawford, Texas, ranch, vowing to stay there until the president would speak with her. Her action unexpectedly resonated with the population, less because of her views on Iraq, which had already been expressed by many activists, than because she communicated the reality of the pain, anger, and love of the situation to so many people. Speaking of the families of the soldiers in the military, she said, "We might not have the same politics, but trust me, we have the same pain."[30]

Chapter Nine

ACTING WITH EQUANIMITY

In April 1968, the night before he was assassinated in Memphis, Tennessee, Martin Luther King Jr. spoke these famous words at the end of his speech:

> Well, I don't know what will happen now. We've got some difficult days ahead. But it doesn't matter with me now. Because I've been to the mountaintop.... And I'm happy, tonight. I'm not worried about anything. I'm not fearing any man.[1]

Part of what we find remarkable about these words is the presence of a deep equanimity in the face of violence. In King's life in general, as well as in the lives of Gandhi, Thich Nhat Hanh, the Dalai Lama, Aung San Suu Kyi of Burma, and many others who are both spiritually grounded and socially engaged, we find a similar equanimity—amid threats and attacks, tension and danger, imprisonment and persecution, criticisms and differences of view, as well as daily ups and downs. This equanimity seems to embody, as in King's speech, emotional and mental balance, imperturbability, deep faith, fearlessness about pain and even death, joy in the midst of danger, and a kind of prophetic vision—all manifested in the very midst of action.

In the teachings of the Buddha, equanimity *(upekkha)* is one of the most important qualities to cultivate. It is one of the Seven Factors of Awakening—one of the attributes of an awakened being and of ourselves when we are aware and present—and one of the ten "perfections" or "virtues" *(paramis)* to be developed in the course of spiritual practice. And it is one of the four divine abodes *(brahmavihara),* along with lovingkindness, compassion, and joy. In each of these groupings, furthermore, equanimity is listed last. It is understood to reflect an advanced spiritual faculty and to be close, in its mature development, to the state of full freedom, or nirvana.

But what is equanimity and how is it cultivated? What are its gifts? What does it mean to be equanimous—in the context of spiritual practice and daily life? What does it mean to be equanimous in the face of pain? When there is injustice or violence? Does equanimity lead to inaction, passivity, or resignation? A well-known activist slogan tells us: "If you're not outraged [and presumably not so equanimous], you're not paying attention." Is equanimity even desirable, given the state of the world?

THE QUALITIES OF EQUANIMITY

In the teachings of the Buddha, equanimity is particularly identified with the qualities of *balance, even-mindedness,* and *imperturbability* and is further linked with *insight and understanding, joy,* and *faith.*

The term *upekkha* literally means "balance." The term suggests both a balanced approach to any experience and a balance of body, heart, and mind in general—a balance between the different energies of our being. The well-known late German monk Nyanaponika Thera, author of *The Heart of Buddhist Meditation,* once wrote that equanimity "is a perfect, unshakable balance of mind, rooted in insight."[2]

In the context of meditation, equanimity can be understood as *even-mindedness,* the ability to be present as fully as possible with *all* experiences—whether we are focused primarily on our internal world or on the external world—with an open heart and clear seeing, without reactivity. This ability is directly cultivated by mindfulness practice, as we continually note how we have been lost in aversion or grasping, and then return to a nonreactive "bare attention" in relation to present experience.

Equanimity in its mature state also connotes *unshakability* and *imperturbability*—in the face of whatever happens to us. The equanimous person has an enormous capacity both to open to any experience and not to react compulsively. The ability to be directly mindful, particularly of difficult experiences, helps avoid, as we shall see later in more detail, some of the possible distortions of equanimity—such as indifference, resignation, or distancing—that rest on an often subtle aversion to experience (one's own or another's).

In a talk to his son, the Buddha likens this unshakable quality of equanimity to the earth's enormous capacity to withstand abuse:

Rahula, develop meditation that is like the earth; for when you develop meditation that is like the earth, agreeable and disagreeable contacts will not invade your mind and remain. Just as people throw clean things and dirty things, excrement, urine, spittle, pus, and blood on the earth, and the earth is not horrified, humiliated, and disgusted because of that, so too, Rahula, develop meditation that is like the earth; for when you develop meditation that is like the earth, agreeable and disagreeable contacts will not invade your mind and remain.[3]

To be unshakable and imperturbable means not to be unduly influenced by what the Buddha calls the "Eight Worldly Winds" (*loka dhamma,* sometimes called the "Eight Worldly Conditions"). The teaching about these "winds" gives us an inventory of eight basic ways in which we become attached (or aversive) to particular experiences or situations.[4] The Buddha identifies four pairs, each made up of a "good" outcome and a "bad" outcome:

Pleasure and pain
Gain and loss
Fame and disrepute
Praise and blame.

Our tendency, not surprisingly, is to be attached to the first member of each pair and aversive toward the second member. We want pleasure, gain, a good reputation, and to be praised, and we don't want pain, loss, a bad reputation, and blame. To be equanimous is to be able to maintain one's intentions, integrity, and nonreactivity in the face of any of these winds.

The Buddha speaks of how Mara, the personification of greed, hatred, and delusion in the Buddhist tradition, once attempted to trick a number of monks (*bhikkhus*) into acting in hateful and prideful ways by manipulating a group of Brahmans living nearby who alternately blamed and praised the monks. The trick did not work; the monks remained equanimous. The Buddha summarizes this teaching of equanimity:

Therefore, bhikkhus, if others abuse, revile, scold, and harass you, on that account you should not entertain any annoyance, bitterness, or dejection of the heart. And if others honor, respect, revere, and venerate you, on that account you should not entertain any delight, joy, or elation of the heart.[5]

In our culture, developing such equanimity in the face of the Eight Worldly Winds is a long and difficult task, for most of us are strongly influenced by praise or blame, by others' perceptions of us, and by whether things go well or not. I remember learning directly about praise and blame some years ago when several of us had organized a six-day Buddhist Peace Fellowship Summer Institute. After several days, we did a brief evaluation of how the gathering was proceeding. Almost all of the fifty or so evaluations were highly positive, but two or three were strongly negative. It was remarkable how seriously I and the other organizers seemed to take those negative evaluations, almost as if the others didn't count. We somehow listened mostly to the blaming, judging voices.

Deep equanimity is also based on *wisdom*—*insight* into and *understanding* of causes and conditions, and the roots of suffering and happiness. At the individual level, it rests on having examined over and over again, for example, the experiences of pain and suffering, of judging negatively and being judged, of blaming and being blamed, of loss. We also investigate continually the tendencies to seek happiness through compulsive grasping. Out of such deep practice arises an ability to see more clearly the causes and conditions of particular situations. When we understand in this way, we tend to blame much less. As the well-known French maxim tells us, "To understand is to forgive." We may experience this especially when, after a conflict with someone close to us, we hear the other person's lived experience in detail. In such an instance, we can often feel a marked softening.

In our social and political lives, we may similarly develop the historical sense that helps us to understand more precisely the causes of pain, suffering, and injustice, and hence the possible causes of freedom and justice. We may see some of the roots of racism, for example, in specific long-term causes and conditions manifesting through centuries-old ideologies and institutions. We may develop a very broad historical perspective about social evolution and the nature of social change.

A number of activists informed by Buddhist practice emphasize the importance of such a long-term perspective, which can coexist with a sense of urgency and the need for immediate action. Gary Snyder often counsels making a "four-thousand-year commitment" to land, community, and spiritual practice. Activist and Zen teacher Taigen Dan Leighton speaks of the importance of this perspective for acting freshly and resolutely in the moment:

> Part of what Buddhist teachings offer to activists is a wider perspective, a perspective that goes back thousands of years, that is not lim-

ited to human history, and that is not limited to the urgency of this moment. That approach is actually helpful for people to be more effective in the complex situation of *this* moment.[6]

Joanna Macy believes that our equanimity is deepened by going back yet further in our understanding, to the very origins of the cosmos and of life:

> If we are not separate from the living world, then we should act our age. We are 4½ billion years old in terms of the origins of life, and 15 billion years old in terms of the Big Bang. Every atom and every molecule in every cell of our body goes back that 15 billion years. The life that is now beating our hearts and breathing our lungs now didn't begin with our conception. Rather, life flows through us. For me, this is a wonderful doorway into equanimity.
>
> We can also feel the presence of future and past generations encircling us, cultivating a sense of our collegiality with them, seeing them as companions on this awesome journey. I would call this an "ordinary person's" version of equanimity; I am just part of this great story. This helps us as activists to give up trying to do it all in our lifetimes, or to succeed as the most effective social change agent the world has ever seen—the peerless defender of the rain forest or the conqueror of the evil empire. Rather, there's a web of life that's much bigger than us; we're part of the story.[7]

Perhaps surprisingly, another important aspect of equanimity is *joy*. Recognizing the joy of equanimity goes against the common view that equanimity is dry, unemotional, and somewhat aloof. For the Buddha, however, mature equanimity is linked with a deep and sometimes subtle joy and happiness, characteristic of a (relative) freedom of mind and heart. Joy naturally arises, the Buddha tells us, when we no longer are hooked by what is agreeable or disagreeable in experience. As we work through our attachments and aversions, we become more and more "purified and bright, malleable, wieldy, and radiant," "peaceful" and "sublime."[8]

It has always been very inspiring for me to find such a deeply rooted joy, a lack of resentment, and a commitment reflecting a powerful equanimity in those persons who know significant pain in their lives. It has moved me deeply, for example, to see images of the equanimity and dignity of older African Americans in the civil rights movement, or of South Africans happily standing in long lines in 1994 to vote for the first time in their lives, for Nelson Mandela. I have been very touched to know friends, old and sometimes young, who have maintained a great joy and equanimity despite serious illnesses or disabilities, as if they were affirming the entirety of life, even as the pain and hurt were present.

Similarly, the well-known Cambodian monk Mahaghosananda, presently the leader of Cambodian Buddhists, is deeply aware of the realities of the "killing fields" of the late 1970s, yet nonetheless communicates both humor and an unstoppable inner radiance. He practiced at a Thai monastery during the 1970s and thus survived. Once he could return safely to his country, where all but three thousand of the fifty thousand monks and nuns had been killed, he devoted himself fully to reconciliation and healing for his country. He began to lead *dhamma yietras* (marches establishing spiritual truth) through areas of Cambodia still full of land mines and bands of Khmer Rouge. I met him several times in Thailand at meetings of the International Network of Engaged Buddhists, in the 1990s. Full of an awareness of both current difficulties and past horrors, his presence nonetheless brought forth laughter, jokes, and great warmth.

Equanimity also expresses a profound *faith*—in the essential goodness of our being, in the ultimate beneficence of the universe, in the spirit of individual and collective evolution toward awakening—despite the sometimes awesome level of pain. Such faith may be personally grounded in regular spiritual practice. The discipline is to enter over and over again into the exploration of suffering and its causes, happiness and its causes, and to be continually tested and deepened through new experiences. In deep equanimity, we might say, faith and insight come together as we rest in being.

Such faith is the fruit, often unexpected and full of "grace," of our committed practice and transformative work. Martin Luther King Jr., for example, went through a deep crisis of faith near the beginning of his work in Montgomery in January 1955. He had been receiving many obscene and threatening phone calls and had recently spent a day in jail. The day after his time in jail, he came home very late after a meeting; his wife and newly born daughter were asleep. Another phone call came, the caller warning him: "Nigger, we are tired of you and your mess now. And if you aren't out of this town in three days, we're going to blow your brains out, and blow up your house." King could not sleep. He made himself a cup of coffee and sat down at the kitchen table. It was around midnight.

He was close to giving up, strategizing about how to end his leadership role and not look like a coward. He contemplated with anguish the possibility of losing his daughter or wife, or his being taken from them. He felt weak but knew that at that point he couldn't even find strength from his parents, away in Atlanta. He later reflected that his only recourse was to call on "that power that can make a way out of no way":

> I bowed down over that cup of coffee. I never will forget it.... I prayed a prayer, and prayed out loud that night. I said, "Lord, I'm down here trying to do what's right. I think I'm right. I think the cause we represent is right. But Lord, I must confess that I'm weak now. I'm faltering. I'm losing my courage.... And it seemed at the moment that I could hear an inner voice saying to me, "Martin Luther, stand up for righteousness. Stand up for justice. Stand up for truth. And lo I will be with you, even until the end of the world."...I heard the voice of Jesus saying still to fight on. He promised never to leave me, never to leave me alone. No never alone. No never alone. He promised never to leave me, never to leave me alone.[9]

King reported that "almost at once my fears began to go. My uncertainty disappeared." A few days later, his home was bombed while he was at church, with his wife and daughter in the house. King was given word of the bombing and spoke briefly at the podium, with his listeners noting with surprise his remarkably steady and calm presence. King later said of the bombing, "My religious experience a few nights before had given me the strength to face it."[10]

DISCERNING THE "NEAR ENEMIES" OF EQUANIMITY

There is a Buddhist teaching that is vital to our development of equanimity in action in the contemporary world. In the practice of lovingkindness, compassion, joy, and equanimity, it is necessary to be able to distinguish the authentic meaning of these qualities from their *near enemies*. The near enemies mimic, as it were, the authentic qualities. Attachment for another mimics lovingkindness; it may look very kind and loving, but there is compulsion and unconsciousness. Pity mimics compassion but is based on a sense of separation and superiority. What appears to be joy may be an excitement that lacks joy's depth.

The near enemy of equanimity mentioned in the classical texts is *indifference*. Indifference is marked by a lack of connection to another's happiness or suffering, which suggests both a self-centeredness and a distance from the experience of the other. Such indifference may be based in a retreat to a kind of fabricated mental world (or, in our times, the virtual world) where I am not touched by anything, and yet I may appear authentically calm and equanimous, perhaps even with a spiritual ambience. I may believe: "I'm equanimous. The sorrows of the world don't really affect me because I'm not attached to how things are." When we look carefully, however, we may find little care and little connection, but rather an indifference based in fear or aversion, that justifies itself by using spiritual language.

In exploring the nature of equanimity in the midst of action in the world, we need to account for and work through not only indifference but also what appear to be a number of related "near enemies" that may masquerade as equanimity. They include the following:

privileged distance
denial
complacency
resignation
acquiescence
numbness
intellectual aloofness
rationalization
cynicism
dogmatism
fear of strong emotions, particularly anger

These near enemies of equanimity rest, in Buddhist terms, on aversion to and distancing from suffering, on the one hand, and grasping after the pleasant qualities of equanimity, on the other. Both in turn depend on an underlying ignorance.

The Near Enemies of Equanimity

A Masked Aversion to Pain and Suffering

For example, many of those in *privileged* positions in a given society maintain what seems like a certain degree of personal and philosophical equanimity that hides aversion. As a well-to-do member of the middle or upper classes, I may typically live and work in neighborhoods separated by physical distance and social boundaries from day-to-day knowledge of and contact with the lives of the poor and oppressed. I may also refuse to look beyond these boundaries and be supported in a kind of *denial* of these lives and realities by the mass media and entertainment industry.

I may say: "Well, I know that others aren't doing so well, but I feel balanced, and my life is going well." I may even cultivate spiritual practices that promise wisdom, love, and equanimity, motivated in part by the desire to create a refuge from a scary world for myself and those close to me, in which I avoid or at least hold at bay awareness of the suffering of the world.

My apparently spiritual equanimity may thus have a significant basis in one or more of the following: *fear, escapism, denial and delusion, complacency, resignation, acquiescence, numbness,* and even *moral insensitivity* in relation to suffering. The increase in suffering in the world and the separation between the "haves" and "have-nots," as the polarization between rich and poor continues to accelerate both globally and in the United States, makes it vital for us to investigate these near enemies.

Grasping after Pseudo-Equanimity

The second broad set of distortions of equanimity occurs when I grasp what seem like the pleasant qualities of equanimity. I may cultivate, for example, an overly *intellectual aloofness* in which I find apparent security and order in a clear and even brilliant interpretation of my experience, a particular situation, or the state of the world. Yet such an attitude may be disconnected from my emotions and from my willingness to be present with what is painful. It may conceal a *cynicism* that, as the psychiatrist Michael Bader tells us, is a kind of defense mechanism to help us hide from the pain of the difficulty or failure of actualizing our basic values, to which our earlier idealism may have led.[11] It may also be built on the creation of a kind of mostly *airtight ideology or belief system* that is significantly removed from contact with much of reality, a set of interwoven views that help me *rationalize* my choices and actions, even if they are deluded.

I may likewise grasp the equanimity associated with my spiritual practices or spiritual environments and stay away from what might threaten the loss of such qualities, from difficult or challenging emotions and situations, and even from everyday life. But this may actually represent a kind of spiritual immaturity, an example of what the late Tibetan teacher Chögyam Trungpa Rinpoche called *spiritual materialism,* the use of spiritual images, principles, and practices to prop up (and obscure from view) self-centeredness and self-image.[12] For example, an apparent equanimity may actually be in part based on a fear of anger, both in oneself and in others. This near enemy is a particular danger for those who think themselves spiritual—calm, centered, wise, and equanimous.

The Importance of Testing Our Equanimity

We may discern the presence of the near enemies particularly when our apparent equanimity is tested—especially by difficult people and challenging circumstances. My friend Thich Minh Duc, a monk and senior teacher in the West Coast Vietnamese Buddhist communities and a dharma heir of Thich Nhat Hanh, for many years worked as a social worker with troubled teenagers in the San Jose, California, area. He would work some thirty hours a week and serve the community as a teacher and leader in various capacities. Most of the teenagers, of course, didn't particularly know or care about his status in the Vietnamese community, and the work with them was often challenging. One year, when Thich Nhat Hanh met with Thich Minh Duc, he compared Minh Duc's action in the world with the lives of monks and nuns in general: "You know, many monks and nuns think that they are somewhat enlightened. They feel peaceful and equanimous. But they live in a protected environment and have not really been tested. You, on the other hand, are being tested regularly, and you can know much more accurately how wise or peaceful or equanimous you really are."

The Buddha tells the story of a housewife named Vedehika, who was reported to be kind, gentle, and peaceful. Yet her maid, Kali, wondered whether these qualities were the result of Kali's good work or part of Vedehika's character. So Kali decided to conduct a series of "tests" by getting up later and later in the day. On the first day, Vedehika was angry and displeased, and a few days later, increasingly enraged, she whacked Kali on the head with a rolling pin, drawing blood. The Buddha counsels his monks (bhikkhus):

> Some bhikkhu is extremely kind, extremely gentle, extremely peaceful, so long as disagreeable courses of speech do not touch him. But it is when disagreeable courses of speech touch him that it can be understood whether that bhikkhu is really kind, gentle, and peaceful. . . . Even if bandits were to sever you savagely limb by limb with a two-handed saw, he who gave rise to a mind of hate towards them would not be carrying out my teaching.[13]

In this sense, it can be very skillful to take on challenges, to learn to grow in equanimity by bringing one's sense of spiritual practice into a more difficult situation, even if we are not quite ready to be sawed apart by bandits.

PRACTICES FOR CULTIVATING EQUANIMITY

There are a number of concrete practices, both traditional and contemporary, that develop equanimity when regularly practiced.

Mindfulness Practice as a Training in Equanimity

Equanimity is the fruit, as we have seen, of regular mindfulness practice. It represents the growing ability to be attentive and compassionate with a wide range of experiences. As we practice, both formally in meditation and more informally in daily life, we note what takes away our equanimity: "Oh, that was a difficult experience. I didn't have much equanimity with that"; or, "Oh, I wanted that situation to turn out this way so badly, and I really got lost for a while." We may also begin to be aware of the near enemies, as we are alert for indifference, denial, resignation, complacency, and the like.

We can thus develop equanimity in very ordinary situations, as we simply keep paying attention. Nor, as many beginning meditators believe, do we even need to be particularly calm or tranquil in our everyday lives in order to be equanimous. I may have a very tempestuous mind, filled with thoughts, and yet be equanimous. I may be incredibly busy and active, and remain equanimous. There can be an equanimity that is the stillness in the midst of activity, the steadiness in the midst of great movement, the calm in the storm.

Nyanaponika Thera calls such profound equanimity the "inner center of the world."[14] It is as if we have in ourselves the counterpart of the Jewish tradition's legendary thirty-six Just Persons, the *Lamed-Vov* (the term simply means "thirty-six"). The *Lamed-Vov* are typically quite ordinary persons wholly dedicated to lives of goodness and service, yet their existence and actions keep the whole universe in balance. They are the "hearts of the world," although they are usually unaware of their roles. But without even one of them, so the legend goes, the universe would lose its center, and the suffering of the world would poison the souls of the newborn.[15]

Formal Equanimity Practice

In the context of the four *brahmavihara,* there are two further traditional ways of practicing equanimity: the cultivation of equanimity by itself and the balancing of equanimity with the other brahmavihara, which we will examine in the next section. Equanimity is typically practiced by itself along with the formal practices of lovingkindness, compassion, and joy. As with these other practices, the meditator develops a phrase or set of phrases that is repeated continually in application to oneself and a range of others. The classical phrase is: "All beings are the owners of their karma. Their happiness and unhappiness depend on their actions, not on my wishes for them."

The meaning of this phrase is that our actions and responses to our present experiences are key to our happiness or unhappiness. As we saw in chapter 3, the Buddha explicates the notion of karma in terms of intention and the possibility of free action in the present moment. So the above phrase can be interpreted as suggesting that it is our response in the present moment that is crucial for happiness, rather than only past events.

Partly because of the ways in which the notion of karma has been misunderstood, Western practitioners have often developed new or modified equanimity phrases to help them navigate some of the complex territory involving equanimity, karma, and action, including the following:

May we all accept things as they are.
May we be undisturbed by the comings and goings of events.
I will care for you but cannot keep you from suffering.
I wish you happiness but cannot make your choices for you.
No matter what I wish for, things are as they are.[16]

Some of these phrases also require some interpretation. For example, if we use a term like *acceptance* to point to an aspect of equanimity, it seems important to distinguish two connotations of *acceptance*. On the one hand, *acceptance* implies recognition: "I accept [that is, I don't deny] that we have an organizational problem." On the other hand, *acceptance* can suggest resignation to the fact or even moral approval: "I accept that there is racism; this is the way that it is and has to be." *Acceptance* in the former sense can lead directly to an intention to make changes, whereas the latter connotation of acceptance may block action or rationalize inaction.

Similarly, to remain "undisturbed" may mean to learn to work through sometimes being disturbed, angry, or upset about what is occurring. To recognize that I "cannot keep you from suffering" and "cannot make your choices for you" is not to deny our interdependence and mutual influence, but it is to affirm a certain degree of individual autonomy and responsibility. To say that "things are as they are," whatever my wishes, is not to say that I should not attempt to transform them in the future.

EXERCISE: Equanimity Practice

Use one of the above traditional or contemporary phrases (or perhaps some other phrase). Work with the phrase first for a "neutral" person, one toward whom you have no particular attraction or aversion. Then, work with the phrase in relation to a benefactor, then a friend, then a "difficult" person, then yourself, and finally all beings.

You may find it helpful to use the technique suggested in chapter 5 for lovingkindness practice: first develop an image of the being (human or nonhuman) toward whom you are cultivating equanimity, then bring your attention to the center of your chest (the "heart center"), then say the phrase, and finally listen for the resonance in your body, heart, and mind.

You may do this practice initially for 10 minutes at a time, before or after your main contemplative practice, or for a period of 30–60 minutes.

Balancing Equanimity, Lovingkindness, Compassion, and Joy

A third way is to develop a balance between equanimity and the other three qualities: lovingkindness, compassion, and joy. This is a particularly helpful and skillful practice in terms of working through the many near enemies of equanimity (as well as the near enemies of the other three qualities). Nyanaponika writes:

> *Lovingkindness* imparts to *equanimity* its selflessness, its boundless nature and even its fervor. For fervor, too, transformed and controlled, is part of perfect *equanimity,* strengthening its power of keen penetration and wise restraint.

> *Compassion* guards *equanimity* from falling into a cold indifference, and keeps it from indolent or selfish isolation. Until *equanimity* has reached perfection, compassion urges it to enter again and again the battle of the world, in order to be able to stand the test, by hardening and strengthening itself....

> *Sympathetic joy* gives to *equanimity* the mild serenity that softens its stern appearance. It is the divine smile on the face of the Enlight-

ened One, a smile that persists in spite of his deep knowledge of the world's suffering, a smile that gives solace and hope, fearlessness and confidence....

Equanimity ... gives to *lovingkindness* an even, unchanging firmness and loyalty. It endows it with the great virtue of patience. *Equanimity* furnishes *compassion* with an even, unwavering courage and fearlessness, enabling it to face the awesome abyss of misery and despair which confronts boundless compassion again and again. To the active side of *compassion, equanimity* is the calm and firm hand led by wisdom—indispensable to those who want to practice the difficult art of helping others. And here again *equanimity* means patience, the patient devotion to the work of *compassion.*[17]

Practices to Cultivate Equanimity in Relational and Collective Contexts

A number of further equanimity practices have been developed in relational and collective contexts. These contemporary practices often reflect a modification of traditional Buddhist practices.

In retreats with my colleague Diana Winston, we have often opened up the territory of equanimity with a short exercise, in which we invite participants to answer the question: "What's difficult for you to accept?" After identifying what's difficult, it is then possible for them to bring mindfulness and inquiry to the area that has surfaced. They typically explore reactivity and unacknowledged pain related to particular states of affairs, assumptions and expectations about what should have happened, and a passion for justice. Such inquiry can help equanimity to arise.

In August 1991, near the end of a six-day Buddhist Peace Fellowship Summer Institute, we heard of the attempted coup on Mikhail Gorbachev, an attempt to end the policies of *glasnost* ("openness" in public discussions about present and past problems) and *perestroika* (economic reform). Some two weeks earlier, I had just returned from a couple of weeks in the Soviet Union, meeting many new friends in Moscow from all over the Soviet Union at a gathering on humanistic and transpersonal psychology and visiting the birthplaces of two of my grandparents in Lithuania, amid barricades and Soviet tanks. The morning we heard of the coup attempt, we told our gathering of about 150 people the breaking news. We invited them to remain in silence for ten minutes, bringing their attention, lovingkindness, and compassion to the people of the Soviet Union and then voicing the names of particular people there, whether friends, acquaintances, or public figures. As tears fell for many, we heard the softly spoken names: "Slava... Grazina... Alexander... Elena... Yasha ... Ernestas... Egle."

Since then, I and others have used variants of this practice many times: as a quiet group meditation to bring attention to what is either difficult or joyous in the participants' lives; in regular BASE meetings as a closing meditation, naming those people and places in difficulty, sometimes with specific details; at a retreat at Auschwitz led by Bernie Glassman, where the names of the dead were chanted; and on the one-year anniversary of September 11, in 2002, when hundreds of participants at Spirit Rock Meditation Center voiced, after a period of silent meditation, the names and situations of those whom they knew who had been significantly affected by the attack.

I believe that this basic practice is a kind of equanimity exercise. It is a tool for groups to be present to difficult events in a balanced and nonreactive manner. It suggests a mature equanimity that may simultaneously express lovingkindness, compassion, or joy and that invokes the larger web of relationships, beyond the separate self, to which Joanna Macy pointed in her discussion of equanimity. It is as if to say, as Sylvia Boorstein suggests: "These are the difficult things happen to people.... They happen. They are bearable. We are not alone. This is part of being human."[18]

EQUANIMITY AND ACTION

The life and teachings of the Buddha, as well as the lives of many of the great engaged spiritual teachers of our time, suggest that it is a serious confusion to interpret or practice equanimity as a separation from action. This confusion is linked to the many near enemies or distortions of equanimity, such as indifference, passivity, resignation, and acquiescence to injustice.

The Buddha, for example, was continuously active as a teacher for forty-five years, offering a way of transformative practice that linked equanimity *and* action. In such practice, as we have seen, one learns to be equanimous and nonreactive about what is happening or has happened, while still acting energetically for awakening, for liberation for oneself and others.

But how do we practice equanimity in our everyday action and in our social action? Here, I mention briefly *four general guidelines* for such action.

First, we need continually to *balance the practice of equanimity with the practices of lovingkindness, compassion, and sympathetic joy.* Without the development of these other qualities, what may look like equanimity will more likely be one or more of its distorted forms. It means very little, for example, to claim to be equanimous about war or racism if we are not deeply present in various ways to the pain and suffering associated with these phenomena, if the equanimity is not suffused with compassion, or if we do not simultaneously deeply want, through our lovingkindness, the well-being of those affected.

This suggests a second guideline: that our practice of equanimity will be in large part a purification practice, in which we *discern and transform the various distortions of equanimity* in ourselves and others. We examine the aversion to suffering that may be behind *indifference,* the myriad forms of attachment to *privilege* that may be expressed in *complacency* and *distancing,* the fear or even self-doubt linked with *acquiescence* or *resignation in relation to injustice and oppression,* or the *denial* or *delusion* that may ground many of the distortions.

Third, *we become students of the causes and conditions* that lead to particular forms of pain and suffering, as well as to possible positive change. We study history; we carry out social analysis; we study our own and others' personal histories and the ways in which our bodies, hearts, and minds work. We develop an ability to know, in a particular situation or in relation to a particular issue, how and when to intervene. Sometimes, an intended outcome is possible and sometimes not, yet in knowing well the broad context (even if we cannot know in advance the outcome), we strengthen our equanimity and our ability to act, whatever the circumstances.

The Buddha, for example, tried three times to stop a war by intervening with the attacking king. However, he did not intervene a fourth time, and war ensued, which led to the defeat of his own people, the Sakyans. The Buddha later acknowledged the great strength of the forces for war, showing an equanimity that manifested itself both in his great efforts to prevent suffering and in an understanding of the power of the causes and conditions of such suffering. Similarly, well after the end of the war in Vietnam, Thich Nhat Hanh remarked that the "conditions for success in terms of a political victory were not present" for the Buddhist movement in Vietnam. Yet at the same time, he did not regret the years of effort dedicated to ending violence and increasing compassion.[19]

This suggests a final, basic equanimity practice: *to act continually and devotedly, yet without attachment to the immediate outcome or fruits of our actions.* This too could be called a purification practice; we are taken through all the difficult territories where we want certain outcomes and don't want others, where we want to "win" and not to "lose," where we want our agendas to be met. Clarifying this last guideline, however, is so basic to our spiritually grounded engagement in the world that we will explore it in the depth that it deserves in the next chapter.

Chapter Ten
COMMITTED ACTION, NON-ATTACHMENT TO OUTCOME

In my first year as a young, full-time teacher of philosophy, I was assigned to teach an introductory class in ethics. Due to the politicized and somewhat bizarre way that undergraduate general requirements had been worked out some twenty years earlier, every student was required to take *either* a two-semester philosophy sequence that usually included Introduction to Philosophy and Ethics *or* two semesters of mathematics. Not surprisingly, few chose the latter option. Consequently, the philosophy department always had very healthy enrollments and a large number of faculty members, with many teaching the introductory sequence.

My section of Ethics in that fall semester met Tuesdays and Thursday at 7:30 PM, for seventy-five minutes. At the first class meeting, I greeted what seemed to me a singularly unenthusiastic group of students, who no doubt were almost all there because the class met a requirement. The group included, I soon saw, a significant number of fairly large football players, perhaps one-third of the class. Each evening, class came after five hours of practice and a sizable meal. Their very natural inclination at the time of the class was to go to sleep, and if this couldn't happen (although it occasionally did), their next inclination was just to "hang out," cracking continual jokes and inviting the rest of the class to join in, sometimes at my expense. Remaining attentive to my earnest ethical inquiries did not seem a viable option.

Of course, *I* was very clear about what I wanted to happen in the class. I wanted the students to be alert, to do the assignments, to prepare for class, not to consider class time primarily as a time for hanging out and joking around, and to treat me respectfully. I wanted them *to learn*! Within a few weeks, as far as I could tell, none of these outcomes was being satisfactorily realized, and I was becoming frustrated. Nothing was working. My attempts at control encouraged more jokes. It didn't help that I didn't look much older than they did.

The conditions were extremely ripe for me to learn something about the spiritual teaching of action without attachment to outcome—or remain at a high level of frustration.

I had read variants of this idea in the Bhagavad Gita, in which Krishna speaks of "non-attachment to the fruits of one's actions":

> Steadfast in the Way, without attachment,
> Do your work, Victorious One,
> The same in success and misfortune.
> This evenness—that is discipline.[1]

I also had read the Taoist writings of Chuang Tzu, who teaches a way of action that he calls "non-action" *(wu wei),* based on an inner stillness: "The non-action of the wise man is not inaction. It is not studied. It is not shaken by anything."[2]

After a few weeks of considerable frustration, however, I began to "get it." I realized that I had an option to let go of my attachment to some of the outcomes, that in many ways the outcomes were out of my control. I reflected: "Here I am in this situation. I will stay here for the duration of the semester. I really don't know what will happen, what the students will learn. But I will still do my best and wisest teaching and give up my expectations that the class will look just like I want it to look."

After that shift in my perspective, it seemed to me that the class improved. It certainly did for me; I was much more relaxed. Many of the students forgot some of their original views about the class. We even studied some of the ethical issues related to sports. After the end of the semester, one student, a football player who had not seemed particularly present during the preceding weeks, told me that he had come to insights during our class that were very important to him. Another told me a year later that the class had affected his outlook on life in ways that he still felt to be very helpful.

THE PRINCIPLE OF ACTING WITHOUT ATTACHMENT TO OUTCOME

We find many different versions of this basic principle of committed action without attachment to outcome, ancient and contemporary, contemplative and activist. The teaching found in the Bhagavad Gita, for example, was at the center of Gandhi's work and life. Gandhi writes of the necessity of acting, with care and focus, yet without attachment to the results:

> This is the unmistakable teaching of the *Gita*. He who gives up action, falls. He who gives up only the reward, rises. But renunciation of fruit in no way means indifference to the result.... He, who...is without desire for the result, and is yet wholly engrossed in the due fulfillment of the task before him, is said to have renounced the fruits of his action.... He who is ever brooding over result often loses nerve in the performance of his duty. He becomes impatient and then gives vent to anger and begins to do unworthy things; he jumps from action to action, never remaining faithful to any.... When there is no desire for fruit, there is no temptation for untruth.... Take any instance of untruth or violence, and it will be found that at its back was the desire to attain the cherished end.[3]

In the Old Testament is the famous story of Job, whose faith in God is severely tested by a series of major misfortunes. At the beginning of this story, Job has a good life. He is prosperous, well respected, and highly pious, full of apparent faith toward God. God says: "There is none like him on the earth, a blameless and upright man, one who fears God and shuns evil" (Job 1:8). Yet things start to go very wrong. All of his children die, and he loses his prosperity and health, as well as his good reputation. Were his faith and spiritual practice dependent only on good outcomes, they would have been shattered by these events. Only when he sees that his initial faith is relatively superficial, predicated on satisfactory outcomes, can he learn spiritually and come to a much more mature faith.

The Buddha's teaching of the Eight Worldly Winds, which we considered in the last chapter, expresses a similar spiritual principle. Its specificity helps us, as we will explore later, by identifying the various ways in which we may get blown off center: by *pleasure* or *pain, gain* or *loss, fame* or *disrepute, praise* or *blame*. These winds continually blow; the conditions of life continually change. The minds of most people, the Buddha tells us, are consumed by such changes, compulsively wanting the first member of each pair to be present and aversive toward the second. We learn, however, how to act wisely and compassionately, whatever the conditions.[4]

Even as we find this spiritual principle expressed in various traditions, it is helpful to remember that it can also be expressed in very simple English: "Do your best, and let the chips fall where they may!"

It is also helpful to remember that this principle is not particularly esoteric. For many parents, for example, a version of the principle guides the skillful raising of children. A good parent is committed to years of care, love, and support, yet does not overly control the child or dictate the child's choices. Similarly, a good teacher, as I found out, needs to be creative and flexible in the light of changing conditions, which do not always match the teacher's preferred scenarios. Skillful and committed activists learn to sustain their energies for the long term, often in difficult conditions in which their desired outcomes seem very far from being realized.

THE CHALLENGE OF ACTING WITHOUT ATTACHMENT TO OUTCOME

Following this principle seems to present us with a radical spiritual paradox whenever we act in the world, whether as a meditator, parent, teacher, or activist: *How can we act decisively, energetically, passionately, wisely, and compassionately while giving up our attachment to the results of our actions?* As we noted in the last chapter, working with this question is a main way to express equanimity and wisdom in the very midst of action. Yet how is committed action without attachment to outcome possible? How do we train to develop the ability to act in this way? What does such action look like? And is it even desirable? Do we need attachment to outcome in order to act, or in order to care?

In the remainder of this chapter, I will explore these questions. I will first ground the meaning of committed action without attachment to outcome in the context of our *individual* practice of mindfulness. I will then catalog some of the ways in which we lose balance in our actions in the world, typically either in attachment to outcome or in the various ways in which we shy away from or are incapable of committed, energetic action. In the final section, we will examine some of the qualities of this way of acting in its mature expressions.

MINDFULNESS PRACTICE AS ACTION WITHOUT ATTACHMENT TO OUTCOME

Mindfulness practice provides an excellent laboratory for us to study this principle. Even though in formal meditation practice we are often sitting and not moving or speaking (at least externally), such practice is still in many ways a very basic form of *action*. We actually are "doing" something. We're training our minds and hearts and bodies. We're cultivating certain competences. We're studying the nature of our personal experience and of experience in general. We're learning about suffering, the roots of suffering, and the possibility of freedom. We have general intentions and expectations—to become wise, peaceful, and compassionate—as well as more modest hopes, such as to work through some of our suffering or to learn to relax a little more.

As we practice, we thus necessarily also learn something about committed action without attachment to outcome. We learn that commitment to practice, to action, is totally necessary if transformation is to occur. Yet we also learn to hold our intentions more lightly in terms of specific day-to-day or week-to-week outcomes. So, for example, I learn not to conclude that my efforts at mindfulness and perhaps even my whole spiritual path are failures because of two weeks of a wildly wandering mind at a retreat, because I got really angry at what I believe is an unjust situation at work and felt out of control and very "unspiritual," or because I've been somewhat depressed for a while about the state of the world.

We can also see how we are commonly attached to hoped-for results, especially in the beginning of our practice. We typically try to know that we are progressing, that we are doing it right. In my own first few years of practice, particularly at retreats, I seemed to need to measure my own "achievements" in meditation especially by several external criteria, so that, I later realized, my "success" would be recognized by my teachers and others. The only problem was that we weren't talking to each other and couldn't easily discern each other's wisdom or compassion. So, as a somewhat competitive meditator, I focused on several external criteria that could help me gauge my spiritual success in relation to others—sitting for longer than most and staying up later than others to meditate.

Through the discipline of ongoing mindfulness practice, we become aware of these attachments to outcomes and external criteria. We learn that it is possible to make a strong effort and have a deep commitment, and *not* be attached to specific outcomes. The training occurs when we keep coming back to being mindful and aware, no matter what has happened. We take refuge, as it were, in coming back to presence in the moment, even if we sometimes don't have the slightest idea what is happening, even when we are sure that what we want to happen *isn't* happening. Yet in our mindfulness practice we also learn that it is possible to take "non-attachment to outcome" too far, so that we lose touch with our deeper intentions and the level of our effort is low. "Oh, it doesn't really matter what happens. It's all just happening perfectly in the moment, whatever it is. That's the teaching, isn't it? In that case it's okay to take it easy. I'll sleep a little more, forget about early-morning meditation, and yes, I will have a second helping of this excellent ginger cake. It's all as it should be." A skillful teacher might well speak to this student about the importance of "wise effort."

As we practice on both sides of the paradox, we enter a mystery. We give ourselves to the present moment over and over again (which reflects our committed action), increasingly without attachment or aversion (which reflects our non-attachment to outcome). Yet we also notice and work skillfully with such attachment and aversion when they arise, in this way making learning possible. The mystery is that this aspiration and effort without expectation is transformative over time.

TRANSFORMING OUR ATTACHMENTS TO OUTCOMES

As we train in formal meditation and extend mindfulness into our daily life activities and the work of community and social transformation, it is helpful to identify the various ways in which we become attached to outcomes in these domains. Much of our growth occurs as we study more intimately the different types of attachment and learn to let go of them.

As we would expect, the personal, relational, and collective forces leading to attachment to outcomes interpenetrate each other. It's helpful to begin by remembering how powerful these collective forces are.

Our Social Conditioning to Be Attached to Outcomes

In contemporary Western societies, and particularly American society, there is clearly *a very strong social and cultural predisposition to be attached to outcomes.* Social theorists from Max Weber to Jürgen Habermas have identified the ways in which in modern secular societies we often become fixated on getting things done, on being pragmatic, often without paying much attention to the deeper value or meaning of what is getting done.

These theorists speak of this tendency as resulting from an overdevelopment of our instrumental rationality, of a means-end rationality in which we focus on finding the best means to achieve a given end or outcome. Much of our everyday work in society is almost exclusively instrumental, focused on figuring out how to achieve a given outcome: attempting to make more money, helping our corporation increase its sales, researching better ways to kill pests, or developing a plan to invade another country. In itself, this thinking about outcomes is a necessary part of our intelligence, helping us to plan, to study cause-and-effect relationships, and to attempt to achieve intended results. However, when this form of rationality becomes predominant, a number of problems arise. For instance, we may continually focus on short-term outcomes, attempting to meet our desires of the moment but finding eventually that continually following such desires, although sometimes quite useful for the growth of the economy, does not lead to a life of wisdom. Or we may spend our entire lives preparing for what comes next and how to get there, preoccupied with planning for immediate outcomes but never arriving anywhere because we are always planning, always concerned with the next plan, the next outcome, always in the future. Most of our lives become an attempt to complete our to-do lists, expecting that some day we will somehow succeed and then relax and do what we really want to do. Our lives may consist of continual, ongoing preparation and, as Yeats once noted, *planning for something that never happens.*[5] We get good grades so we can get into good schools, so that we can get good jobs, so we can have enough money to raise our children and send them to good preparatory schools, so that they can get into good colleges, so that they can find good jobs, so that they can have enough money to raise their children and have a comfortable retirement...and die, just like us, having been successful in achieving all the desired outcomes—except, of course, for death.

Or we may, in our work, meetings, and actions, become preoccupied with attaining *outcomes* at the expense of attention to the *process*—to how we treat others and to our own and others' actual experiences at any given moment.

Or we may sometimes be so preoccupied by the means and the immediate outcomes that we never reflect on the ends and whether they are the right ones.

One summer, when I worked as an intern in the House of Representatives while in college, I found a great preoccupation among the House members, not surprisingly, with getting elected. In many cases, a direct and open inquiry into fundamental issues seemed impossible because of political considerations. Interestingly, I found that those staffing the congressional committees in relatively nonpartisan ways knew exactly what needed to be done to resolve a critical issue. But the politicians themselves felt constrained against acting in wise or skillful ways, or even suggesting certain ideas, because of political pressures and a long list of taboo topics.

Bearing in mind how these social and cultural forces strongly condition our attachments to outcomes, we can go on to identify the concrete ways in which such attachments manifest themselves in our experience, whether more individually or in our relational and collective lives.

What are some of the particular types of attachment to outcomes? Here, I identify three basic forms: (1) being attached to specific outcomes, (2) trying to control outcomes, and (3) owning an outcome as "mine."

Becoming Attached to Specific Outcomes

When we act, we typically want and expect particular outcomes and don't want other outcomes. I want to arrive at my meeting this evening, rather than have my car or the bus break down. I want my protest to have an effect on other citizens and even on those in power, rather than have them ignore us. I intend my work to help bring about a new environmental law that will succeed, rather than fail.

Of course, our lives are full of experiences in which we see that our intended outcomes, small and large, don't happen, or they don't happen the way we want them to happen, or unwanted outcomes *do* happen. In our training in committed action with non-attachment to outcome, we begin by noticing our reactions in relation to these kinds of situations.

The teaching of the Eight Worldly Winds suggests how we get attached to outcomes. As we saw in chapter 6, attachment for the Buddha is a compulsive and often unconscious state in which we grasp on to (or push away) a person, an object, an experience, or a view, somehow believing that doing so will bring us long-term happiness. How do we practice with the Eight Winds? First, we need to be as mindful of their presence as possible, particularly when they appear with some force. Second, when one of the winds appears, we can explore its nature, textures, and where it leads. What is the experience of loss like? What occurs when I am praised or when others hold me in disrepute? Third, we can examine those situations in which we experience suffering because of the winds or find ourselves acting somewhat unethically to ensure an outcome. How do I sulk for hours, disappointed in not having accomplished a particular task?

How do I become attached to the meeting's ending with this or that result or that successful vote? How do I become depressed when my local legislature doesn't act the way I wanted them to, despite my having I lobbied them for a year?

Trying to Control Outcomes

Our attachment to a particular outcome typically leads us to attempt to control situations, other people, and ourselves. We may find ourselves becoming manipulative and insensitive to others, maneuvering to obtain what we want. We may, when we look carefully, see that we have imagined ourselves, in our work as activists or helpers, as all-powerful controllers.

Justine Dawson speaks of how, in her work at a home for women and children in transition, she has had to examine, through mindfulness and reflection, such a self-centered tendency to find security in control, especially in difficult situations:

> Ironically, direct service work can sometimes become very egocentric; it can center on *me* as the responsible one, the one who responds. I can believe, "I've always got to do everything. I've always got to do this or that. I, I, I!" I've learned to ask myself a lot of questions.
>
> Sometimes, it's helpful to ask, "What is happening right now?" I'll walk into a room to find a total circus—the kids are going crazy. I'll say to myself, "Oh, here's the circus." Then I try to be aware of my own tendencies, like "I have this great need to change and control the situation." I often go t hrough a kind of internal debate: "Well, on the one hand, I'm legally responsible for these kids. And there is a standard in the household that we want to maintain. On the other hand, it's just a circus."
>
> I ask myself: "What is triggering me in this situation? What is it bringing up personally? How do I need to work with the 'internal' material that is coming up in order to respond more appropriately to the 'external' situation?"[6]

"Owning" Particular Outcomes

The Eight Winds, particularly those of praise and blame and fame and disrepute, remind us of a further complication: identifying a particular outcome, consciously or unconsciously, with our self-images and identities. Of course, such a link goes back to very early conditioning in the family context, in which a child's given behavior is typically defined as good or bad and often made the basis of the child's very "goodness" or "badness." Over time, such conditioning connects deep aspects of our identities with praise and blame (and more broadly fame and disrepute), and we come to internalize the standards of praise, so that external praise and blame may scarcely be needed.

Hence, to examine closely attachment to outcome is for most of us also to carry out a deep and penetrating investigation into the very contours of our constructed selves and self-images, including the areas where we are confused and wounded. Such practice over time has the potential to deconstruct such identities and images, freeing our action from the pressures, constraints, and distortions that arise when they implicitly (and sometimes explicitly) carry the objective of confirming and sustaining our identities and images.

We can notice such ownership of actions in various ways. We may notice thoughts in which we congratulate ourselves, or how we subtly shift the conversation so as to receive praise or confirmation. We may exaggerate or inflate our relationship to a given outcome, much as the beaver does in telling the muskrat by the Hoover Dam: "It's not that I built it. They just picked up one of my ideas."

When we do this in the context of transformational work, whether that of individual spiritual practice or social change, the contradictions can be particularly poignant. One of the most difficult issues in any community or organization is how credit and ownership of actions, particularly successes, are given, both from inside and outside. In our current historical setting, with its strong tendencies to identify charismatic leaders and stars, in which, we might say, the prevailing ideology is that ownership of outcomes is desirable, some individuals often receive public credit in ways that can be in significant tension with attempts to expand leadership, question prevailing models of power, and empower communities and individuals.

We may also appropriate our supposed spiritual achievements for the glorification of self and the solidification of identity and image. As long as we see ourselves as separate, we miss the irony and even humor of our situation, *crediting ourselves for our transcendence of ourselves, strengthening our self-image because we have cut through our self-images, and taking credit for ourselves for our selfless service.*

A Jewish story illustrates the wonderful absurdity of this dynamic. In a synagogue one day, the rabbi suddenly was struck by religious fervor linked to a powerful experience of humility in relationship to God. He went down on the floor, prostrating himself, saying, "I'm nobody. I'm nobody." Soon the cantor was beside the rabbi, possessed by the same realization, "I'm nobody. I'm nobody." A moment later, the *shamus* (or custodian) was similarly inspired, repeating, "I'm nobody. I'm nobody." At this point, however, the rabbi turned to the cantor and complained, "Look who thinks he's nobody."[7]

EXERCISE: Identifying and Working with Your Attachments to Outcomes

What are the main ways in which you get attached to outcomes? Reflect in particular on how you are influenced by the Eight Worldly Winds. In what parts of your life (for example, your personal life, your spiritual practice, your relationships, your work, or your social change work) are the attachments to outcomes easiest to notice? Reflect especially on moments of suffering in these domains, for usually such suffering can be traced to attachments to outcomes. Reflect also on how you attempt to control outcomes, or how you take credit for outcomes. Devote a week to examining attachment to outcome in a specific part of your life. Take notes and produce an inventory of your various attachments. Explore what it might mean to "let go" in some of these areas.

SHYING AWAY FROM COMMITTED ACTION

Attachments to outcomes often register in a very obvious way in our psyches, notably as suffering when our preferred outcomes don't occur! The complementary imbalance, of a lack of committed action expressing our deeper intentions, is often harder to discern and more subtle in its manifestations. Yet we also need to bring to light the various ways in which this imbalance appears in our lives.

Losing Sight of Our Deeper Intentions

In a society so structured by attachment to immediate outcomes, it is easy, as we saw, to forget more fundamental intentions and aspirations, especially as we move into the adult world of jobs, family, and planning for retirement. In other words, we may be quite active and busy while *not* expressing our deeper commitments. We may even speak of this process as a movement to "maturity," understood as the outgrowing of one's youthful and surely naive idealism.

When I was teaching at Kenyon College in the late 1980s, I would often ask soon-to-graduate seniors whether they would accept a very modest, basic middle-class salary if they could do the kind of work that they most wanted to do. Most, but not all, said that they *would* happily choose such an option (a minority were more interested in making a lot of money). Then I asked, "How many of you actually have that option?" Almost no one raised a hand; they all felt as if their options were severely constrained, and that they could not do work that matched their deeper intentions. No doubt within a few years, many or most forgot those original intentions, which moved beneath the surface of consciousness, often only to appear, if at all, in a midlife crisis (or during other types of crisis) or even later in life, perhaps at the time of retirement.

Even when we are more consciously attuned to our deeper intentions, it still remains a great challenge to keep them alive in the midst of the details, deadlines, pressures, busyness, and sometimes tedium of daily life. This is why it is so crucial to find activities—such as a daily spiritual practice, periods of reflection, community gatherings and rituals, travel, and periodic retreats—that cut through the dulling of consciousness that can occur amid the repetitions of daily life, to reinspire us, to renew our visions and intentions.

Fear of Acting Authentically

Another primary reason that we don't act according to our deeper intentions, or don't act at all, has to do with fear. We can be fearful, of course, about many things. We can become passive because we fear certain challenges or conflicts—whether personal or social—that arise when we act. We may be fearful of questioning authorities and those in power, fearful of threats to our personal security and well-being, which of course often can be quite real. We can be fearful of what others will think of us and of the possibility of isolation and rejection. We may be fearful of failure and of not realizing our intentions or our intended outcomes. We may be fearful of pain—physical, emotional, and mental. In other words, we tend to be especially fearful of the four unpleasant winds in ways that can be paralyzing and pervasive.

Despair, Burnout, and a Sense of Powerlessness

Often we are emotionally overwhelmed to the point of despair by what seems to be the immensity of the task of transformation, whether individual, relational, or collective. We may be deeply discouraged by how those who are intent on transformation themselves have internalized and often express the very problems that we are seeking to remedy. We may, as we saw in chapter 5, experience burnout, for a variety of reasons. Or we may have a sense that we are not really having any effect and feel quite powerless. Most of us involved in long-term transformation in any domain have to work through such difficulties.

"Spiritual" Suspicions about Committed Action

A final way in which we tend to avoid committed action is perhaps more subtle—it is the way that we marshal supposedly spiritual insights as reasons to avoid committed action. We may think that our real work is to awaken through inner work, and that action in the world is not important, or is merely part of the relative world. We may believe that committed action requires plans and a sense of the future, undermining our intention to be "in the moment."

Such apparently spiritual reflection may conveniently provide a cover for our fears and difficult emotions, a way for us to stay safe and avoid the actual messiness of action. For meditation teacher and activist Christopher Titmuss, the very use of the concept of non-attachment has its hazards:

The Achilles heel of Buddhists, their shadow, is their lack of engaging. The danger is that sitting on the cushion, which potentially helps us to see things clearly and develop the energy and passion to respond, can become a kind of zone of security. Meditation then becomes navel gazing, trying to keep the self comfortable. We have to risk moving consciousness away from its safety zone, again and again and again, as part of practice, to live the insecurity of it all.[8]

EXERCISE: Committed Action: What Makes It Difficult? What Makes It Possible?

Reflect on the ways in which you have difficulty acting fully, in a committed way. What makes such committed action difficult for you? To what extent are you acting out of your deeper intentions? To what extent are you doing too many things? What qualities of mind and heart (perhaps despair, confusion, self-judgment, or distraction) undermine your ability to act fully?

Think of when you have acted most fully, with the most commitment. What was such action like? What were some of the inner and outer conditions that made such action possible?

THE QUALITIES OF COMMITTED ACTION AND NON-ATTACHMENT TO OUTCOME

As we observe and work through our attachments to outcomes and our difficulties in acting fully, a number of qualities develop in us. Here, I want to identify several of these, in part through the stories of spiritual activists. Some of these qualities express a sense of committed action over the long haul, in any circumstance; others express the sense of non-attachment to outcome.

Appreciating the Journey

As we become less attached to outcomes, we can appreciate and enjoy the whole process of working for personal and social transformation. We may come to see this process more as a drama, with the outcome in doubt, and we may experience poignancy and mystery much as if we were witnesses to a work of theatrical art.

Centered in the present moment more, we know that our actions matter, yet we also develop an equanimity in relation to what happens. This is similar to athletes who before a big game sometimes talk about appreciating the challenge, beyond the immediate outcome, even though the stakes are very high.

There Is No Failure

As we develop in our wise commitment, with a broader sense of the whole journey of learning and transformation, we are less likely to attempt to fit every action into the boxes of success and failure, creating some kind of personal or organizational scorecard. When we can learn from outcomes that reflect failures, mistakes, or what didn't work, in a sense there is no failure. Rather, there is a deeper commitment to the whole process as one of spiritual growth. Dr. A. T. Ariyaratne, the founder of Sarvodaya in Sri Lanka, reflects on over fifty years of dedicated work grounded in spiritual practice:

> When I do something with good intentions and I "fail," I do not take it as a failure. It may be a failure to others, but to me it is not a failure, because that "failure" may have taught me equanimity or detachment or renunciation. In learning to accept failure, in a sense, I succeed. Every action that I carry out carries an internal reason, which is always beneficial to me.[9]

"Failure," when understood in this spirit, may thus temper our arrogance, self-centeredness, and beliefs about our ability to control things or thoughts about the way that things have to be. As mythologist and story-teller Michael Meade points out, in this sense, "The soul loves failure." Without such a perspective, we tend to cover over or hide our failures, avoiding the vulnerability that makes transformation possible.

Increased Awareness of the Web of Causes and Conditions

As we move away from an egocentric sense of control, we come to recognize the vast web of causes and conditions that determine success or failure. We typically intervene in the midst of forces that have a long history and momentum, whatever our immediate wishes.

Justine Dawson speaks of learning to discern better the broader set of conditions and how this has lessened her attachment to particular outcomes, in her work with children and women in transition:

> I reflect at times on the limits of what I can do, given the forces at work. This reflection helps bring a certain amount of equanimity. For example, there have been times when I've felt a deep urge to protect the kids. I've wanted to take them all into my bedroom and hide them away. Yet there is only so much that I can do, and things are as they are right now for everyone. Sometimes I realize that the things are going on in the house are really old patterns that are playing themselves out. If I intervene, it might have an effect in the moment, but it's not necessarily going to change the underlying behavior. But this is often a struggle for me. I find myself craving the relief of quiet and ease, even if it's momentary.

Developing a Long-Term Perspective

As we deepen our commitment and decrease our attachment to outcomes, we often express a long-term perspective, especially in working for collective transformation. We may become more aware that the forces, for example, of militarism, violence, racism, and ecological degradation have been in motion for thousands of years, even as they manifest themselves in current events.

For the Vietnamese monk Thich Minh Duc, who was a student and teacher in Vietnam during the war and participated in the Buddhist demonstrations against the war in Saigon in the 1960s and 1970s, awareness of the causes and conditions of the war and a long-term perspective were vital to sustained action:

> During the Vietnam War, we knew that we were going against two huge and powerful forces— those Vietnamese who benefited from the war and the Americans. We did not think that by demonstrating we'd turn things around immediately. Rather, we had to look to the long-term process of practice *(tu)*. *Tu* means to transform bad to good—today one inch, tomorrow another inch. We might not be successful right away, but perhaps in ten years we would succeed.
>
> That's how we thought; that was the policy of the Buddhist church, communicated verbally by other young people and by local monks and nuns. For one hundred years, we were controlled by the French, and then the other religions took over. We knew that it would take years to untie the knot.[10]

We find a similar long-term perspective in the work of Dr. Ariyaratne and Sarvodaya. They have, for example, advanced a five-hundred-year peace plan to address the causes and conditions of the civil war in Sri Lanka, maintaining that since the causes and conditions for violence arose over several centuries, through long periods of colonialism, racism, injustice, and misunderstandings between Sinhalese and Tamils, so must the causes and conditions for peace.

"Success" Depends on Particular Conditions

With a long-term perspective, we can realize more clearly, to use the language of Michael Nagler, a leading scholar of nonviolence, that spiritually grounded transformative practice always *works,* in the sense of leading to learning and development, but only sometimes *"works,"* in the sense of leading to success in a conventional sense.[11]

When we don't engage in reflection and practice, we commonly look for immediate change and are discouraged when our preferred outcomes don't occur. With maturity, in part through an understanding of causes and conditions, we realize that the success of particular outcomes is highly dependent on the alignment of conditions. Thich Minh Duc sees the work of the Buddhist movement during the war in Vietnam as akin to planting seeds of peace and then supporting the conditions for the seeds to grow, not knowing exactly what would lead to the "success" of the seeds:

As Buddhists, we thought that we were planting seeds. The best and only thing that we could do was to create favorable conditions for the seeds to become fruitful. We didn't know how long it would take. Sometimes if you plant a banana seed it may take a certain number of months for the plant to produce bananas, but if you plant a coconut seed it may take longer.[12]

"Devotedly Do"

Continual, committed action becomes a way of life, a basic orientation. One of my personal inspirations has been the life of a friend and colleague, Zen teacher and activist Maylie Scott (1935–2001), with whom I worked for ten years on Buddhist Peace Fellowship projects, including coleading the first BASE program in 1995. Maylie typically invoked a phrase she coined, "Devotedly do," in speaking of her own life, her Zen practice, and her activism, as well as in encouraging others. Many of those she mentored speak of remembering this phrase in their own difficult moments—in the midst of conflict, despair, or fear.

Maylie was persistent and committed in her activism, serving for years as a social worker, for decades regularly taking part in demonstrations and acts of civil disobedience against international arms trafficking at the Concord Naval Weapons Station near San Francisco; teaching in prisons; demonstrating against continued development of nuclear weapons at Lawrence Livermore Laboratory in California, at Los Alamos, and elsewhere; and taking part in interfaith groups concerned with the issues of the homeless. All the while she was immersing herself in Zen, eventually receiving "transmission"—the invitation from her teacher to become a publicly recognized Zen teacher.

For Dr. Ariyaratne, this spirit of devoted action is linked to patience and courage and to an ability not to be discouraged, either by events or by criticisms:

I've been working nearly forty-seven years with Sarvodaya. I have never become disheartened or disappointed. I never get discouraged. Even at times when I failed in certain ways and everybody was ungrateful, I never got discouraged. Newspapers have called me all kinds of things, but I have never become discouraged or tried to reply to all the comments. Today there is hardly any criticism; everybody now says that I am doing good work. Time is a great healer if you are able to be patient and courageous.[13]

Recognizing the Mysterious Nature of Change

Even as we open more to the complex set of causes and conditions that lead to change, we may acknowledge that how and when and whether there is change is sometimes quite mysterious, hard to fathom. Remembering this mysterious aspect and the fact that every action matters can help us to keep our effort full and help develop a healthy skepticism about our assumptions about what will or won't change.

Daniel Ellsberg tells the story of meeting activist, poet, and Zen practitioner Gary Snyder by chance at a bar near the Zen monastery of Ryoanji in Kyoto, Japan, in 1960. Ellsberg was living in Tokyo, working on nuclear weapons policy for the Office of Naval Research, through the Rand Corporation. Snyder was then midway through a nearly ten-year period of Zen practice, staying at or near Zen monasteries for the bulk of that time. Ellsberg had gone to see the Zen garden at Ryoanji because he had read about it in Jack Kerouac's *The Dharma Bums,* in which Snyder was the lightly fictionalized major figure. The impact and memory of Ellsberg's conversations with Snyder at the bar and the next day at Snyder's cottage, Ellsberg later reported, played a significant role in his later decision, *some nine years later,* to divulge the Pentagon Papers, the secret history of the planning of the Vietnam War. Ellsberg's action was a major contribution to the turn against the war in public opinion and political discussions in the United States.[14]

This may remind us that change is always possible, that forces operate in ways not always known to us, even when we may think that things are stuck or that change is impossible.

Weathering Difficult Conditions

The principle of committed action and non-attachment to outcomes or results can be particularly helpful and inspiring in difficult times, when things are not going well, when our intended outcomes can seem remote, when our efforts can seem futile, or when others criticize or disparage us.

The Czech playwright and former President Václav Havel, who worked as a political activist for many years despite imprisonment and decades of repression under the Communist regime, helps to illuminate the principle further by making the distinction between *hope* and *optimism.* Optimism, according to Havel, depends on a happy outcome, on getting what we want. Hope, on the other hand, depends on giving all of one's energy to the work, whatever the outcome. He wrote at a particularly difficult time:

The kind of hope I often think about (especially in situations that are particularly hopeless, such as prison) I understand above all as a state of mind, not a state of the world.... It is a dimension of the soul, and it's not essentially dependent on some particular observation of the world or estimate of the situation....

Hope, in this deep and powerful sense, is not the same as joy that things are going well, or willingness to invest in enterprises that are obviously headed for early success, but, rather, an ability to work for something because it is good ... regardless of how it turns out.[15]

Resting in Paradox

Speaking of committed action and non-attachment to outcome points beyond our conventional understanding—that committed action requires attachment. It leads us to the territory of paradox, to an awareness of existential ambiguity and irony, to the humor of deep understanding, to the landscape of the poets, artists, and tricksters.

Gary Snyder speaks of this principle in a variety of paradoxical ways. We have to act, he tells us, both as if our heads are on fire—the situation is urgent—and as if we have all the time in the world. Mature action is rooted in familiarity with paradox: "Knowing that nothing need be done, is where we begin to move from."[16]

Cornel West speaks of African American blues artists as expressing what he calls "tragicomic hope," the paradox of creativity and joy arising out of oppression. Such hope "expresses righteous indignation with a smile and deep inner pain without bitterness or revenge."[17]

I think of some activists as being tricksters familiar with humor, with the blues, with paradox. Deeply committed, in a way they are impossible to defeat, like mythical tricksters such as Coyote or Raven, who continually arise from the dead.

I think, for example, of the thirteenth-century Japanese Zen teacher Ikkyu, a critic of institutional corruption, going on his begging rounds and visiting a rich family in his shabby clothes; soon after, he was kicked out of the home. Later, as a spiritual teacher invited to a feast, he met the same family, who this time bowed to him. At that point Ikkyu took off his monastic robes, said, "You are bowing only to the robes, not to me," and left.

I think of Myles Horton founding the Highlander School, working amid difficult conditions for decades, and immediately rebuilding the school after it was closed in 1960 by the state of Tennessee and then burned to the ground. Nowadays, some fifteen years after Horton's death, the school remains a primary locale for training for social change.

Conclusion

FINDING OUR INDIVIDUAL DIRECTIONS, DISCERNING OUR NEXT STEPS

W e may feel drawn to the vision of a seamless, integrative spirituality suggested in this book and to the principles and practices that support us in walking a spiritual path guided by this vision. Still, we all have to embody very personally such a vision and such a path within very particular lives, with our own idiosyncratic expressions. To walk a spiritual path is to know more universal insights and enact basic practices, but it is also to know and express what the universal means more personally. To neglect either the universal or the personal is to go astray.

Here, in this concluding chapter, I point to the very personal dimension of walking this path, first inquiring into how we might each come to know better how to walk such a path in our own ways—in touch with the mystery and preciousness of our lives. Then I'll look at how we elicit our core intentions and specific next steps on this path.

YOU DON'T HAVE TO DO EVERYTHING

In exploring how we each might personally act in the world, it is first very important to realize that what the world most needs are our unique contributions, our own individual ways of living an engaged spiritual life, rather than our performances of some imagined set of uniform duties. The great African American mystic and activist Howard Thurman once counseled a young man: "Don't ask yourself what the world needs. Ask yourself what makes you come alive, and go do that, because what the world needs is people who have come alive."[1]

Yet we can be very confused about our personal choices as to how to act and even how to live. In conducting retreats on connecting individual spiritual practice with action in the world, I often hear: (1) "I feel isolated"; (2) "I'm not doing enough"; and (3) "I don't know what to do." These perceptions and emotions can soon lead to guilt, burnout, despair, and withdrawal.

I have often responded by giving a model of three types of transformative action, developed by Joanna Macy.[2] First, there are "holding actions" such as protests, political and legislative work, and civil disobedience; the aim is to prevent further harm. Second, there is the development of alternative institutions—such as in health and medicine, education, or economics—based in part on an analysis of the structural roots of problems. Third, there are practices, such as meditation, art, and immersion in the wilderness, to name a few, that shift the way we experience and understand ourselves, others, and the world. If our current moral, political, and ecological problems in many ways reflect a crisis of our habitual modes of perception, then we need, as William Blake suggests, to "cleanse the doors of perception," to develop new ways of seeing.

All three types of action are very much needed. We might respond deeply to the present situation primarily by developing an alternative school in our community. Or teaching yoga and a different way of experiencing our bodies. Or working full-time for an environmental organization. Or organizing protests against particular policies. Or doing a long meditation retreat. When we ground whatever we're doing in an understanding of transforming suffering and how the three forms of action mentioned by Macy are deeply interrelated, we can feel closely connected with others who are doing very different work—knowing that all of us are contributing in important ways to the same larger transformations.

My retreatants typically emit sighs of relief upon hearing of this model. We don't have to do everything! We can be active in ways that express our callings and our gifts and that respect our cycles of inner work and outer action.

To honor such cycles in our lives means that sometimes we need times of refuge, reflection, and renewal, often for an extended period. There is also an important role in social transformation for contemplatives like Buddhadasa or Thomas Merton—receiving activists at their monasteries and writing about spiritual responses to social ills.

At other times, we need to go outward, to bring forward our work for the healing and transformation of the world, however we do this. Sometimes we need first to gather tools, competences, and support in order to go forth skillfully.

Sometimes life events call—the need for education and training, an illness, caring for another, a birth, a death, a call to balance our lives in some way, a vision, the demands of beauty. Following these calls, we may not seem to be carrying out inner or outer transformation in ways that fit the old models, and may sometimes feel confused, unworthy, or somehow off the path. At these times, it is very helpful to keep focused on the fundamental transformative principles and how they are being developed, and on the ways that they can guide us in *all* domains, in *all* activities. Taking refuge in this large vision of the seamless whole of spiritual life can remind us, contrary to some of our internalized voices: We don't have to do everything all the time!

LISTENING FOR ONE'S CALLING, EXPRESSING ONE'S GIFTS

One important way to talk about finding what makes each of us come alive is to invite ourselves to know better our callings, our vocations. To hear one's calling is to know one's gifts and how best to be and act in the world, given one's background, abilities, and passions. It is to point to one's distinct personal manifestation while following a path shared with others.

The ideas of calling and vocation (the latter term also relates etymologically to hearing a voice—*vox* in Latin) have deep roots in Jewish and Christian traditions. In Jewish tradition, the call is from God, both to Israel as a whole and to certain individuals to take specific roles—particularly important communal roles, such as military leader, king, priest, or prophet. Jesus gives a call to individuals to enter the kingdom of God; the word in the New Testament for church, *ekklesia,* literally means an assembly of those who are called *(kletos).*

In the modern world, the notions of calling and vocation have often been both secularized and psychologized. At times, to receive guidance from a vocational counselor might be simply to see how we best can match the occupational demands of society, the possible roles available, given our ethnic, class, and gender backgrounds. All too often this can simply feel like being told to be a cog in the machine (a machine sometimes working in questionable ways). Yet for many in the contemporary world there still remains the hope of finding meaning in one's vocation, paradoxically combining the free choice of an individual with a response to something higher. If the call of God is no longer heard, then at least one might listen for the call from the inner self. Carl Jung writes:

> True personality always has vocation, which acts like the Law of God from which there is no escape. Who has vocation hears the voice of the inner man; he is called. . . . The greatness and the liberating effect of all genuine personality consists in this, it subjects itself of free choice to its vocation.[3]

I believe that many of us genuinely feel called to a vision of our lives in which inner and outer transformation are connected. Knowing that we don't have to do everything, that there are many aspects to transformation, frees us further to listen for a calling, a vocation, for the very specific ways in which we might live this vision. As we have seen, we don't all have to be on the frontlines, in every demonstration, or attending directly to those in great need, in order to be of great help. We can follow a vocation that might not be seen as that of an activist—say, teaching children or gardening—yet that vocation can represent a deep response to the suffering of our society.

In this sense, a multitude of vocations can be linked with the vision of this book. What is most important is that we follow, in our own unique ways, the basic transformative principles and practices. What also is vital is that we be aware of the interpenetration of domains, of how the individual, relational, and collective aspects are present in whatever we are doing. I may not be on the frontlines, but I can know that I am part of the same basic work—that all of our contributions are necessary, and that all are connected.

Some seem to know their vocations all their lives, or from a very early age on, and others find multiple vocations in one life. Some have powerful experiences in which they come to know their callings through spiritual experiences, as in traditional vision quests, or through intense immersion in an activity, at the end of which they "know" or are reminded. Others are guided by elders and mentors, perhaps by becoming apprentices, and are initiated into a calling. For others, to come to know one's calling requires at times a deep listening, an ability to let go of distractions and busyness and focus on what might come in silence and stillness.

A genuine calling or vocation seems to be a way to express one's gifts, the abilities and interests that bring energy, passion, and commitment.

At times, we may need to listen carefully for what brings us alive, for what these gifts are. We may need to unearth buried gifts, develop gifts that are not yet manifest, or remember one's purpose, as the French writer Albert Camus once suggested, by rediscovering "those one or two images in the presence of which . . . [one's] heart first opened."[4] To explore a wide variety of types of work and ways of being seems important for many of us, in order to be able to come to know our own gifts. Eventually, we discover ourselves afresh, as a new kind of being, as is said in the African American church song:

> I looked at my hands, and my hands looked new.
> I looked at my feet, and they did, too.
> I started to talk, and I had a new talk.
> I started to walk, and I had a new walk.[5]

EXERCISE: Listening for Your Calling

Reflect on your sense of calling or vocation and on your perception of your gifts. How would you express your calling in one sentence? What are your most important gifts? When you are most inspired, what is your calling?

If you believe that you know your calling and resonate with the vision of integrating inner and outer transformation, reflect on your calling in the light of this vision.

If you are not aware of your calling, then reflect on those experiences in which you felt most alive or inspired, or in which you felt your heart open, or your mind open. You can also simply set up periods of quiet meditation, in which you listen, without much active thinking, inviting some further clarity about your vocation to be present. Another way is to take part in a retreat, leaving some time at the end to be quiet and invite clarity and directions about your vocation to be present.

At times, giving a short narrative about your life to others can help in the listening process. In many of the groups with which I work, we begin a months-long or yearlong process, inviting each person to tell a fifteen- to twenty-minute story bringing out his or her main values, formative experiences, and current learning edge, followed by a chance for others to ask questions.

INTENTIONS AND NEXT STEPS

Given this path of engagement and a sense of calling, each of us can also ask a series of guiding questions to help formulate a sequence of learning and development. Often, it is helpful to reflect on questions like these, writing down our responses and keeping a record, or engaging in dialogue with a friend or mentor:

EXERCISE: What Are Your Next Steps?

What personal qualities do you most need to develop?
What abilities do you most need to develop?
What kinds of support do you need to ask for?
What obstacles are you likely to put in your own way in walking this path?
How will you overcome these obstacles?
What can you do in the next week to help you develop further in this path?
What can you do in the next twenty-four hours—no matter how small—to help you develop further?[6]

It can also be very helpful to be in touch with your visionary self, through this visualization exercise:

EXERCISE: Visualizing Yourself in Ten Years

Visualize yourself ten years from now, having moved into a considerably more mature form of spiritually grounded action in the world, in your own way. Bring to mind how you look, the qualities of your presence, your body, the way you move. Imagine yourself in a particular setting. Where are you? Who are you with? What are you doing? Then ask further: What have you learned in these years? What did you need to go through or learn to bring out further your abilities and your inspiration? What projects did you carry out? What sustains you on an everyday basis at this time?

IN CLOSING

To walk this path of engagement is to wake up while in the world. It is to awaken in the midst of both suffering and beauty. It is to find a home everywhere, even when there is pain and danger.

Such a path seems both a full-hearted response to the great needs of our times, expressing an emerging contemporary vision, and a way of realizing ancient and timeless insights.

It is a path led by the heart of compassion, much as the Buddha counseled, near the end of his life: "Wander forth...for the welfare of the multitude, for the happiness of the multitude, out of compassion for the world."[7]

It is a path, as we have seen, in which we act so as to bring about changes but are in many ways not dependent on particular results. It is more of a way of being, a way of walking, of appearing in the world, even when things are difficult.

It is very much as the Czech playwright Václav Havel wrote of hope, several years before the end of the Communist dictatorship in his country: "Hope is not prognostication. It is an orientation of the spirit, an orientation of the heart."[8]

On this path, the success of action may be measured, as Thich Nhah Hanh writes, less by outer victory than by whether love and nonviolence have been furthered.[9]

To walk this path is thus to prepare for the long haul. The qualities necessary for the long haul are the focus of this book: impeccable ethics, mindfulness, clarity of intentions, compassion and ability to be present with suffering, self-knowledge and self-care, equanimity, and understanding of interdependence, among others.

Yet on this path, as in individual spiritual practice, we are present for the long haul while also remaining open to immediate insight, transformation, and change. Individually and collectively, such change sometimes comes unexpectedly and swiftly, for better or for worse, as we know when considering the end of apartheid in South Africa, the breakup of the Soviet Union, or the possibility of rapid economic and ecological changes.

On this path, therefore, as the Buddha taught, every moment of mindfulness matters! Every moment of kindness and compassionate action matters! When we are mindful with the nearby trees or respond skillfully to a sarcastic word from a coworker, we are "stopping the war." We are transforming ourselves and the world.

In walking the path, we may remember the words of the second-century rabbi Tarfon: "It is not upon you to finish the work. Neither are you free to desist from it."[10]

There is an image in my study that inspires my own walking of this path: a photograph of the Dalai Lama, seemingly walking slowly on a path through the forest, probably in India. His head bowed forward, he extends his right arm and touches firmly the middle of a large rifle, held vertically by a soldier at alert. It is as if his heart reaches out, as he walks, to touch the gun with kindness, to touch the violence of the world with compassion and understanding.

In closing, let us dedicate whatever is helpful and fruitful in this book to others—knowing that we walk this path both for ourselves and for others, as we transform ourselves and the world. Let us dedicate our efforts and projects to the healing, the peace, the transformation, the liberation, and the awakening of all beings!

NOTES

The following abbreviations of the discourses of the Buddha will be used in the notes:

AN   Anguttara Nikaya
Dhp Dhammapada
MN   Majjhima Nikaya
SN   Samyutta Nikaya
Sn   Sutta Nipata

The particular translations used will be indicated in the notes. To be faithful to some English translations, I have at times retained the use of gendered language, particularly the use of "he" to refer to *bhikkhu* (monk). Were I rendering these passages, I would use inclusive language, much as some translators render *bhikkhu* as "practitioner." This latter usage has a basis both in the tradition itself, where sometimes *bhikkhu* has been used explicitly to refer to any sincere practitioner, and in much of contemporary Western Buddhist practice, which is generally equally open to males and females, as well as to monastics and laypersons. I invite the reader to consider these passages with inclusive language in mind, as well as the quotations from other authors who wrote prior to the widespread use of inclusive language.

INTRODUCTION: CONNECTING INNER AND OUTER TRANSFORMATION

1. Thomas Merton, ed., *Gandhi on Non-violence: A Selection from the Writings of Mahatma Gandhi* (New York: New Directions, 1965), 64.

CHAPTER ONE: ESTABLISHING THE CONDITIONS FOR SAFETY NEAR AND FAR: ETHICAL PRACTICE

1. Martine Batchelor, "The Buddhist Precepts: An Introduction," *Tricycle* 13 (Winter 2003): 36.
2. William Shannon, *Thomas Merton's Dark Path: The Inner Experience of a Contemplative* (New York: Penguin Books, 1982), 116.
3. Batchelor, "Buddhist Precepts," 36.

4. Sn 394, in *The Group of Discourses (Sutta-Nipata)*, trans. K. R. Norman, rev. ed. (Oxford: Pali Text Society, 1992), cited in *An Introduction to Buddhist Ethics*, by Peter Harvey (New York: Cambridge University Press, 2000), 69.

5. Vasubandhu, *Dasabhumika-sutra*, cited in the introduction of *Inner Peace, World Peace: Essays on Buddhism and Nonviolence*, ed. Kenneth Kraft (Albany: State University of New York Press, 1992), 5.

6. MN 51.14. Bhikkhu Nanamoli and Bhikkhu Bodhi, trans., *The Middle Length Discourses of the Buddha: A New Translation of the Majjihima Nikaya* (Boston: Wisdom Publications, 1995), 448–49. Cited in *Introduction*, by Harvey, 69, with a different translation. References to the Nanamoli and Bodhi translation of the *Majjihima Nikaya* will henceforth be indicated by MN, with identifying number and page numbers of this edition; in a few cases, it will be noted that other versions of a given passage are used.

7. *Milindapanha* 185, in *Milinda's Questions*, trans. I. B. Horner, 2 vols. (London: Pali Text Society, 1964), cited in *Introduction*, by Harvey, 69.

8. Thich Nhat Hanh et al., *For a Future to Be Possible: Commentaries on the Five Wonderful Precepts* (Berkeley: Parallax Press, 1993), 13.

9. Ibid., 14.

10. Sulak Sivaraksa, *Seeds of Peace: A Buddhist Vision for Renewing Society* (Berkeley: Parallax Press, 1992), 74.

11. Sn II.14.19 (394). H. Sadhatissa, trans., *The Sutta-Nipata* (Richmond, Surrey, Great Britain: Curzon, 1985), 44. Italics added. References to this translation of *The Sutta-Nipata* will henceforth be indicated by Sn, with the identifying section, sutta, verse (with the verse of the Pali Text Society edition in parentheses), and page number of this edition.

12. G. W. F. Hegel, *Introduction to the Philosophy of History*, trans. Leo Rauch (Indianapolis: Hackett Publishing Company, 1988), 24.

13. Dhp 5, in *Teachings of the Buddha*, ed. Jack Kornfield, rev. ed. (Boston: Shambhala, 1966), 15. Future references to the Dhammapada will be indicated by Dhp, with the identifying verse.

14. Donald Rothberg, "A Thai Perspective on Socially Engaged Buddhism: A Conversation with Sulak Sivaraksa," *ReVision* 15 (Winter 1993): 122.

15. Thich Nhat Hanh, *Being Peace* (Berkeley: Parallax Press, 1987), 98–99, 92.

16. Sn II.14.20 (395), 44. Italics added.

17. MN 27.13. I have given my own version of the text.

18. AN V.198. Thanissaro Bhikkhu, trans., *A Handful of Leaves*, vol. 3, *An Anthology from the Anguttara Nikaya* (Santa Cruz, CA: Sati Center for Buddhist Studies & Metta Forest Monastery, 2003), 190. References to this translation of the *Anguttara Nikaya* will henceforth be indicated by AN, with the identifying section, sutta, and page number of this edition.

19. Charles Lane, "Justices Hear Widow's Plea in Torture Case," *San Francisco Chronicle*, March 19, 2002, sec. A4.

20. Thich Nhat Hanh, *Love in Action: Writings on Nonviolent Social Change* (Berkeley: Parallax Press, 1993), 66–67.

21. Peter Ackerman and Jack DuVall, *A Force More Powerful: A Century of Nonviolent Conflict* (New York: St. Martin's Press, 2000), 326–27.

22. Sn II.14.24 (399), 45.

23. AN VIII.39, 252.

24. Thich Nhat Hanh et al., *For a Future to Be Possible*, 62.

CHAPTER TWO: MINDFULNESS IN ACTION

1. Joanna Macy, "The Meditation That Can End a War," *Inquiring Mind* 19 (Fall 2002): 20–21.

2. MN 10.4, 145. I take the translation "attending with mindfulness" from the work of Analayo, *Satipatthana: The Direct Path to Realization* (Birmingham, Great Britain: Windhorse Publications, 2003), 29.

3. Bhikkhu Bodhi, ed., *Abhidhammattha Sangaha: The Comprehensive Manual of Abhidhamma* (Seattle: BPS Pariyatti Editions, 2000), 86 (II.5.2).

4. Sylvia Boorstein, *It's Easier Than You Think: The Buddhist Way to Happiness* (San Francisco: HarperSanFrancisco, 1997), 60.

5. I thank Gil Fronsdal for this account of the pictogram.

6. MN 10.4. I have given my own version of the passage. *Parimukham* literally means "around" *(pari)* "the mouth or face" *(mukham)*. It can also mean "around or about any person." I take it to mean "here and now" and therefore in the present.

7. Gary Snyder, *The Real Work: Interviews and Talk, 1964–1979* (New York: New Directions, 1980), 96.

8. For an excellent account of the four yogas, see Huston Smith, *The World's Religions* (San Francisco: HarperCollins Publishers, 1991).

9. For further information on *tonglen*, see the work of Pema Chödrön, for example, *Awakening Loving-Kindness* (Boston: Shambhala, 1996), 123–42.

10. Alan Senauke, interview by author and Sara Schedler, Berkeley, CA, August 18, 2004.

11. Thich Nhat Hanh, *Peace Is Every Step* (New York: Bantam Books, 1991), 91.

12. Christopher Queen, "Glassman Roshi and the Peacemaker Order," in *Engaged Buddhism in the West*, ed. Christopher Queen (Boston: Wisdom Publications, 2000), 105.

13. Taigen Dan Leighton, interview by author and Sara Schedler, Berkeley, CA, August 2, 2004.

14. Thich Nhat Hanh, *Being Peace* (Berkeley: Parallax Press, 1987), 80.

CHAPTER THREE: CLARIFYING AND SETTING INTENTIONS

1. Dhp 1–2. *Teachings of the Buddha,* ed. Jack Kornfield, rev. ed. (Boston: Shambhala, 1996), 4.
2. AN VI.63.5. I have given my own version of the passage.
3. MN 135.4, 1053.
4. See Jonathan Watts, "Buddhist Responses to Modern Violence: Storytelling, Structural Analysis, Ethical Praxis," www.bpf.org/tsangha/tsm03report/longreport.html.
5. SN 36.21. Bhikkhu Bodhi, trans., *The Connected Discourses of the Buddha: A New Translation of the Samyutta Nikaya,* 2 vols. (Boston: Wisdom Publications, 2000), 1279. References to the Bodhi translation of the *Samyutta Nikaya* will henceforth be indicated by SN, with the identifying chapter, sutta, and page number. Stephen Batchelor pointed out this text to me.
6. Diana Winston and Donald Rothberg, *A Handbook for the Creation of the Buddhist Alliance for Social Engagement (BASE),* 2nd ed. (Berkeley: Buddhist Peace Fellowship [P.O. Box 4650, Berkeley, CA 94704], 2001), 15–16, also available at www.bpf.org/html/current_projects/base/base.html.
7. Diana Winston, "Intersection Point: Buddhist Activism at the WTO," *Turning Wheel: The Journal of the Buddhist Peace Fellowship* (Spring 2000): 42.
8. James Washington, ed., *A Testament of Hope: The Essential Writings of Martin Luther King, Jr.* (New York: Harper & Row, 1986), 537–38.

CHAPTER FOUR: OPENING TO SUFFERING, OPENING TO COMPASSION

1. SN 36.6, 1264.
2. Anita Barrows and Joanna Macy, trans., *Rilke's Book of Hours: Love Poems to God* (New York: Riverhead Books, 1996), 112.
3. Rachel Naomi Remen, *Kitchen Table Wisdom: Stories That Heal* (New York: Riverhead Books, 1996), 114–18.
4. Thomas Merton, ed., *Gandhi on Non-violence: A Selection from the Writings of Mahatma Gandhi* (New York: New Directions, 1965), 46.
5. Thich Nhat Hanh, *Being Peace* (Berkeley: Parallax Press, 1987), 91.
6. Thich Nhat Hanh, *Love in Action: Writings on Nonviolent Social Change* (Berkeley: Parallax Press, 1993), 39.
7. See Joanna Macy and Molly Young Brown, *Coming Back to Life: Practices to Reconnect Our Lives, Our World* (Gabriola Island, British Columbia: New Society Publishers, 1998), 101–4.
8. Larry Yang, interview by author and Sara Schedler, Berkeley, CA, November 4, 2004.

9. Timothy Ash, "The Truth about Dictatorship," *New York Review of Books* 45 (February 19, 1998): 40.

10. Donald Rothberg, "Truth, Justice, and Reconciliation in South Africa: A Conversation with Bongani Blessing Finca," *Turning Wheel: The Journal of Socially Engaged Buddhism* (Fall 2001): 29.

CHAPTER FIVE: TAKING CARE OF MYSELF, I TAKE CARE OF THE WORLD

1. Myles Horton, with Judith Kohl and Herbert Kohl, *The Long Haul: An Autobiography* (New York: Teachers College Press, 1998), 227–28.

2. Christina Maslach and Michael Leiter, *The Truth about Burnout: How Organizations Cause Personal Stress and What to Do About It* (San Francisco: Jossey-Bass, 1997).

3. Thomas Merton, *Conjectures of a Guilty Bystander* (Garden City, NY: Doubleday Image, 1968), 86.

4. Juliet Schor, *The Overworked American: The Unexpected Decline of Leisure* (New York: Basic Books, 1992).

5. Jürgen Habermas, *The Theory of Communicative Action,* vol. 2, *Lifeworld and System: A Critique of Functionalist Reason,* trans. Thomas McCarthy (Boston: Beacon Press, 1987), 356ff.

6. Taigen Dan Leighton, *Faces of Compassion: Classic Bodhisattva Archetypes and Their Modern Expression,* rev. ed. (Boston: Wisdom Publications, 2003), 33.

7. Cornel West, *Democracy Matters: Winning the Fight against Imperialism* (New York: Penguin Press, 2004), 20–21.

8. Cornel West and Davey D, "Street Knowledge," talk in Oakland, CA, February 14, 2004.

9. Bhikkhu Nyanamoli, trans., Bhadantācariya Buddhaghosa, *The Path of Purification (Visuddhimagga),* 2 vols. (Berkeley: Shambhala, 1976), I:323 (9.10).

10. Justine Dawson, interview by author and Sara Schedler, Berkeley, CA, November 23, 2004.

11. Taizan Maezumi Roshi and Francis Dojun Cook, trans., Dogen, "Genjo Koan," modifying Chotan Aitken Roshi-Kazuaki Tanahashi's translation (Los Angeles: Zen Center of Los Angeles, 1977), 2.

12. S I.8.1, 3–5 (143, 145–47). Metta Sutta. The translation here is from the Amaravati Sangha at the Amaravati Buddhist Monastery in Great Britain.

13. Tempel Smith, interview by author and Sara Schedler, Berkeley, CA, September 13, 2004.

14. SN 47.19, 1649.

15. Justine Dawson, interview by author and Sara Schedler.

16. David Brazier, *Zen Therapy* (London: Constable and Company, 1995), 53.

CHAPTER SIX: NOT KNOWING BUT KEEPING GOING

1. Louis Fischer, *Gandhi: His Life and Message for the World* (New York: New American Library, 1954), 95; Narayan Desai, videocassette, *A Force More Powerful* (Alexandria, VA: PBS, 2000). See also Peter Ackerman and Jack Duvall, *A Force More Powerful: A Century of Nonviolent Conflict* (New York: St. Martin's Press, 2000), 77–111.

2. Wing-Tsit Chan, trans., *The Way of Lao Tzu* (Indianapolis: Bobbs-Merrill, 1963), 97.

3. Seng-tsan, "Verses on the Faith Mind," in *Teachings of the Buddha*, ed. Jack Kornfield, rev. ed. (Boston: Shambhala, 1996), 143–44.

4. Fischer, *Gandhi*, 53.

5. C. G. Jung, *Memories, Dreams, Reflections* (New York: Vintage Books, 1963), 170.

6. MN 2.8, 93.

7. Thich Nhat Hanh, *Being Peace* (Berkeley: Parallax Press, 1987), 89–91.

8. Seng-tsan, *Teachings of the Buddha*, 117.

9. Ibid., 118.

10. Stephen Batchelor, *Verses from the Center: A Buddhist Vision of the Sublime* (New York: Riverhead Books, 2000), 109 (Nagarjuna, *Mulamadhyamaka-karika* [MMK] 16.9).

11. Ibid., 103 (MMK 13.8).

12. Christopher Titmuss, interview by author, Inverness, CA, September 23, 2005.

13. The Carter Center, www.cartercenter.org/doc181.htm.

14. Thich Nhat Hanh, *Creating True Peace: Ending Violence in Yourself, Your Family, Your Community, and the World* (New York: Free Press, 2003), 22.

15. Rainer Maria Rilke, *Letters to a Young Poet*, trans. M. D. Herter Norton (New York: W. W. Norton, 1954), 35. The italics are in the original.

16. Sir Richard Burton, *The Kasîdah of Hâjî Abdû El-Yezdî*, chapter 2, section 6, www.etext.library.adelaide.edu.au/b/burton/Richard/b97k/.

CHAPTER SEVEN: INTERDEPENDENCE

1. James Joyce, *Dubliners* (New York: Modern Library, 1954), 134. I first heard this story from Jack Kornfield.

2. Stephen Batchelor, *Verses from the Center: A Buddhist Vision of the Sublime* (New York: Riverhead Books, 2000), 115–16.

3. James Washington, ed., *A Testament of Hope: The Essential Writings and Speeches of Martin Luther King, Jr.* (San Francisco: HarperSanFrancisco, 1986), 290.

4. Peter Schumann, *St. Francis Preaches to the Birds* (San Francisco: Chronicle Books, n.d.).

5. Cecilia Garibay, " 'Following the Chocolate Chain' Exercise," personal communication.

6. Sasaki Roshi, "Who Pollutes the World?" *Zero: Contemporary Buddhist Life and Thought* 2 (1979): 151–57.

7. Sam Keen, *Faces of the Enemy: Reflections of the Hostile Imagination; The Psychology of Enmity* (San Francisco: Harper & Row, 1986).

8. Thomas McDonnell, ed., *A Thomas Merton Reader*, rev. ed. (Garden City, NY: Doubleday, 1974), 276.

9. Justine Dawson, interview by author and Sara Schedler, Berkeley, CA, November 23, 2004.

10. The quote is a composite of three citations: Louis Fischer, *The Life of Mahatma Gandhi* (New York: Harper & Row, 1950), 77; Thomas Merton, ed., *Gandhi on Non-violence: A Selection from the Writings of Mahatma Gandhi* (New York: New Directions, 1965), 28; and D. G. Tendulkar, ed., *Mahatma*, vols. 1–8, 2nd ed. (Ahmedabad, India: Navajivan Publishing House, 1960), 4:291.

11. Washington, *Testament of Hope*, 88, 47.

12. Stephen Batchelor, trans., Shantideva, *A Guide to the Bodhisattva's Life* (Dharamsala, India: Library of Tibetan Works and Archives, 1979), 6.107, 74.

13. Diana Winston, "Seven Reasons Why It's Better Not to Hate Them (even if they really are horrible, greedy, corrupt, and completely deserve it…)," *Tricycle* 14 (Fall 2004): 86–89.

14. *An Interrupted Life: The Diaries of Etty Hillesum* (New York: Washington Square Press, 1985), 258.

CHAPTER EIGHT: TRANSFORMING ANGER

1. My approach in this chapter has been helped tremendously by the work of Robert Masters and my conversations with him. See particularly his "Compassionate Wrath: Transpersonal Approaches to Anger," *Journal of Transpersonal Psychology* 32, no. 1 (2000): 31–51; and "Until the Fire Is but Light: An Interdisciplinary, Psychospiritual Investigation of Anger" (Ph.D. diss., Saybrook Graduate School, 1999).

2. Dhp 221–33. Gil Fronsdal, trans., *The Dhammapada: A New Translation of the Buddhist Classic with Annotations* (Boston: Shambhala, 2005), 59–61.

3. Stephen Batchelor, trans., Shantideva, *A Guide to the Bodhisattva's Life* (Dharamsala, India: Library of Tibetan Works and Archives, 1979), 6.73, 68.

4. Ibid., 6.1, 56.

5. See, for example, Thubten Chodron, *Working with Anger* (Ithaca, NY: Snow Lion Publications, 2001); and Robert Thurman, *Anger* (New York: Oxford University Press, 2005).

6. The Dalai Lama, *Healing Anger: The Power of Patience from a Buddhist Perspective* (Ithaca, NY: Snow Lion Publications, 1997), 7. The main term translated as "anger" is the Pali word *kodha* (*krodha* in Sanskirt). *Kodha* has no positive consequences in the moment of anger, and has numerous negative consequences when it is the basis for action. In the *Kodhana Sutta,* the Buddha speaks of a number of reasons why *kodha* is a problem, some related to the lived experience of *kodha,* most related to its consequences. An angry person is ugly, sleeps poorly, does "damage with word and deed," "takes pleasure in bad deeds as if they were good," destroys wealth and status, is unable to have spiritual insight, and ultimately suffers "as if burned with fire" (AN 7.60, 233). The connotations of *kodha* and of other Pali and Sanskrit terms sometimes translated as "anger" (including *dosa*) always refer to the afflictive emotions, which by definition are entirely negative.

At times, *patigha, vyapada,* and *dosa* are also translated as "anger," although these terms are more general. *Patigha* is more often translated as "irritation" and often said to be synonymous with *vyapada* and *dosa. Vyapada* is usually translated as "ill will" or "aversion," although sometimes as "hatred" or "anger." It is the general term that appears as one of the five "hindrances" *(nivarana)* to spiritual practice and is one of the ten fetters *(samyojana)* preventing awakening or enlightenment. *Dosa* is also commonly translated as "ill will" or "aversion," although perhaps more frequently as "hatred." It is one of the three roots *(mula),* along with greed and delusion, that lead to suffering and is said to cover the whole range from mild irritation to the most intense hatred.

7. Cited in *The Prophets,* by Abraham Joshua Heschel vol. 2 (New York: Harper & Row, 1962), 61.

8. Ibid., 76.

9. Richard Lattimore, trans., *The Iliad of Homer* (Chicago: University of Chicago Press, 1961), 59.

10. Aristotle, *Nicomachean Ethics,* trans. Martin Ostwald (Indianapolis: Bobbs-Merrill, 1962), 4.5 (1125b–26a), 100–102.

11. Thomas Aquinas, *Summa theologica* I–II, 47, 1, ad. 1, www.cin.org/users/james/ebooks/master/aquinas/acommo5.htm.

12. Thomas Paine, "Common Sense," in *Paine: Key Writings,* ed. Harry Hayden Clark (New York: Hill and Wang, 1961), 25, 34.

13. Eugene Kamenka, ed., *The Portable Karl Marx* (New York: Penguin Books, 1983), 117, 119.

14. Mohandas Gandhi, *An Autobiography: The Story of My Experiments with*

Truth (Boston: Beacon Press, 1957), cited in *Psychology for Peace Activists,* by David Adams (New Haven, CT: Advocate Press, 1987), 10; *Young India*, September 15, 1920, 6, www.mkgandhi.org.

15. Dorothy Day, *The Long Loneliness: An Autobiography* (New York: Harper & Row 1952), 72ff., cited in *Psychology for Peace Activists,* by Adams, 12.

16. Martin Luther King Jr., *Stride toward Freedom: The Montgomery Story* (New York: Harper & Row, 1958), cited in *Psychology for Peace Activists,* by Adams, 12.

17. The story was told by Michael Nagler at the "Conference on Spiritual Activism," Berkeley, CA, July 20–23, 2005.

18. Cited by Roger Gottlieb, *A Spirituality of Resistance: Finding a Peaceful Heart and Protecting the Earth* (Lanham, MD: Rowman & Littlefield, 2003), 152.

19. Cornel West, *Race Matters* (New York: Vintage Books, 1994), 136.

20. Robert Masters, "Compassionate Wrath," 39.

21. Batchelor, trans., Shantideva, *A Guide to the Bodhisattva's Life,* 5.48, 45.

22. Harvey Aronson, *Buddhist Practice on Western Ground: Reconciling Eastern Ideals and Western Psychology* (Boston: Shambhala, 2004), 114.

23. Marshall Rosenberg, *Nonviolent Communication: A Language of Compassion* (Encinitas, CA: PuddleDancer Press, 2000), 144–45.

24. Starhawk, "The Road Forward," November 4, 2004, www.starhawk.org/activism/activism-writings/theroadforward.html.

25. *Flashpoints,* radio program, KPFA, Berkeley, CA, June 2, 2003.

26. *Reaching Out,* television series, 1998, www.reachingout.org/community_viewguide_text.html#welcome.

27. Thich Nhat Hanh, *Love in Action: Writings on Nonviolent Social Change* (Berkeley: Parallax Press, 1993), 82, 84.

28. Taigen Dan Leighton, interview by author, Berkeley, CA, September 4, 2005.

29. Cited in Michael Nagler, *Is There No Other Way? The Search for a Nonviolent Future* (Berkeley: Berkeley Hills Books, 2001), 101.

30. Amy Goodman, "Democracy Now," August 26, 2005, www.democracynow.org/article.pl?sid=05/08/26/1350207.

CHAPTER NINE: ACTING WITH EQUANIMITY

1. James Washington, ed., *A Testament of Hope: The Essential Writings and Speeches of Martin Luther King, Jr.* (San Francisco: HarperSanFrancisco, 1986), 286.

2. Nyanaponika Thera, "The Four Sublime States," in *The Vision of Dhamma: The Buddhist Writings of Nyanaponika Thera* (York Beach, ME: Samuel Weiser, 1986), 193.

3. MN 62.13, 529–30.

4. AN 8.6, 242–44.

5. MN 22.39, 234.

6. Taigen Dan Leighton, interview by author and Sara Schedler, Berkeley, CA, August 2, 2004.

7. Joanna Macy, interview by author and Sara Schedler, Berkeley, CA, August 24, 2004.

8. MN 140.20, 1092; MN 152.4, 1148.

9. David Garrow, *Bearing the Cross: Martin Luther King, Jr., and the Southern Christian Leadership Conference* (New York: Vintage Books, 1988), 56–58.

10. Ibid., 60.

11. Michael Bader, "The Psychodynamics of Cynicism," *Tikkun* 11 (May/June 1996): 33–34, 76.

12. Chögyam Trungpa, *Cutting through Spiritual Materialism* (Berkeley: Shambhala, 1973).

13. MN 21.10, 21.20, 220, 223.

14. Nyanaponika Thera, "Four Sublime States," 199.

15. André Schwarz-Bart, *The Last of the Just* (New York: Bantam Books, 1961), 5.

16. Sharon Salzberg, *Lovingkindness: The Revolutionary Art of Happiness* (Boston: Shambhala, 1997), 152. The last phrase was provided by Sharda Rogell, a colleague at Spirit Rock Meditation Center. I thank Gil Fronsdal for helping to clarify the understandings of equanimity phrases in relation to the issue of karma.

17. Thera, "Four Sublime States," 196–98.

18. Sylvia Boorstein, *Pay Attention, for Goodness' Sake: Practicing the Perfections of the Heart—the Buddhist Path of Kindness* (New York: Ballantine Books, 2002), 271.

19. Thich Nhat Hanh, *Love in Action: Writings on Nonviolent Social Change* (Berkeley: Parallax Press, 1993), 47.

CHAPTER TEN: COMMITTED ACTION, NON-ATTACHMENT TO OUTCOME

1. Ann Stanford, trans., *The Bhagavad Gita: A New Verse Translation* (New York: Seabury Press, 1970), 2.48, 20.

2. Thomas Merton, ed., *The Way of Chuang Tzu* (New York: New Directions, 1965), 80.

3. M. K. Gandhi, "The Message of the Gita," 16, *Young India*, June 8, 1931, 15–18, in *Truth Is God [Gleanings from the Writings of Mahatma Gandhi*

Bearing on God, God-Realization, and the Godly Way], comp. R. K. Prabhu (Ahmedabad: Navajivan Publishing House, 1955), www.forget-me.net/en/Gandhi/truth.txt.

4. AN 8.6, 242–44.

5. Cited in David Loy, *A Buddhist History of the West: Studies in Lack* (Albany: State University of New York Press), 171.

6. Justine Dawson, interview by author and Sara Schedler, Berkeley, CA, November 23, 2004.

7. Ram Dass and Paul Gorman, *How Can I Help? Stories and Reflections on Service* (New York: Knopf, 1985), 28–29.

8. Christopher Titmuss, interview by author, Inverness, CA, September 23, 2005.

9. A. T. Ariyaratne, interview by author, Woodacre, CA, September 27, 2005.

10. Thich Minh Duc, interview by author, Sunnyvale, CA, September 5, 2005.

11. Michael Nagler, *Is There No Other Way? The Search for a Nonviolent Future* (Berkeley, CA: Berkeley Hills Books, 2001), 122.

12. Thich Minh Duc, interview by author.

13. A. T. Ariyaratne, interview by author.

14. Daniel Ellsberg, "The First Two Times We Met," in *Gary Snyder: Dimensions of a Life*, ed. Jon Halper (San Francisco: Sierra Club Books, 1991), 331–39.

15. Václav Havel, "An Orientation of the Heart," in *The Impossible Will Take a Little While: A Citizen's Guide to Hope in a Time of Fear*, ed. Paul Rogat Loeb (New York: Basic Books, 2004), 82.

16. Gary Snyder, *Turtle Island* (New York: New Directions, 1974), 102.

17. Cornel West, *Democracy Matters: Winning the Fight against Imperialism* (New York: Penguin Press, 2004), 19.

CONCLUSION: FINDING OUR INDIVIDUAL DIRECTIONS, DISCERNING OUR NEXT STEPS

1. Howard Thurman, cited in Gil Bailie, *Violence Unveiled: Humanity at the Crossroads* (New York: Crossroad, 1997), xv.

2. Joanna Macy and Molly Young Brown, *Coming Back to Life: Practices to Reconnect Our Lives, Our World* (Gabriola Island, British Columbia: New Society Publishers, 1998), 17–24.

3. Carl Jung, "The Development of Personality," in *The Development of Personality: Papers on Child Psychology, Education, and Related Subjects: Collected Works*, vol. 17 (Princeton: Princeton University Press, 1954), 175–76. The original essay was written in 1934. Cited in "Initiation into a Life Calling:

Vocation as a Central Theme in Personal Myth and Transpersonal Psychology," by Greg Bogart (Ph.D. diss., Saybrook Graduate School, 1992), 43.

4. Albert Camus, cited in *Men and the Waters of Life: Initiation and the Tempering of Men,* by Michael Meade (San Francisco: HarperSanFrancisco, 1993), 10.

5. Michael Kernan, "Conveying History through Song," *Smithsonian* (February 1999), www.smithsonianmag.si.edu/smithsonian/issues99/feb99/mall_feb99.html.

6. I thank Joanna Macy for several of the last questions. See Macy and Brown, *Coming Back to Life,* 171–72.

7. SN 4.5, 198.

8. Václav Havel, "An Orientation of the Heart," in *The Impossible Will Take a Little While: A Citizen's Guide to Hope in a Time of Fear,* ed. Paul Rogat Loeb (New York: Basic Books, 2004), 82.

9. Thich Nhat Hanh, *Love in Action: Writings on Nonviolent Social Change* (Berkeley: Parallax Press, 1993), 47.

10. *Pirke Avot* 2.19, heard in a version adapted from Charles Taylor, trans., *Sayings of the Jewish Fathers,* 2nd ed. (Cambridge: Cambridge University Press, 1897), 41.

FURTHER RESOURCES

CONNECTING SPIRITUAL AND
SOCIAL TRANSFORMATION: GENERAL

Armstrong, Karen. *The Battle for God: A History of Fundamentalism*. Rev. ed. New York: Ballantine Books, 2001.

Dass, Ram, and Mirabai Bush. *Compassion in Action: Setting Out on the Path of Service*. New York: Bell Tower, 1992.

————, and Paul Gorman. *How Can I Help? Stories and Reflections on Service*. New York: Alfred A. Knopf, 1985.

Day, Dorothy. *The Long Loneliness*. San Francisco: Harper & Row, 1952.

Gandhi, Mohandas. *An Autobiography: The Story of My Experiments with Truth*. Boston: Beacon Press, 1957.

Gottlieb, Roger. *Joining Hands: Politics and Religion Together for Social Change*. Boulder, CO: Westview Press, 2002.

Ingram, Catherine. *In the Footsteps of Gandhi: Conversations with Spiritual Social Activists*. Berkeley: Parallax Press, 1990.

Lerner, Michael. *Spirit Matters*. Charlottesville, VA: Hampton Road Publishing, 2000.

Nagler, Michael. *The Search for a Nonviolent Future: A Promise of Peace for Ourselves, Our Families, and Our World*. Makawao, HI: Inner Ocean Books, 2004.

O'Sullivan, Edmund. *Transformative Learning: Educational Vision for the 21st Century*. London: Zed Books, 1999.

Washington, James, ed. *A Testament of Hope: The Essential Writings and Speeches of Martin Luther King, Jr.* San Francisco: Harper San Francisco, 1986.

ETHICAL PRACTICE

Aitken, Robert. *The Mind of Clover: Essays in Zen Buddhist Ethics*. San Francisco: North Point Press, 1984.

Dalai Lama. *Ethics for the New Millennium*. New York: Riverhead Books, 1999.

Harvey, Peter. *An Introduction to Buddhist Ethics: Foundations, Values and Issues*. New York: Cambridge University Press, 2000.

Lakoff, George. *Moral Politics: How Liberals and Conservatives Think.* 2nd ed. Chicago: University of Chicago Press, 2002.

Nhat Hanh, Thich. *Interbeing: Fourteen Guidelines for Engaged Buddhism.* 3rd ed. Berkeley: Parallax Press, 1998.

————, et al. *For a Future to Be Possible: Commentaries on the Five Wonderful Precepts.* Berkeley: Parallax Press, 1993.

MINDFULNESS PRACTICE

Analayo. *Satipatthana: The Direct Path to Realization.* Birmingham, Great Britain: Windhorse Publications, 2003.

Boorstein, Sylvia. *Don't Just Do Something, Sit There.* San Francisco: HarperSanFrancisco, 1996.

Goldstein, Joseph, and Jack Kornfield. *Seeking the Heart of Wisdom: The Path of Insight Meditation.* Boston: Shambhala, 1987.

Kornfield, Jack. *A Path with Heart: A Guide through the Perils and Promises of the Spiritual Life.* New York: Bantam Books, 1993.

Nhat Hanh, Thich. *The Miracle of Mindfulness: A Manual on Meditation.* Boston: Beacon Press, 1976.

LOVINGKINDNESS PRACTICE

Brach, Tara. *Radical Acceptance: Embracing Your Life with the Heart of a Buddha.* New York: Bantam Books, 2003.

Chödrön, Pema. *Awakening Loving-Kindness.* Boston: Shambhala, 1996.

Kornfield, Jack. *The Art of Forgiveness, Lovingkindness, and Peace.* New York: Bantam Books, 2002.

Salzberg, Sharon. *Lovingkindness: The Revolutionary Art of Happiness.* Boston: Shambhala, 1997.

OPENING TO SUFFERING, OPENING TO COMPASSION

Bloom, Pamela, ed. *Buddhist Acts of Compassion.* York Beach, ME: Conari Press, 2000.

Macy, Joanna, and Molly Young Brown. *Coming Back to Life: Practices to Reconnect Our Lives, Our World.* Gabriola Island, British Columbia: New Society Publishers, 1998.

Mitchell, Donald, and James Wiseman, eds. *Transforming Suffering: Reflections on Finding Peace in Troubled Times.* New York: Doubleday, 2002.

Young-Eisendrath, Polly. *The Resilient Spirit: Transforming Suffering into Insight and Renewal.* Cambridge: Perseus Publishing, 1996.

THE BODHISATTVA

Leighton, Taigen Dan. *Faces of Compassion: Classic Bodhisattva Archetypes and Their Modern Expression*. Rev. ed. Boston: Wisdom Publications, 2003.

Shantideva. *A Guide to the Bodhisattva's Way of Life* (several translations).

SOCIALLY ENGAGED BUDDHISM

Aung San Suu Kyi, with Alan Clements. *The Voice of Hope*. New York: Seven Stories Press, 1997.

Boucher, Sandy. *Turning the Wheel: American Women Creating the New Buddhism*. Rev. ed. Boston: Beacon Press, 1993.

Eppsteiner, Fred, ed. *The Path of Compassion: Writings on Socially Engaged Buddhism*. Rev. ed. Berkeley: Parallax Press, 1988.

Glassman, Bernie. *Bearing Witness: A Zen Master's Lessons in Making Peace*. New York: Bell Tower, 1998.

Jones, Ken. *The New Social Face of Buddhism: A Call to Action*. Boston: Wisdom Publications, 2003.

Kaza, Stephanie, ed. *Hooked! Buddhist Responses to Consumerism*. Boston: Shambhala, 2004.

Kaza, Stephanie, and Kenneth Kraft, eds. *Dharma Rain: Sources of Buddhist Environmentalism*. Boston: Shambhala, 1999.

Khong, Chan. *Learning True Love: How I Learned and Practiced Social Change in Vietnam*. Berkeley: Parallax Press, 1993.

Kraft, Kenneth. *The Wheel of Engaged Buddhism: A New Map of the Path*. New York: Weatherhill, 1999.

Macy, Joanna. *World as Lover, World as Self*. Berkeley: Parallax Press, 1991.

Maha, Ghosananda. *Step by Step: Meditation on Wisdom and Compassion*. Berkeley: Parallax Press, 1992.

Moon, Susan, ed. *Not Turning Away: The Practice of Engaged Buddhism; 25 Years of Turning Wheel*. Boston: Shambhala, 2004.

Nhat Hanh, Thich. *Being Peace*. Berkeley: Parallax Press, 1987.

———. *Love in Action: Writings on Nonviolent Social Change*. Berkeley: Parallax Press, 1993.

———. *Creating True Peace: Ending Violence in Yourself, Your Family, Your Community, and the World*. New York: Free Press, 2003.

Queen, Christopher, ed. *Engaged Buddhism in the West*. Boston: Wisdom Publications, 2000.

Queen, Christopher, and Sallie King, eds. *Engaged Buddhism: Buddhist Liberation Movements in Asia*. Albany: State University of New York Press, 1996.

Snyder, Gary. *The Practice of the Wild*. San Francisco: North Point Press, 1990.

Winston, Diana, and Donald Rothberg. *A Handbook for the Creation of the Buddhist Alliance for Social Engagement (BASE)*. Berkeley: Buddhist Peace Fellowship, 2000 (also available online at www.bpf.org/html/current_projects/base/base.html).

TRANSFORMATIVE VISIONS AND STRATEGIES

Gottlieb, Roger. *A Greener Faith: Religious Environmentalism and Our Planet's Future*. New York: Oxford University Press, 2006.

Lerner, Michael. *The Left Hand of God: Taking Back Our Country from the Religious Right*. San Francisco: HarperSanFrancisco, 2006.

Loy, David. *The Great Awakening: A Buddhist Social Theory*. Boston: Wisdom Publications, 2003.

Starhawk. *Webs of Power: Notes from the Global Uprising*. Gabriola Island, BC, Canada: New Society Publishers, 2002.

Wallis, Jim. *God's Politics: Why the Right Gets It Wrong and the Left Doesn't Get It*. San Francisco: HarperSanFrancisco, 2005.

West, Cornel. *Democracy Matters: Winning the Fight against Imperialism*. New York: Penguin Press, 2004.

SELECT ORGANIZATIONS

Buddhist Peace Fellowship (United States): P.O. Box 3470, Berkeley, CA 94703, (510) 655-6169, www.bpf.org

Community of Mindful Living: www.iamhome.org (international network connected with the work of Thich Nhat Hanh)

Insight Meditation Society: 1230 Pleasant Street, Barre, MA 01005, (978) 355-4378, www.dharma.org/ims (offers retreats in mindfulness and lovingkindness practice)

International Network of Engaged Buddhists: 666 Charoen Nakorn Road, Klong San, Bangkok 10600, Thailand, 662-860-2194, www.sulak-sivaraksa.org/network22.php

Prison Dharma Network: P.O. Box 4623, Boulder, CO 80306, (303) 544-5923, www.prisondharmanetwork.org/

Sarvodaya: No. 98, Rawatawatta Road, Moratuwa, Sri Lanka, 94 11 264-7159, www.sarvodaya.org/ (a network of 15,000 villages that uses Buddhist and Gandhian principles and practices)

Saybrook Graduate School: 747 Front Street, 3rd floor, San Francisco, CA 94111, (800) 825-4480, www.saybrook.edu (offers an eighteen-month certificate program in socially engaged spirituality that I direct)

Spirit Rock Meditation Center: P.O. Box 169, Woodacre, CA 94973, (415) 488-0164, www.spiritrock.org/ (offers classes and retreats in mindfulness and lovingkindness practice, and in 2007 will offer a two-year program called "The Path of Engagement")

Think Sangha: www.bpf.org/think.html (international network that provides " 'Buddhist' intellectual practice tools for integrating spirituality and social change work")

Tikkun: 2342 Shattuck Avenue, no. 1200, Berkeley, CA 94704, (510) 644-1200, www.tikkun.org/ (a multifaith international community connecting spirituality and social changes that publishes a magazine and has developed a "Network of Spiritual Progressives")

Zen Peacemakers: 177 Ripley Road, Montague, MA 01351, (413) 367-2048, www.zenpeacemakers.org/ (connected with the work of Roshi Bernie Glassman)

For my comprehensive listing "Resources on Socially Engaged Buddhism," including English-language books, journals, organizations, and Web sites, as well as a link to my teaching schedule and a listing of my events and writings, please visit www.beacon.org and go to the author's page for this book.

ACKNOWLEDGMENTS

Writing this book has been a great lesson in many of the principles explored in the book, particularly interdependence. Indeed, *The Engaged Spiritual Life* has been born into the world only because of the support, kindness, and wisdom of so many people.

Sara Schedler helped immeasurably with the development of the book, working closely with me for the last year and a half of its genesis. It is hard for me to imagine the book's completion without her contributions. She read and commented at length on virtually the entire manuscript, co-conducted with me and transcribed most of the interviews, and discussed in great detail with me the themes of the book. I thank her so much for her vision, dedication, hard work, and passion for the book.

I thank those friends and colleagues who have read and/or discussed parts of the book and offered me their suggestions and feedback. Many thanks to Sylvia Boorstein, Kathy Cheney, Dan Frank, Gil Fronsdal, Robert Masters, Bonnie Morrissey, Bernice Rothberg, Richard Shankman, Heather Sundberg, and Diana Winston. I also thank Chenée Fournier for her help in transcribing several of the interviews. For last-minute heroics, I have much gratitude for Linda Peckham.

I thank Beacon Press for its great support and integrity. Amy Caldwell, my editor, has believed deeply in the book and offered her considerable skills, wisdom, and energy in making the book better. I also appreciate Christopher Queen's help in connecting me with Beacon Press.

I give special thanks to my good friend and longtime colleague Diana Winston. The vision for the book and many of the ideas came out of our work and our teaching classes and retreats together over the last eleven years. Indeed, the basic framework for the book, the identification of core principles and practices for connecting our inner and outer lives, grew out of our collaboration.

I also appreciate the dedication of those retreatants, members of my ongoing meditation groups, students from classes, and participants in the Buddhist Peace Fellowship BASE programs with whom I have worked over the years. It has been their great interest and energy in exploring and applying the principles and practices presented in the book that have made possible the maturation of my understanding and the collection of a large body of stories and experiences, both vital for the book.

Similarly, for their camaraderie and help over the years, I thank my many friends and colleagues in several organizations: the Buddhist Peace Fellowship, with its office in Berkeley, California; the International Network of Engaged Buddhists, based in Thailand; the Socially Engaged Spirituality Program at Saybrook Graduate School in San Francisco; and the Spirit Rock Meditation Center in Woodacre, California.

I thank especially Jürgen Kremer and Ann Masai, my colleagues in the Socially Engaged Spirituality Program, for their inspiration, great support, and many discussions over the last years. I also thank my sister, Elizabeth Rothberg, and brother, Frederick Rothberg, for much over the years that has made the book better.

I also want to give a big hug and much appreciation for the generosity of my mentors over the last years: Sylvia Boorstein, Gil Fronsdal, Joanna Macy, Huston Smith, and John Travis. Thanks also to Sylvia, Joanna, and Huston, as well as Jack Kornfield and Michael Lerner, for their championing of the book in its early stages. A big thanks also to Jack for writing the foreword.

Last, I want to thank my parents, Bernice and Simon, for their enormous support and kindness. They have helped in the development of the book in so many ways—from attending many of my talks related to the book and giving feedback, to commenting on the manuscript, to offering funds for an assistant during the writing of the book, to their own sustained interests in social justice, living with integrity, and balancing the inner and the outer, which were imparted to me from the beginning.

My mother, Bernice, provided perspectives from her own activism and political involvement going back to her youth in New York, and leading to working with Head Start in Maryland, race relations in Virginia, and the League of Women Voters. She has always been eager to discuss the themes of the book and their application to contemporary issues, and has continually encouraged me and given unconditional support during the writing process.

I especially want to acknowledge the contributions of my father, Simon, who died in October 2005, just before the completion of the manuscript. He exemplified many of the qualities that are the focus of this book, particularly equanimity in the face of adversity. Despite many difficult circumstances, including injury in World War II, blindness in the last twenty years of his life, and several bouts with cancer in the last twenty-seven years of his life, he kept an incredibly positive outlook and complained very little. These challenges didn't stop his career as a research biochemist, extensive publications, participation in scientific meetings until the very end of his life, and active civic involvement at the neighborhood, city, and state levels.

In the last few weeks of his life, his conversations with me often focused on his happiness at the completion of this book. "Wonderful!" he would say upon being given the news of another chapter completed. Even in his last days, he taught us all so much, dying at home with great peace, lucidity, and equanimity, surrounded by love.

On my desk is a name block with "Dr. Rothberg" printed on it, which he passed on to me when I received my own doctorate. On the bottom, he wrote a short message, speaking of how the name block had always reminded him of his "continuous pursuit of truth, knowledge, and wisdom." May this book help sustain such a pursuit for all of us.

Berkeley, California

INDEX

African Americans: 2, 53, 73; blues
and hope of, 204; Christian prophetic
tradition and, 100; church song of,
211; in civil rights movement, 59,
173; collective shadow and, 78;
images of, 140; internalized oppression and, 104–5; in Nashville, 29–
30; in prisons, 33; structural violence
and, 77. *See also* civil rights movement; King, Martin Luther, Jr.;
Malcolm X; Parks, Rosa; racism;
Thurman, Howard; West, Cornel
ahimsa, 13. *See also* nonviolence
Aitken, Robert, 14
Albareda, Ramon, 137
American Revolution, 154
Analayo, 215n. 2
anger: activists and, 54, 73, 93, 107,
141, 149–50, 154–55, 164–68; attachment to views and, 119; Buddhism
and, 150–52, 220n. 6; burnout and,
5, 93; Christian views of, 153–54;
confusion and ambivalence about,
151–55; fear of, 176–77; Greek views
of, 153; Jewish views of, 152–53;
justice and, 123, 153, 154–55; love
and, 123, 152, 158, 160, 161; mindfulness of, 80, 126, 146–47, 155–57,
159–61; Nonviolent Communication
and, 162–64; opponents or enemies
and, 143, 144, 145, 146; pain and,
14, 75, 84, 160, 165, 166, 167, 168;
reflecting on, 161–62; transforming,
157–68; translation issues and,
152, 220n. 6; Truth Mandala and,

85, 86; types of, 152–54, 158; violence
and, 13, 53
anti-Semitism: responding to, 163–64.
See also Nonviolent Communication
Arendt, Hannah, 2
Argentina, 168
Aristotle, 2, 153–54
Ariyaratne, A. T., 35–36, 199, 201, 202
Armstrong, Guy, 103
Aronson, Harvey, 159
Ash, Timothy, 88
Asoka, 16
attachment: and clinging or grasping,
117; and lovingkindness, 175; to not
knowing, 126–27; to outcomes, 191–
96; to pleasure, 171; to privilege, 184;
suffering and, 43–44; types of, 117; to
views, 113, 116–20, 121–24, 145. *See
also* commitment; non-attachment
Augustine, Saint, 154
Aung San Suu Kyi, 169
Auschwitz, 183
autonomy, 45, 130–32, 180. *See also*
individualism; interdependence; self
Avalokiteshvara, 97. *See also* Kwan Yin
awareness. *See* mindfulness

Bader, Michael, 177
Baldwin, James, 100
Batchelor, Martine, 69
Batchelor, Stephen, 216n. 5
bearing witness, 50–51, 87
Bellah, Robert, 132
Berlin Wall, 120
Bernstein, Dennis, 164

233